BYRON AS CRITIC

BYRON AS CRITIC

BY

CLEMENT TYSON GOODE, A. M., Ph.D.

PROFESSOR OF ENGLISH IN MERCER UNIVERSITY

HASKELL HOUSE

Publishers of Scholarly Books

NEW YORK

1964

published by

HASKELL HOUSE

Publishers of Scholarly Books

30 East 10th Street • New York, N. Y. 10003

Library of Congress Catalog Card Number: 65-15893

PRINTED IN UNITED STATES OF AMERICA

ACKNOWLEDGMENT

It is a privilege to acknowledge my obligations, in the preparation of this work, to so distinguished a scholar and considerate a friend as Professor Joseph Q. Adams of Cornell University.

Macon, Georgia
June 1, 1923

CLEMENT TYSON GOODE

CONTENTS

Chapter I

INTRODUCTION

There will be much new talk about Byron, but we should like to know who is better worth talking about in these de pressed days.—*Academy*, August 11, 1900.

Byron has perhaps been taken less seriously as a critic than any other great figure in modern literature. One or two opinions of well known writers, among the great number that might be cited, may be quoted to show the usual estimate.

His critical faculty, if I may steal one phrase from a treasury that may well spare me the loan, was " zero, or even a frightful *minus* quantity " ; his judgment never worth the expense of a thought or word.[1]

The chief of these gifts is criticism—a department in which Byron, for all his shrewdness, simply does not count, because of the waywardness, egotism, and personal prejudice which tinge every one of his critical utterances, eulogistic or depreciatory. . . .

Suffice it to say, that to take him seriously as a critic is impossible.[2]

But there is scant evidence that any thorough study of Byron as a critic has ever been made. Apparently opinion has been formed from merely a cursory examination of his more emphatic critical writings, which represent him more as a controversialist than as a critic.

Such treatment, though undeserved, is not altogether surprising. Independently as a critic, Byron is not one of

---

[1] A. C. Swinburne, *Essays and Studies*, 251.
[2] George Saintsbury, *A History of Criticism* III, 110 & 282.

the great names. And his criticism, such of it as is well
known, has suffered unduly from contrast with his poetry.
He is universally regarded as having written in accordance
with one creed, and as having criticised dogmatically in
another.

Byron the critic and Byron the poet were two very different
men.[1]

It was thus natural for him to pose as the spokesman of two
ages—as a critic and as an author.[2]

Lord Byron protested against the new movement, while he
followed it; upheld to the last the models which it was the
fashion to decry, confessed to the last, in poetry as in morals,
"Video meliora proboque, deteriora sequor."[3]

In the universal approval of his poetry, it has followed
too often, consciously or not, that his criticism, as set up
in opposition, is negligible. But the general acceptance of
his poetry, instead of being a cause for a summary rejection
of his criticism, should be a stimulus to a sympathetic study
of it. A great artist has, or should have, a right to be
heard in his opinions of his art.

Moreover, the influence which Byron's achievements gave
him is ample reason for an attitude not of tolerance merely
but of interest toward his criticism. It is difficult indeed
for the present age to conceive the almost despotic power
which he possessed over the literary world of his day.

He had a wider influence at the time than Goethe.[4]

This morning I looked over my ledger, and I find £75,000 has
passed over that counter from Lord Byron's pen alone. Can any
one in the trade say as much? And then look at the time it
was done in—ten years. I think that proves he was a great poet.[5]

[1] T. B. Macaulay, *Lord Byron*, 33.
[2] John Nichol, *Byron*, 206.
[3] Charles Kingsley, *Fraser's Magazine*, November, 1853.
[4] Sir Oliver Elton, *English Literature*, 1780—1830, II, 135.
[5] John Murray, reported by Trelawny, *Records*, 185.

I suppose no man who ever lived has possessed the extraordinary celebrity of Lord Byron in such an intense, haunting,
almost maddening degree. And this celebrity extended all over
the continent to as great an extent as in England. . . . All
Europe was so enthralled with the magic of the man's very
name that the sensation he made even discounted, to some
extent, the sensation of Waterloo.[1]

Y nuestra edad, el principio del siglo, al descubrir la cabeza
apolina de Byron, cruzada de rayos y de sombras, podrá ex-
clamar: " Hé ahí mi imágen, hé ahí mi simbolo." [2]

A knowledge of the critical opinions of such a figure would
seem to be imperative for a complete understanding and
appreciation of the literature of the time.

A difficulty confronts the student of any aspect of Byron's
work or career—his much emphasized inconsistencies.
Byron prided himself on these "inconsistencies," and from
his pride in them they have been exaggerated, as have
other particulars of his life and character.

In Lord Byron, however, this sort of pivot of Character was
almost wholly wanting. Governed as he was at different
moments by totally different passions, and impelled sometimes,
as during his short access of parsimony in Italy, by springs
of action never before developed in his nature, in him this
simple mode of tracing character to its sources must be often
wholly at fault; and if, as is not impossible, in trying to solve
the strange variances of his mind, I should myself be found
to have fallen into contradictions and inconsistencies, the extreme difficulty of analysing, without dazzle or bewilderment,
such an unexampled complication of qualities must be admitted
as my excuse.[3]

Byron may almost be said to have had no character at all.
Every attempt to bring his virtues or his vices within the

---

[1] Jane Clermont, reported by William Graham, *Last Links*, 13 f.
[2] Emilio Castelar, *Vida de Lord Byron*, 163.
[3] Thomas Moore, *Life* VI, 229.

boundaries of a theory, or to represent his conduct as guided by any predominant principle of good or evil, has been accompanied by blunders and perversions. His nature had no simplicity or unity. He seems an embodied antithesis,—a mass of contradictions,—a collection of opposite frailties and powers . . . in short, a man continually busy in giving the lie to his thoughts, opinions, tastes and conduct.[1]

This journal is a relief. When I am tired—as I generally am—out comes this, and down goes every thing. But I can't read it over ; and God knows what contradictions it may contain. If I am sincere with myself (but I fear one lies more to one's self than to any one else), every page should confute, refute, and utterly abjure its predecessor.[2]

If such statements were to be taken literally, the student well might be deterred from any systematic study of Byron. And yet there is some truth in them. Byron has his complexities, which recommend caution. The difficulty of dealing with them is evident in the various treatises on his poetry, although his poetry as the product of his *alter ego* is least affected by them. As much is manifest in his biographies, where each biographer finds a different interest in his manifold nature. And popular opinion holds these complexities to be so plentiful in his criticism as to nullify the whole body of it. But the saving salt in his critical opinions is that they were made impulsively, and from their dependence upon his deeper nature which controlled his reactions, they show a consistency, as I hope will appear in the course of this study, that is surprising, from what we know, or imagine we have known, of Byron.

A very nice question arises, in a study of Byron's criticism, whether or not in his letters and journals, which contain the richest store of his critical opinions, he was sincere.

[1] E. P. Whipple, *North American Review*, January, 1845.
[2] Journal, *L. & J.* II, 366.

There is no doubt about the quality of those compositions. They are indeed "among the best in our language." And opinion is nearly unanimous upon their naturalness and lifelike character.

They give the truest portrait of the man.[1]

They contain the only natural expression of his feelings freely poured forth in the very circumstances that excited them, with no view at the time to obtain or keep up a particular character, and therefore with no restraint upon his own character.[2]

Since Saint Simon we have not seen more lifelike confidences.[3]

If the epistolary style of Lord Byron was artificial, it was a rare and admirable instance of that highest art which cannot be distinguished from nature.[4]

After a certain period in his career, Byron had a right to expect that his letters would be preserved and published.[5] But from his native fearlessness, his reckless disregard of consequences, and his lack of prevision, there is little probability that anticipations of the kind affected his utterances at all materially.

Finally, Byron's criticism in its reactionary character need not be regarded as the anomaly that it seems. The age itself was pretty much mixed in its opinions and ideas of literature. It was the aftermath of Pope and Johnson, and it produced Coleridge and Byron.

¿ Cuál era el estado de aquellos dias primeros del siglo, en las obras de Byron contenido, representado? Era la incertidumbre.[6]

It is not surprising then that, as the best representative

---

[1] R. E. Prothero, Preface to *L. & J.* I, vi.

[2] R. C. Dallas, *Recollections*, 46,—specifically of Byron's letters to his mother.

[3] H. A. Taine, *History of English Literature* IV, 6.

[4] T. B. Macaulay, *Lord Byron*, 4.

[5] Cf. *L. & J.* I, 44, 335, and V, 379-80, 559.

[6] Castelar, *Vida de Lord Byron*, 146.

which the time produced of its own conglomerate character, Byron should appear sometimes as two-fold.[1]

But whatever system his criticism professes to follow, it is always vigorous and individual.   And,

> [Literary criticism] is a creative art and has few bounds but those of personality. . . .   It is too obvious to need saying that good criticism, like any other good thing, depends first of all on mental vigor.[2]

The *rôle* of the impressionist is by no means a contemptible one . . . and he has the lion's share of the critical labors of the present.[3]

Byron as a critic, whatever class or rank he may be adjudged to represent or fill in his criticism, undoubtedly has a unique place in our literature.

---

[1] See W. L. Phelps, *The Beginnings*, etc., for a like conscious classicism and unconscious romanticism in such figures as Walpole, McPherson, Thomson, and others.

[2] W. T. Brewster, *The Logic of Literary Criticism*.

[3] W. P. Trent, *The Authority of Criticism*, 29.

CHAPTER II

EQUIPMENT

HEREDITY AND TRAINING

I own myself the child of *Folly*,
But not so wicked as they make me.
        —" Egotism," *Hours of Idleness.*

Ancestry   Byron's family history has been unusually
              attractive to writers on his life and works.[1]
His intimate friend and biographer, Thomas Moore, taking
a cue doubtless from his subject's pride of ancestry, has
emphasized the strong hereditary strain in the make-up of
the man.[2]   Almost every writer since, following Moore's
example, has felt the need of tracing the influences of blood
in the poet-peer's complex character and genius.[3]

The object of all these enquiries into Byron's lineage has
been to find the source, however unconvincing and remote,
of the poetical genius in Byron.   But it is reasonable to say
that all such endeavors must remain a part of the romance

[1] " Independently of any scientific reminders, Byron has always
seemed to his biographers an obvious illustration of the blend of good
and bad bequeathed by one's forefathers." — J. Wright Duff, *Byron's
Selected Poetry*, Introduction, x.
[2] " It cannot fail to be remarked how strikingly he combined in
his own nature some of the best and, perhaps, worst qualities that
lie scattered through the various characters of his predecessors."—
The Life and Works of Lord Byron I, 7.
[3] " Never was poet born to so much illustrious and to so much
bad blood."—John Nichol, *Byron*, 12.   " In his character, as finally
developed, were concentrated many of the historic qualities of an
ancient family."—Courthope, *A History of English Poetry* VI, 232.
" In unexampled measure the good and evil of his nature was inborn."—
Albert Brecknock, *The Pilgrim Poet*, 12.

b

which arises from Byron's strange nature and envelops his spectacular career. All that science presumes to account for in heredity is approximately regular and normal qualities.[1] Poetical genius is too rare among family or even racial characteristics to pretend to any regularity. Its presence in the individual is an independent phenomenon. On the contrary, temperament or talent of any kind may safely be traced through common properties that extend far back of the possessor. Any search then into the ancestry of Byron—unbroken as it was in caste from the Conquest— for influences that might tend to make him a warrior, a churchman, a statesman, an adventurer, or a scholar and man of letters—and consequently a critic, rather than a poet—would probably be rewarded with success.

The character of the blood which Byron inherited was, by a long process of refinement from exclusive marriage within itself, such as would normally have produced in him, as in the last heir of the House of Usher, an essential quality of the critical art, to wit, a delicate susceptibility and taste. Then if his intellectual possessions proved adequate, his native equipment for the critical rôle was complete, and there was required to perfect it but the conventional training of original talent and the opportunity in life for its exercise and use.

He had a pride, as great as it was honest, in his patrician descent,[2] and he believed that an advantage in sensibilities,

---

[1] "Extrana historia y extrana genealogia la suya." — Emilio Castelar, *Vida de Lord Byron*, 150. Byron himself has prescribed a wholesome caution in matters of the kind, though remarked in his " quietly facetious " mood:—

" It would not be fair
From sire to son to augur good or ill."—*Don Juan* I, 51.

[2] Jeaffreson says (*The Real Lord Byron*, Chapters I-IV) that Byron's pride in his descent has been overrated by his biographers, and ridicules his habit of deriving his qualities from the distant founders of his house, rather than from nearer representatives and from strains from

as in personal privilege, descended to him from it. He was
ready, as well, to relieve himself of responsibility for fault
or foible in his nature and actions, by appeal to the same
authority.[1] But his poetical talent, he believed, originated
with himself.[2] In this belief, indeed, he was more nearly
right than are many of his biographers.

maternal sides. It is true that he is often unscientific in his processes
of the kind, but as a peer of England he would be expected to have
an interest in his forbears mainly on his father's side (Cp. *Correspondence*
II, 166), a fact which Jeaffreson seems not to understand, or ignores.
The well authenticated stories of " Dominus," " Old English Baron,"
" The House of Lords, Sir," and such passages as,

> " I can boast a race as true
> To monarchs crowned, and some discrowned,
> As ever Britain's annals knew,"

prove his pride in his lineage. Cf. *L. & J.* V, 99.

[1] " It is not that I may not have incurred
For my ancestral faults or mine, the wound
I bleed withal."—*Childe Harold's Pilgrimage* IV, 133.

" I trust I shall go through the process with a creditable *sang froid*
and not disgrace a line of cut-throat ancestors."—*L. & J.* I, 306.

" You 'know, or you do *not* know, that my maternal Grandfather
(a very clever man, and amiable, I am told) was strongly suspected
of Suicide (he was found drowned in the Avon at Bath), and that
another very near relative of the same branch took poison, and was
merely saved by antidotes. For the first of these events there was
no apparent cause, as he was rich, respected, and of considerable
intellectual resources, hardly forty years of age, and not at all addicted
to any unhinging vice. It was, however, but a strong suspicion, owing
to the manner of his death and to his melancholy temper. The *second
had* a cause, but it does not become me to touch upon it; it happened
when I was far too young to be aware of it, and I never heard of it
till after the death of that relative, many years afterwards. I think,
then, that I may call this dejection *constitutional.* I had always been
told that in *temper* I more resembled my maternal Grandfather than
any of my *father's* family,—that is, in the gloomier part of his temper,
for he was what you call a goodnatured man, and I am not."—*L. & J.*
V, 370f. Cf. *Correspondence* I, 147.

" What is the reason why I have been, all my lifetime, more or less
ennuyé ? and that, if anything, I am rather less so now than I was at
twenty, as far as my recollection serves ? I do not know how to answer
this, but presume that it is constitutional,—as well as the waking in
low spirits, which I have invariably done for many years."—*L. & J.*
V, 155 f.

[2] Cf. *infra*, Chapter IV.

His family was Norman in origin. It is traceable in England back to the Conquest and extends in legend all the way to Scandinavia. With the Conqueror there were " two potent barons of the name "—Byron or Burun (-on, -en), orthography was not fixed till the reign of Henry II [1]— Erneis and Ralph, of unknown relationship. The poet is descended from the latter, who held estates in Nottingham and Derby. Newstead is in the former shire, hence the family is associated with one place from its beginnings in England.[2] Hugh de Burun, son of the founder, gave " the Church of Ossington to the monks of Lenton," thus becoming, though it may have been only remotely in his purpose and sympathies, a patron of learning.[3] His son, Hugh the second, became a monk of the order in the hermitage of Kersale, so initiating the long and richer-growing family interest in letters that was to culminate in the single really great scion of the house, the Sixth Lord, centuries later. The fourth of the line in England, Sir Roger de Buron, continued this support of religious houses, and hence of learning, in his donations of land and estates to the monks of Swinstead. With the following dozen generations before

---

[1] Apparently pronunciation varied in Byron's own day. Mrs. Byron's usage seemingly was Byr-rone (*L. & J.* I, 46, 48). Leigh Hunt says: —" This reminds me of the disputes respecting Lord Byron's pronunciation of his name; some maintaining that he called it Bȳron, with a short *y*, others Bȳron with a long one. The truth is, he pronounced it both ways, but in general the former. Captain Medwin says that in speaking of Lady Byron, he pronounced it ' Byrn '; but this is a mistake. The Captain's ear might not have discerned the second vowel, but it was discernible to others. ' Byrn ' is *Byron*, pronounced shortly, with the northern burr. But he called himself Byron sometimes; and the Italians always called him so; at least as nearly as they could. They made it *Bairon*, as I have noticed in Madame Guiccioli."—*Lord Byron*, 178 f. Cf. *L & J.* II, 264.

[2] " The poet killed the family of which he was abundantly proud."— Jeaffreson, *The Real Lord Byron* I, 14. And in 1817 he disposed of the ancestral estate at Newstead, despite his many declarations that he would never do so.

[3] Cf. *Don Juan* X, 36.

the barony in 1643, there is a lack of evidence, in the general meagerness of information, of any very pronounced literary sympathies or inclinations. The family leanings, as far as they were conspicuous at all, were more toward martial life and statecraft [1] than toward art or learning. But the family was famed for its landed property, and from this fact and the return gift of Newstead, which came with the barony, it is natural to suppose that ecclesiastical patronage was continued.

" From Charles the Second's restoration the Newstead Byrons had taken an interest in letters and the fine arts." [2] But the first in the peerage, " who had a taste, if not actually a turn for literature," [3] was not the First Lord but his nephew William, who became Third Lord Byron in 1679. He was a writer of verse, and an admiring patron of at least one poet.[4] His son (1669–1736), the Fourth Lord Byron, gave evidence of artistic gifts in a taste for painting, like his mother Elizabeth Chaworth, and produced some landscapes, which Sir William Musgrave found worth reproducing in etching.[5] The Fourth Lord's son (who was a brother of " the wicked Lord," of Isabella Carlisle, and of the poet's grandfather, " Foul-weather Jack ") exhibited the family traits in two ways—by taking holy orders, and by a skill in painting that was sufficient to impose upon a

---

[1] Byron's early ambitions were doubtless fired by a knowledge of this side of his family history. " My earliest dreams (as most boys' dreams are) were martial."—*L. & J.* V. 426. " My qualities were much more oratorical and martial, than poetical."—*L. & J.* V. 453. Cf. *ibid.* I, 126.

[2] Jeaffreson, *The Real Lord Byron*, 19.

[3] Francis Gribble, *The Love Affairs of Lord Byron*, 3.

[4] " Er war mit einem untergeordneten Poeten Thomas Shipman befreundet, der ihn und die Seinigen mehrfach angesungen hat; ja in Shipman's ' Carolina; or, Loyal Poems ' (1683) findet sich sogar ein Gedicht von ihm, und es geht auch sonst daraus hervor, daß er selbst ein Versmacher war."—Karl Elze, *Lord Byron*, 4.

[5] Jeaffreson, *The Real Lord Byron*, 19 f.

connoisseur purchaser a copy of a Rembrandt landscape for the original painting.[1]

From this point the inquiry is among the immediate predecessors of the poet, from whom he would most probably derive his qualities. Among his immediate forbears a literary turn is so frequent as to be almost a common possession of the family, and in some it is distinguished. The poet's grandfather, Admiral Byron or " Foul-weather Jack," is the author of the *Narrative of the Honorable John Byron*,[2] a work justly celebrated among the many books of travel of the English race. Its freshness and narrative power have won for it a comparison with Sir John Mandeville's works, and its descriptive force ranks it with the best writings of Defoe.[3] The Admiral's sister, Isabella Carlisle, the poet's grand-aunt, was an accomplished writer of rhymes.[4] And her son, Lord Carlisle, the poet's guardian,[5] was a writer of " verse, tragedies, and pamphlets," some of which won the critical approval of both Walpole and Dr. Johnson.

Byron's biographers do not ordinarily acknowledge anything of worth as coming to him from his own rakish father. Indeed from Captain Byron's life and character little merit of any kind could be expected to come. But from him more than from any other Byron inherited his " tumultuous passions "—so described by his Trinity College

---

[1] Jeaffreson, *The Real Lord Byron*, 19 f.

[2] " One of the most interesting books of the kind which the language contains."—Geo. Clinton, *Memoirs*, 24.

[3] Nichol, and others. Cf.

> " His hardships were comparative
> To those related in my grand-dad's ' Narrative.' "
>   —*Don Juan* II, 137.

[4] " She also wrote beautiful poetry, and after adorning the fashionable world for many years, she left it without any apparent cause."—J. W. Lake, *Life of Lord Byron*, x.

[5] Cf. " The paralytic puling of Carlisle."—*English Bards and Scotch Reviewers*. Byron himself recognized later the injustice of his criticism and attempted to correct it, after long solicitation from his sister.

tutor [1]—and his passions, by his own explicit declaration, time and again, were the source of his poetry.[2]

Popular opinion holds, as well, that he could have received, from his maternal side immediately, little good of any kind. The notion comes from a greater interest in the poet's own selfish point of view [3] and the statements of his apologists than frcm a just interpretation of the facts as they stand. Mrs. Byron's constant boast was her descent from James I of Scotland, who sang his own romance in the *King's Quair*, and through the meter employed gave to the language the term Rime Royal. And Catherine Gordon herself was an extraordinary person, even if not admirable. Her unique character included an interest in letters, specifically in qualities that forecast criticism [4] more than any other literary form, to wit, shrewdness, discrimination, and

[1] *L. & J.* I, 156. This strain, according to Jeaffreson (*The Real Lord Byron*, Chapter III), descended from the line of the Berkeleys on a maternal side three generations back, not from the parent stock of the Byrons.

[2] Cf. Chapter V, 87 f.

[3] The reader is asked to compare Byron's letters to his sister, 1804-6, with some of his mother's to Hanson and others at about the same time.

[4] " Catherine Gordon—destined to be the mother of a great poet— was all her life particularly fond of reading, and read good literature; she wrote vivid, though inelegant, letters; and she could criticise shrewdly, in after years, not only her son's poem's (those which she saw, for she died before his notable works were published), but the discrepant reviews of them."—E. C. Mayne, *Byron* I, 4.

" She was fond of books, subscribed to the Southwell Book Club, copied passages which struck her in the course of her reading, collected all the criticisms on her son's poetry, made shrewd remarks upon them herself . . . and corresponded with her friends upon literary subjects."— R. E. Prothero, Byron's *Letters and Journals* I, 3.

Moore acknowledges as much, notwithstanding his obvious hostility toward the mother :—" She had got bound together in a volume, which a friend of mine once saw, a collection of all the literary notices, that had then appeared, of his early Poems and Satire,—written over on the margin, with observations of her own, which to my informant appeared indicative of much more sense and ability than, from her general character, we should be inclined to attribute to her."—*Life* II, 36. The account is given also in Moore's *Memoirs* (V, 295), where the friend and informant is named, to wit, William Harness.

fondness for contemporary writing.[1] But she was as notoriously lacking in the great essential, philosophical calm, as was her son after her. She made no pretensions to writing other than " epistolary communications," which, in Byron's own phrase, were " very concise and much to the purpose." [2] These qualities are cardinal virtues in criticism.

From the foregoing facts of the family temper and racial history of the Byrons—of an interest in letters displayed early, and growing stronger and more prevalent till it became almost a family trait—it is not surprising that a turn for letters was prominent among the characteristics which Byron had a right to expect by inheritance; not indeed a genius for creation, which is not explicable in terms of heredity, but a power of quick and sure discernment, of discrimination, and of appraisement of artistic things. In brief, he inherited the elements of a delicate and refined taste in as large measure as anything else that came to him through the channels of his aristocratic blood.[3] With his

---

[1] "You seem to be a mighty reader of magazines : where do you pick up all of this intelligence, quotations, etc., etc. ? "—*L. & J.* I, 283.

[2] " She was not without a taste for books, and her letters are sensible and to the point."—E. H. C., *Encyclopedia Britannica.*
For the variety of stops that Mrs. Byron was able to command in her correspondence with her incorrigible son, compare the following :—
" At last you have a *decent* specimen of the dowager's talents for epistles in the *furioso* style."—*L. & J.* I, 66. " I sent back to the Epistle, which was couched in *elegant* terms, a severe answer."—*L. & J.* I, 81. " At last in answer to a *Furious Epistle,* I returned a *Sarcastick* Answer." —*L. & J.* I, 83. " The *Details* of her *Generosity* in allowing me part of my *own property* would be continually *thundered* in my ears, or *launched* in the *Lightening* of her letters."—*L. & J.* I, 88. " Her soft warblings must have delighted her auditors, her higher notes being particularly musical, and on a calm moonlight evening would be heard to great advantage."—*L. & J.* I, 101.

[3] " To this must be added his exquisite delicacy of taste."—Otto Matthiae, *Characteristics of Lord Byron,* 20.
" He differed also from the majority of young people in the delicacy of his sensibilities."— Jeaffreson, *The Real Lord Byron,* 51.
" El tiene, sobre todo y ántes que todo, la sensibilidad, esa sensibilidad que se conmueve y se riza al menor soplo del aire, que cambia de matices al menor reflejo de la luz, que presiente las tempestades futuras, asi

great intellectual powers early in evidence, everything else in the equipment of the critic could be acquired.

Byron is as good a subject for a study of the effects of environment as he is of the influences of heredity.[1] His keen **Environment** sensitiveness, descending to him from his birth, told inestimably upon his development through the powerful impressions which he received from surroundings. From their fortunate excellence he derived standards of beauty and taste, which remained with him for life.

He was born in London, but the first ten years of his life were spent in Scotland, where the fine Highland scenery about Aberdeenshire had a powerful effect upon his boyish

del Universo como de la sociedad, y que siendo uno de los mayores dones de la naturaleza, es tambien uno de los mayores tormentos de la vida."—Castelar, *Vida de Lord Byron*, 142.

[1] His biographers are as nearly unanimous in tracing the influences of environment on the *quality* of his poetry as they are in their zeal to account for the presence of his genius from the characters of his ancestors.

" He was, undoubtedly, delicately susceptible of impressions from the beauties of nature, for he retained recollections of the scenes which interested his childish wonder, fresh and glowing, to his latest days; nor have there been wanting plausible theories to ascribe the formation of his poetical character to the contemplation of those romantic scenes." — John Galt, *Life of Byron*, 14.

" The savage grandeur of nature around him; the feeling that he was upon hills where ' Foreign tyrant never trod ' . . . blended with the wild supernatural fictions peculiar to remote and thinly-populated districts, were admirably calculated to foster that poetical feeling innate in his character."—J. W. Lake, *Byron*, ix.

" Immediatamente que tocais estas playas, os sentís movido, segun vuestro temperamento, si sois fuerte y nervudo, al trabajo; si sois emprendedor, al comercio; si sois filósofo, á pensar; y á sonar si sois poeta."—Castelar, *Vida de Lord Byron*, 3.

" To the wildness and grandeur of the scenes, among which his childhood was passed, it is not unusual to trace the first awakening of his poetic talent. But it may be questioned whether this faculty was ever so produced."—Moore, *Life* I, 22. Captain Medwin quotes directly from conversation with Byron:—" Probably the wild scenery of Morven and Loch-na-gar, and the banks of the Dee, were the parents of my poetical vein, and the developers of my poetical boss."—*Conversations with Lord Byron*, 63.

imagination.[1]   These years and scenes were the richest of all
in the moulding and refining influences which environment
had to offer.   He himself has left ample evidence, in his
poetry, and in more straightforward and unimpassioned
way in his prose, of the effect on his character and temperament of this period of his life in its wonderful setting.[2]

[1] " On the shores of *Aberdeenshire*, Lord Byron seems from infancy
to have accustomed himself to delight in the expanse, the roll, and the
lonely roar of the Northern Ocean! "—Sir Egerton Brydges, *Letters
on Lord Byron*, 120.
  " The early life he spent in Scotland, amongst wild and mountainous
scenery helped to develop his mental faculties, and to impress upon
his strong imagination those natural beauties which he described so
vividly in his writings.   As a boy he loved to wander alone amid the
wild and lonely hills of the Highlands, from which his soul drew its
inspiration, and gathered memories and traditions which remained with
him to the last days of his life."—A. Brecknock, *The Pilgrim Poet*, 14.
  [2] " Lachin y Gair," addressed to " one of the most sublime and
picturesque amongst our ' Caledonian Alps,' " is acknowledged the best
of his juvenile poems, while " When I Roved a Young Highlander,"
with its tribute to " Morven of snow," is a close second.   These poems
were the earliest results of the inspiration which be derived from his
surroundings.   Cf., " I suppose you will soon have a view of the eternal
snows that summit the top of Lachin y Gair, which towers so magnifi-
cently above the rest of our Northern Alps.   I still remember with
pleasure the admiration which filled my mind, when I first beheld it,
and further on the dark frowning mountains which rise near Invercauld,
together with the romantic rocks that overshadow Mar Lodge, a seat
of Lord Fife's, and the cataract of the Dee, which dashes down the
declivity with impetuous violence in the grounds adjoining to the
House."—*L. & J.* I, 77.   A year before his death he could write with
the same feeling :—

> " Long have I roamed through lands which are not mine,
> Adored the Alp, and loved the Apennine,
> Reverred Parnassus, and beheld the steep
> Jove's Ida and Olympus crown the deep ;
> But ' twas not all long ages ' lore, nor all
> *Their* nature held me in their thrilling thrall ;
> The infant rapture still survived the boy,
> And Lach-na-gar with Ida looked o'er Troy,
> Mixed Celtic memories with the Phrygian mount
> And Highland linns with Castalie's clear fount.
> Forgive me, Homer's universal shade !
> Forgive me, Phoebus ! that my fancy strayed ;
> The North and Nature taught me to adore
> Your scenes sublime, from those beloved before."
>   —*The Island* II, xii.

His innate appreciation, awakened thus by such potent means, became a dominating force in his later conduct [1] and works. It enhanced the joy and profit of his travel incalculably, and these in turn reacted powerfully on his esthetic nature and bore fruit in his artistic modes and beliefs.[2]

Upon his return to England in 1798 the impressionable young peer was surrounded by less inspiring natural scenery, but the somewhat serious lack was made up for by the

"When very young, about eight years of age, after an attack of the scarlet fever at Aberdeen, I was removed by medical advice, into the Highlands. Here I passed occasionally some summers, and from this period I date my love of mountainous countries. I can never forget the effect, a few years afterward, in England, of the only thing I had long seen, even in miniature, of a mountain, in the Malvern Hills. After I returned to Cheltenham, I used to watch them every afternoon, at sunset, with a sensation which I cannot describe."—Note to *The Island.*

[1] "As long as I retain my feeling and my passion for Nature, I can partly soften or subdue my other passions and resist or endure those of others."—*L. & J.* VI, 89.

[2]   " To me
High mountains are a feeling."—*Childe Harold* III, 72.

"Are not the mountains, waves, and skies, a part
Of me and of my Soul, as I of them ? "—*Ibid.*, 75.

" My altars are the mountains and the Ocean,
Earth—air—stars,—all that springs from the great Whole."
                                   —*Don Juan* III, 104.
"And made him friends of mountains; with the stars
And the quick Spirit of the Universe
He held his dialogues: and they did teach
To him the magic of their mysteries."—*The Dream.*

"And I have loved thee, Ocean! and my joy
Of youthful sports was on thy breast to be
Borne, like thy bubbles, onward: from a boy
I wantoned with thy breakers—they to me
Were a delight; and if the freshening sea
Made them a terror—'twas a pleasing fear,
For I was, as it were, a Child of thee,
And trusted to thy billows far and near,
And laid my hand upon thy mane—as I do here."
                                   —*Childe Harold* IV, 184.
Cf. *Childe Harold* II, 37; *ibid.* III, 13; and *L. & J.* I, 295, *ibid.* V, 99.

richer traditions of some of the objects, and these on their part were well adapted to soften and subdue the stronger effects of the Scottish wilds. Newstead Abbey [1] and its surroundings—the fine old memories of the place, the statuary and paintings, the shadowy halls and picturesque architecture, and the romantic legends of Sherwood Forest close by, echoing of both Robin Hood and King Richard — were not the least influences in training and correcting his native artistic turn and temper.

The next great set of associations, with new and changing natural scenery, belongs to the first pilgrimage, where the enjoyment and profit for the unusually susceptible youth were multiplied at every turn by the experience he had had amid the scenes of his earlier life. But this period comprehends so much more in his training and equipment, than the mere shift of location to new surroundings, that it is reserved for a special study.[2]

It would be unreasonable to insist upon the origin of poetic genius among the associations of its possessor's early environment, be those associations what they may. Yet it would be uncritical not to acknowledge them, in instances of delicately moulded natures like Byron's, as primary influences in the development of a fine estheticism and a consequent ready and accurate discernment in works of literature and art.

School and College When the school period includes residence in the elementary and preparatory institutions, as well as in the college, the influence upon the individual is proportionately more vital. Such

---

[1] " The possession of this lordly and historic domain was an inspiration in itself."—*Encyclopedia Britannica*.

"A half-ruined palace, indeed, but spacious, magnificent, inspiring, and the impression for good and for evil was indelible."—E. H. Coleridge, Introductory Memoir, *Byron's Poems.* Cf., " Elegy on Newstead Abbey," " Newstead Abbey," and *Don Juan* XIII, 55-72.

[2] See Chapter III.

was true of the English system a century ago,[1] a fact often not understood by the American student. And Byron's case was typical. Indeed he hardly knew a home outside of school walls during the whole of his boyhood.[2] And yet his entire scholastic career, long as it was, was, in what it professed to offer, a much less important influence in his life than either his birthright or his early environment. The curricula and discipline of those " exclusively classical institutions " chafed rather than stimulated his free spirit. At Dulwich, Harrow, and Cambridge he had the narrow range of subjects administered to him with all the pedantic exactions and dry literalness that belonged to the time, till there is little wonder that the boy rebelled against the regïme.[3] The result is, his school record, interpreted only in a decorous and scholarly light, is unflattering.[4]

[1] " One of the most striking results of the English system of education is, that while in no country are there so many instances of manly friendships early formed and steadily maintained, so in no other country, perhaps, are the feelings toward the parental home so early estranged, or, at the best, feebly cherished."—Moore, *Life* I, 65.

[2] "You must excuse my being a little cynical, knowing how my *temper* was tried in my Non-age; the manner in which I was brought up must necessarily have broken a meek Spirit, or rendered a fiery one ungovernable; the effect it has had on mine I need not state."— *L. & J.* II, 13. Cf. *L. & J.* I, 43, and Cp. *ibid.*, 44, 53.

[3]   " I abhorred
  Too much to conquer for the Poet's sake,
  The drilled dull lesson, forced down word by word
  In my repugnant youth."—*Childe Harold* IV, 75.

[4] His indifference has the customary applause from his biographers. " He was a great lover of sports, and preferred hockey to Horace, relinquished even Helicon for ' duck-puddle,' and gave up the best poet that ever wrote hard Latin for a game of cricket on the common."— J. W. Lake, *Life*, x f., reported from an unnamed school fellow. " He was above studying the poetics, and held the rules of the Stagyrite in as little esteem as in after-life he did the 'invariable principles' of the Reverend Mr. Bowles."—*Ibid.* Such habits bode ill for the accurate scholar, if well for the original genius.

Moore is more charitable still:—" Nor is it genius only that thus rebels at the discipline of the schools. Even the tamer quality of Taste,

His schooling began in his fifth year, with results that resembled Oriental attainments, from their dependence upon
sheer memory.[1] He next passed through the hands of a very
" decent, clever, little Clergyman " by the name of Ross,
under whom he began to acquire that delight in history,[2]
which later became so marked with him.   His third preceptor was a " very serious, saturnine, but kind young man "
named Paterson, with whom he began and continued Latin,[3]
while he was yet under six years of age.   It was here that
the classics, which were at the root of his avowed critical
system, began their effects.   From what has already been
learned of his responsive nature, the ultimate results are
not surprising.

He was just on the threshold of his seventh year when he
was placed in the Aberdeen Grammar School.   There he
threaded his way to the fourth form, without distinction,
but with a reputation for mental alertness and a delight
in history and romance.   After one of the most mixed

which it is the professed object of classical studies to cultivate, is sometimes found to turn restive under the pedantic *manège* to which it is
subjected."—*Life* I, 198.

[1] " I was sent at five years old, or earlier, to a school kept by a Mr.
Bowers, who was called ' *Bodsy* Bowers ' by reason of his dapperness.
It was a school for both sexes.   I learned little there, except to repeat
by rote the first lesson of Monosyllables—' God made man, let us love
him '—by hearing it often repeated, without acquiring a letter.   Whenever proof was made of my progress at home, I repeated these words
with the most rapid fluency ; but on turning over a new leaf, I continued
to repeat them, so that the narrow boundaries of my first year's accomplishments were detected, my ears boxed (which they did not deserve,
seeing that it was by *ear* only that I had acquired my letters), and my
intellects consigned to a new preceptor."—" My Dictionary," *L. & J.*
V, 406.

[2] " The moment I could read, my grand passion was *history* ; and
why, I know not, but I was particularly taken with the battle near
the lake Regillus in the Roman History, put into my hands the first."—
" My Dictionary," *L & J.* V, 406.

[3] " He was the son of my Shoemaker, but a good Scholar, as is
common with the Scotch.   He was a rigid Presbyterian also.   With him
I began Latin in Ruddiman's Grammar, and continued till I went
to the ' Grammar School.' "—" My Dictionary," *L. & J.* V, 407.

school careers, which was to continue in much the same way afterwards, he was recalled to England by the accidental circumstances which brought him his title.[1]

Byron's English schooling was really the important one with him. It meant a real severance of home ties, or all that he had known as home ties, and the new relationships of school had to take their place. Moreover, he now occupied the totally different station of a peer of England, and his own purposes and training, so far as the latter could be exceptional, had to be modified accordingly.

Because of his malformed limb his schooling for the first year after his return was only incidental to other interests. At his own request, however, he read Cicero and Virgil under a tutor by the name of Rogers, "a pensioned American royalist," much to the satisfaction of both master and pupil. But at the end of the summer vacation, 1799, he was placed in residence in a preparatory school at Dulwich. He remained there for the better part of two years, but was subjected to many and causeless interruptions by Mrs. Byron, until by her importunities Lord Carlisle was prevailed upon to remove him from the school. He left Dulwich with a record for omnivorous reading, particularly in poetry, for the maintenance of his fondness for history, for a familiarity with the Bible, and for his " first dash into poetry."[2]

His change from Dulwich to Harrow was immediate, only a brief summer vacation intervening. The selection of the new school was fortunate. His training there, in a strictly

[1] " I went to the ' Grammar School ' (*Scotice* ' Schule '—*Aberdonice* ' Squeel '), where I threaded all the Classes to the *fourth*, when I was re-called to England (where I had been hatched) by the demise of my Uncle."—" My Dictionary," *L. & J*. V, 407.

[2] *L. & J*. V, 449. Significant of future critical power at the time is a remark by John Hanson, the shrewd solicitor for the estates of the young ward, in a letter to Mrs. Byron early in the Dulwich period :— " He has Ability and a quickness of Conception, and a correct Discrimination that is seldom seen in a youth."—*L. & J*. I, 10, footnote 1.

academic way, must be regarded as the most important of his life. He needed a great public school to make up for the deficiencies of his earlier desultory training, one that could command his respect and at the same time enlist his sympathy.[1] His residence at Harrow was longer, more intimate, and less interrupted, than his residence at any other institution. Furthermore, he was happier there, for at least a part of the time, than at any other place, perhaps than at any other period of his life.[2] It was as nearly a real home as he ever knew.[3] The result was that his scholastic echoes in after life were more of Harrow, except for a few larger perquisites which only the University could offer, than of Trinity College itself.

On the whole, Byron made good at Harrow his Dulwich reputation.[4] The classics, which he had begun early and

---

[1] " Its ' aristocratic ' character was developed under Dr. Drury, who was master in Byron's time."—Robt. Pitcairn, *Harrow School.* This character was not the least cause of Byron's satisfaction in the school. Harrow was in its greatest period at the time. " The greatest number of scholars that ever was upon the establishment at the same time was in 1804, when Dr. Drury had under him 353 students, of whom one was Byron."—Finden's *Illustrations of the Life and Works of Lord Byron,* III.

[2] " I believe no one could, or can be, more attached to Harrow than I have always been, and with reason ;—a part of the time passed there was the happiest of my life."—*Childe Harold* IV, note to stanza 75.

[3]   " Ah ! sure some stronger impulse vibrates here,
    Which whispers friendship will be doubly dear
    To one, who thus for kindred hearts must roam,
    And seek abroad, the love denied at home.
    Those hearts, dear *Ida,* have I found in thee,
    A home, a world, a paradise to me."—*Childish Recollections.*

[4] For the last very few months of his residence at Harrow, after the change of headmasters, which he greatly resented, " he behaved in a rebellious, high-spirited, poetical fashion " (J. F. Williams, *Harrow,* 75), but this was not characteristic of his whole career. The outgoing headmaster, Dr. Drury, who was in charge of the school for almost the whole of Byron's career there, and for fifteen or more years before, had " won the wayward reverence of the future Sultan of English Literature, Lord Byron " (*Ibid.,* 74). But even Dr. Drury at one time thought of sending him away. See *L. & J.* I, 52, note.

pursued for a while at his own election, in their complete usurpation of the school curriculum,[1] and in the painful, uninspired way in which they were taught, failed to hold his interest,[2] and he found attraction in the wider range of English literature and in attaining a command of French. These new interests constituted an acquisition which was none the worse for the critic, if worse for the traditional scholar.

At no part of the time, and in no subject, was he a deep or accurate scholar,[3] either from deliberate choice or from a wilful lack of application,[4] in accordance with what seems

---

[1] See Appendix C, I, J. F. Williams, *Harrow*, 210, for a "Week's Business in Dr. Drury's Time."

[2] Cf., " That harmonious plagiary and miserable flatterer, whose cursed hexameters were drilled into me at Harrow."—*L. & J.* IV, 103 f. " Not from dislike to the poet, but a well-founded horror of hexameters. Indeed, the public school penance of ' Long and Short ' is enough to beget an antipathy to poetry for the residue of a man's life."—*Hints from Horace*, prose note to 226.

> " Then farewell, Horace—whom I hated so,
> Not for thy faults, but mine : it is a curse
> To understand, not feel thy lyric flow,
> To comprehend, but never love thy verse."
> —*Childe Harold* IV, 77.

" I wish to express, that we become tired of the task before we can comprehend the beauty; that we learn by rote before we can get by heart; that the freshness is worn away, and the future pleasure and advantage deadened and destroyed, by the didactic anticipation, at an age when we can neither feel nor understand the power of compositions which it requires an acquaintance with life, as well as Latin and Greek, to relish, or to reason upon. . . . I certainly do not speak on this point from any pique or aversion towards the place of my education."—*Childe Harold* IV, note to 75.

[3] His Latin and Greek texts were marked and underlined here and there, with the English equivalents written over often very ordinary words. Cf. Moore, *Life* I, 88. And, " He absorbed a good deal of scholarship without ever becoming a good scholar in the technical sense."— Gribble, *The Love Affairs of Lord Byron*, 17.

[4] " I was not a slow, though an idle boy."—*Childe Harold* IV, note to 75.

" He could run level with Sir Robert Peel, who afterward took a sensational double first at Oxford."— Gribble, *The Love Affairs*, etc., 17. Peel later became Prime Minister.

c

to have been a certain kind of Harrovian ideal at the time.[1] Dr. Drury discovered " mind in his eye " upon a first impression of him. In one academic attainment, declamation, he rose to distinction, from his proficiency in which he long entertained the notion of entering a parliamentary career.[2] In brief, at Harrow he displayed just those qualities for which his criticism is noted, to wit, quickness of perception, nice discernment, ready reactiveness, but never persistent application.[3] His criticism is the natural outgrowth of his school life there and elsewhere, but as such it was derived more from native than from acquired elements in him.

Byron proceeded to Trinity College, Cambridge, from Harrow, after the summer vacation of 1805, with his academic habits pretty well fixed. Doubtless he went with the aim of acquiring knowledge—he was too alert mentally to be satisfied with complete indolence—yet with

---

[1] See Jeaffreson, *The Real Lord Byron*, Chapter VII. A particular phase of this ideal—indifference to spelling in the mother tongue—Byron exemplified very fully.

> " I don't much pique myself upon orthography,
> So that I do not grossly err in facts."—*Don Juan* VIII, 74.

Moore says: " Spelling, indeed, was a very late accomplishment with him."—*Diary*, Jan. 22, 1828.

[2] " My qualities were much more oratorical and martial, than poetical; and Dr. D., my grand patron (our headmaster), had a great notion that I should turn out an Orator, from my fluency, my turbulence, my voice, my copiousness of declamation, and my action. I remember that my first declamation astonished him into some unwonted (for he was economical of such), and sudden compliments, before the declaimers at our first rehearsal. My first Harrow verses (that is, English as exercises), a translation of a chorus from the Prometheus of Aeschylus, were received by him but cooly (sic) : no one had the least notion that I should subside into poesy."—" Detached Thoughts," *L. & J.* V, 453. Cf. *ibid.*, 414 f., and II, 338-9.

[3] " Notwithstanding his backwardness in the mere verbal scholarship, on which so large and precious a portion of life is wasted, in all that general and miscellaneous knowledge which is alone useful in the world, he was making rapid and even wonderful progress."—Moore, *Life* I, 89.

The Countess Guiccioli says, on the authority of D'Israeli, that he was " a studious boy," misunderstood by his masters and fellow students.—*Recollections*, 107.

the notion pretty clearly settled in his mind of playing
the rôle of the typical young undergraduate nobleman, of
profiting from the larger privileges wherever it suited his
native craving to do so, but of maintaining at least an air
and semblance of disdain for the routine of work as unworthy
of his rank and pretensions. And this is just about what
Lord Byron did in his university career.[1]

The curriculum of Cambridge at the time comprised not
much more than the classics, some history, theology, logic,
philosophy, and the elements of mathematics. Greek and
Latin were the great essentials. The requirements of residence and attendance upon lectures were slight enough for
the regular candidates for the classical bachelor's degree;
for the nobleman's degree,[2] which presumably was Byron's
aim from his entrance, they were hardly more than nominal. Byron's work in the regular subjects, or in any
assigned duty or task, as may be supposed, was performed

[1] His habits there, as has been waggishly remarked, are best described
in the titlé he chose for his first regular volume of verse, " Hours of
Idleness." But allowance must be made for exaggeration in any
attempt at self-portraiture which he makes. At the beginning of his
career he says :—" College improves in everything but Learning.
Nobody here seems to look into an Author, ancient or modern, if they
can avoid it. The Muses, poor Devils, are totally neglected, except
by a few musty old *Sophs* and *Fellows*, who, however agreeable they
may be to *Minerva*, are perfect Antidotes to the *Graces*. Even I (great
as is my *inclination* for Knowledge) am carried away by the Tide."—
L. & J. I, 83. " Improvement at an English University to a Man of
Rank is, you know, impossible, and the very Idea *ridiculous*."—
L. & J. I, 95. Cf. *ibid.*, 84.

Mrs. Byron speaks equally as disparagingly toward the end of his
second year :—" I do not know what to say about Byron's returning
to Cambridge. When he was there, I believe he did nothing but drink,
gamble and spend money."—Letter to Hanson, *L. & J.* I, 129, footnote.
Cf. *L. & J.* I, 133.

[2] " The preponderance of external considerations with the acade-
micians of that day, may be seen in the favor shown to men of rank
in taking degrees : a favor which had long been occasionally bestowed,
but was looked on as a great abuse. It was now established by statute."
—*The English Universities* I, 329, Huber-Newman. This was in the
time of Elizabeth. The action followed her visits to the two great
universities.

in an indifferent spirit and a perfunctory way, as was becoming to his nature.[1]

But his attainments in Latin and Greek must not be rated too cheaply, from the less prominent position of these subjects in American curricula to-day.[2] His juvenile poems show an acquaintance with more classical authors than the modern bachelor of arts could name offhand.[3] His *Hints from Horace*, upon which he set considerable store at one time in his life, and his resort to Latin for the purposes of conversation at times in his travel abroad, prove that he was not ill-grounded in the subjects, if he was somewhat lacking in a full technical knowledge of them.

He received the Master of Arts degree from Trinity College in the spring of 1808.[4] He was entitled to this distinction, having fulfilled the formal requirements. For almost the whole of the year previous to his taking the degree, he was absent in London.

If there was a single achievement of his entire Cambridge

---

[1] His neglect of duties is not to be attributed too much to his preference for Oxford,—an excuse he made later, and one that his biographers are too prone to accept. His own testimony at the time disproves any objection that he could have felt to the choice of Cambridge instead :—" Mr. H. Recommends Cambridge ; Lord Carlisle allows me to chuse for myself, and I must own I prefer Oxford. But, I am not violently bent upon it, and whichever is determined upon will meet with my concurrence."—*L. & J.* I, 56. Cf. *L. & J.* V, 122, 445. He was simply " constitutionally " unhappy at being away from Harrow, and would have been equally so at Oxford.

[2] " Of the classics, I know about as much as most schoolboys after a discipline of thirteen years."—*L. & J.* I, 172. " I make no pretensions to a Knowledge of any thing but a Greek Grammer (*sic*) or a Racing Calendar."—*L. & J.* I, 139.

[3] Hodgson represents Byron at the time as an indifferent classical scholar, and says his reading of the Latin and Greek authors, Livy, Tacitus, Thucydides, Xenophon, Plutarch, etc. must have been done in translations. (See *Memoirs*, etc., II, 206). Hodgson was a tutor in Cambridge for the full time of his acquaintance with Byron there.

[4] "*Alma Mater* was to me *injusta noverca*; and the old beldam only gave me my M. A. degree because she could not avoid it.—You know what a farce a noble Cantab. must perform."—*L. & J.* I, 218. Cf. *ibid.*, footnote 2, and *ibid.*, 172.

career that was worthy of his great powers, it was the production of his *Hours of Idleness.* The volume contains in a small way some actual criticism, and thus marks his appearance as a critic.

Byron's study at Cambridge was precisely the kind of work one would expect as preparation for his criticism. It was always privileged and impressionistic. But even in his desultory way he submitted to the regime on its purely academic side sufficiently to make his critical system a thing apart from his creative practice. If he had led a more studious and exemplary life, it is not unreasonable to suppose that he might have become a confirmed classicist, which inevitably would have been to stultify his poetry. If he could but have come to possess the deeper knowledge, which only faithful study and close application can bring, and kept his spirit free to make his criticism one with his great poetry, his career would have been eventful in criticism as it was in poetry. But such a thing was impossible with his exquisitely formed nature. His poetry is as free as Ariel and as great as it is free. His criticism is the same free spirit pent in the oak of his classical training. It is well that during his school career he followed his own instinctive guidance in his pursuit of knowledge.

Friendships If Byron was indifferent to the requirements of the several schools he attended, he was keenly alive to some of their privileges. His home relations were pathetically inadequate, but the compensation to him in school friendships was as nearly ample as such things could be. Some of the earlier attachments of the kind seem downright sentimental in their ardor and effusiveness. Later in his college career, with one or two exceptions, they were more manly in character, were longer in duration, and consequently they exerted a greater and more wholesome influence on his life and habits of thought.   His friends were never ill-chosen, they were often beneath him in rank, and apparently they always reciprocated his feelings fully.   The circle was never large,[1] owing to a natural shyness on his part, but the ties were strong.[2] And the time at which they occurred, the most susceptible years of an ever susceptible and responsive life, makes them forces to be reckoned with in any analysis of his character.[3]

But for such friendships as would tend to make him a critic, the elementary school associates [4] may be ignored, and the attention centered on the university group.   It was indeed an assemblage of talent, as rich in quality as the celebrated " Apostles " of Tennyson-Hallam fame a few years later.   The members were few,[5] but the personnel was as distinguished perhaps as ever was found in a group at a university.   By a congeniality of temperaments they developed into a literary coterie, confessed or not, which

---

[1] Cp., " Of *Friends* I've known a *goodly Hundred*—
  For finding *one* in each acquaintance,
  By *some deceiv'd*, by others plunder'd,
    Friendship, to me, was not *Repentance.*"—" Egotism," 9,
in *Hours of Idleness.*

[2] " My school friendships were with *me passions* " (" Detached Thoughts," *L. & J.* V, 455), he declared in 1821, when all youthful exaggeration was past.   The overpowering sensation he felt on meeting the Earl of Clare in Italy in the same year, whom he had not seen for a number of years, proves the strength of some of those ties.   See " Detached Thoughts," *L. & J.* V, 455, 463, " To the Earl of Clare " in *Hours of Idleness*, etc.

[3] "Wir sind also wohlberechtigt zu sagen, daß der Einfluß der Schulfreunde auf Byrons Lehren äußerst wichtig war."—F. A. Milledge, *Byrons Beziehungen*, etc.

[4] To mention *en passant*: Peel, the later Prime Minister; Long, who went with Byron to Cambridge but withdrew at the end of the first year and was drowned in 1809, too early for fame to have come to him; the Earl of Clare, who became Governor of Bombay; Bryan Waller Procter, though less intimately, the well-known " Barry Cornwall " later; and certainly the eminent Dr. Drury, who was to Byron the first of all Harrovians (Cf. *L. & J.* I, 49 f., *C. H.* IV, 75, footnote, etc.).

[5] Jeaffreson gives only six, including Byron—*The Real Lord Byron*, Chap. IV.

exercised an influence on the individual members that was incalculable. Byron's responsive nature cannot have resisted the elevating influences of such associations.

The real character of the group can be judged only from the later achievements of the individuals.[1] William Harness [2] became the well-known scholar and editor of Shakespeare and other Elizabethan dramatists, a sermon writer of renown, and an able biographer. Francis Hodgson, with whom friendship was formed rather late at Cambridge, " rhymed with an ease that almost rivals that of Byron," [3] in Latin as well as in English, and in both original and translated works. The amount of his poetry was great, and its quality was inferior only to the really great poetry of the day. William Bankes, who " ruled the roast, or rather the *roasting* " [4] at Trinity College, produced a notable work of archeological research, made and published a translation of Finati's Italian *Narrative*, and occupied a seat in Parliament for a number of sessions. Charles Skinner Matthews, whom Byron calls the idol of his admiration at College, was by common consent the genius of the group, as gifted a man as ever enrolled in either of the great English

---

[1] "There is hardly one of my School and College contemporaries that has not turned out more or less celebrated."—*L & J.* V, 68. "You will see some of our old college contemporaries turned into lords of the Treasury, Admiralty, and the like,—others become reformers and orators,—many settled in life, as it is called,—and others settled in death."—*L. & J.* IV, 378. By " contemporaries " in both passages he means friends and acquaintances.

"Whatever he did or failed to do, he made friends who were worthy of his choice."—*Encyclopædia Britannica*, referring specifically to his Cambridge period.

[2] Friendship with Harness began at Harrow, but a coolness between them arose over a literary matter, and their intimacy was not reestablished until just before the close of Byron's Cambridge career, from which time their friendship continued uninterruptedly. Cf. *L. & J.* I, 218.

[3] *L. & J.* I, 195, footnote 1.

[4] *L. & J.* V, 123.

universities. He died by accident in 1811, too early for his
great talent to have begun to fulfil its fine promise. But he
was already productive in a literary way, as we know from
the body of manuscript which almost certainly he left at his
death.[1] John Cam Hobhouse, who was associated with
Byron longer and more intimately than any other person,
produced a creditable volume of verse two years after
Byron's *Hours of Idleness,* directed many of the artistic
excursions in *Childe Harold,* wrote and published various
works,[2] and was indeed, to borrow Byron's own correct critical phrase, " a much better proser and scholar than I am."[3]
Finally, Scrope Berdmore Davies, whom Byron called " one
of the cleverest men I ever knew," was occupied, according
to report, for a number of years in writing up recollections
of his illustrious friends, but he died without having produced the work, and his notes were not recovered.

To the list must be added the chorister Edleston, who
was Byron's almost constant companion at Cambridge for
the first year and a half of residence.[4] He won his place
in Byron's esteem by an artistic talent that was entirely
different from the others, his musical voice. But like some
of the other friends, who had the fortune, or fate, to come
intimately into the poet's life for awhile, he died too early
for fame to have come to him. Byron's fondness for music

[1] "What became of his *papers* (and he certainly had many), at the
time of this death, was never known."—*L. & J.* I, 153. For Byron's
estimate of the man compare *L. & J.* I, 150—160, 324 f., 338; II, 8,
29, 33; and V, 116 f., 121-8; *Childe Harold* I, note 19, etc. Byron
showed a really subservient spirit, consistently so, to only one man,
William Gifford. If there was a second, it was Matthews.

[2] Cf., " Oh thou with pen perpetual in thy fist."—" Farewell
Petition to J. C. H., Esqre."

[3] *L. & J.* III, 178.

[4] " I rejoice to hear you are interested in my *protégé*; he has been
my *almost constant* associate since October, 1805, when I entered
Trinity College. His *voice* first attracted my attention, his *countenance*
fixed it, and his *manners* attached me to him for ever."—*L. & J.*
I, 133-4.

later was, to some extent certainly, cultivated by his association with Edleston.

Imagination is prone to picture Byron as the center of this brilliant group, and as the soul which drew it together and enlisted its interest in artistic subjects. But in all probability, he was the least compelling force in the whole body, as he was certainly the least assertive member of its sub-committee—Bankes, Davies, Matthews, Hobhouse, and Byron. He was made of more impressionable material than any, and consequently was affected most, and in a way that bore directly upon criticism.

Second in importance only to the University group were a few select personages outside, who came intimately into the poet's life at about the same time with the brilliant student fraternity. John and Elizabeth Pigot, of Southwell, were both deeply interested in literary matters, and encouraged the young poet's muse through the Cambridge vacations. The former had a turn for verse-making, and at one time held a correspondence with Byron in verse.[1] The Rev. John T. Becher, later the author of three sociological works of temporary importance, was a wholesome critic of Byron's early poems. He rhymed fluently himself, expostulated kindly but firmly with Byron over a too strong amatory strain in some of his verses,[2] prevailed upon him to destroy the worst offenders, and happily guided the early lyrical flights. Robert Charles Dallas, a kinsman by marriage, was a poet and novelist of limited fame before Byron's appearance. Coming into the chosen circle after the *Hours of Idleness*, he wrought for a higher moral tone in Byron's subsequent poetry, conducted the *English Bards*

---

[1] Cf., " Reply to Some Verses of J. M. B. Pigot, Esq.," and " To the Sighing Strephon," in *Hours of Idleness*.

[2] See *L. & J.* I, 182 f. Cf., " Egotism, A Letter to J. T. Becher," in *Hours of Idleness*.

and Scotch Reviewers through its chequered growth, and discovered *Childe Harold.*[1]

Among the Southwell friends were the Leacrofts, who demand mention not for any literary influence which they exerted but for their interest in another great branch of art, with which later Byron was associated in various capacities.[2] The private theatricals of the autumn of 1806, in which Byron found such delight, were given under their favor and patronage. Byron was "chief mover of the project," developed into "the star of the company," and in the several performances "repeatedly brought down the house with his acting."[3] The vocal quality of his poetry is doubtless the effect of the same talent and training. Certainly his expanding artistic sense received a happy stimulus from the experience.

Byron left England almost immediately after the appearance of his satire, and by so doing virtually closed the door to the further refining influences of gifted friends during his plastic years. Hobhouse accompanied him on the trip, remained with him for the greater part of the time abroad, and directed many of his interests on the way. But there is no evidence that any new friendships were formed that could have made any very ennobling and lasting impressions upon him. Soon after his return in the summer of 1811, he found himself famous, and thus was brought into contact with such "leaders in art and letters" as "Sir Humphrey Davy, the Edgeworths, Sir James Mackintosh, Colman the

---

[1] Byron acknowledged his indebtedness to Dallas by dedications and the profits arising from copyrights of several of his works.

[2] See Chapters V, 106 f. and VIII, 252 f.

[3] See *L. & J.* I, 117 f. Apparently two plays, Cumberland's *Wheel of Fortune* and Allingham's *Weathercock*, comprised the repertoire of the company. Byron's name appears first on the list of characters in each play, as Penruddock in the first and as Tristram Fickle in the second. His interest in amateur theatricals was continued at Newstead. See *L. & J.* I, 189.

dramatic author, the elder Kean, Monk Lewis, Grattan, Curran, and Madame de Staël," [1] and we must add, pre-eminently, among "the better brethren," Sheridan, Thomas Moore and Samuel Rogers. But by this time he was several years in his majority, celebrated enough to attract illustrious friendships, and mature enough to exert a critical influence greater than he in turn could feel. His friends thereafter were talented and artistic,[2] but his growth had been attained, hence they are not to be reckoned as permanently affecting his tastes and temper in his equipment for a critical career.

It is noteworthy that his formative friendships were with men of talent and wit, and it is remarkable that this talent and wit, almost without exception, was displayed conspicuously in a literary way, while he, with "qualities much more oratorical and martial, than poetical," [3] was contemplating a parliamentary career. Such influences at such a time may have gone far in attracting him into a literary life at all. But if his poetical character was pre-determined by other and more elemental causes, still his constant and close association with such choice spirits could not but have heightened his artistic ideals, and given him those habits of judgment that are vital to criticism.

Reading If nature gave Byron a single indispensable critical asset, it was a good memory.[4] But almost equal to his great memory, and certainly necessary for the fullest development, was his quickness of perception, a quality noted by all his tutors and associates.[5] To add

---

[1] Nichol, *Byron*, 78.

[2] " The intimates of Byron through life were persons distinguished for their talents and wit."—Roden Noel, *Byron*, 64.

[3] " Detached Thoughts," *L. & J.* V, 453.

[4] " Having a memory only less retentive than Macaulay's."—Nichol, *Byron*, 27.

[5] His " rapid eye and retentive memory."—Moore, *Life* VI, 87. For Byron's characterization of his own eyesight, see *L. & J.* V, 409-10.

a third, a desire to know,[1] and give him the means and leisure with which to gratify it, all of which Byron had abundantly, was to make the Baconian "full man," in his instance, an assured product.[2]

Byron freely indulged almost from infancy in the habit of reading, but the time of its greatest importance to him was the period of his youth and adolescence. Reading was then his mental and esthetical meat and drink. His natural craving for it was doubtless whetted by the narrow range of studies at both school and college. His native independence taught him to seek it, and his " will, that walked astray," [3] rebelling at academic restraint, led him to turn to it often at the expense of the delegated task, thus marring the exact scholar perhaps, but not the poet and critic.

Before he left Scotland he had read far more than the average boy of his age.[4] At Dulwich the amount was immense, including a formidable set of the English poets from Chaucer to Churchill.[5] At Harrow it was enormous. The list of his reading up to the time is given by himself " hastily and promiscuously scribbled out " from memory, with several omissions. The whole catalogue must be given in full for the reader to appreciate its great variety and astonishing extent.

<hr>

[1] " Great as is my *inclination* for Knowledge."—*L. & J.* I, 83.

[2] It may be interesting to note that Byron took occasion more than once to correct Bacon in his historical references.   See *L. & J.* V, Appendix VI, 597 f., and *Don Juan* V, 147, footnote.

[3] " Epistle to Augusta," stanza 4.

[4] "A surprising list of books read by him before he was ten."— Roden Noel, *Byron*, 33.

[5] " In my study he found many books open to him, both to please his taste and gratify his curiosity; among others, a set of our poets from Chaucer to Churchill, which I am almost tempted to say he had more than once perused from beginning to end."—Dr. Glennie, reported by Moore, *Life* I, 46.   The set comprised one hundred and nine volumes. See L. Fuhrmann, *Die Belesenheit des jungen Byron*.

LIST OF HISTORICAL WRITERS WHOSE WORKS
I HAVE PERUSED IN DIFFERENT LANGUAGES.

History of England.—Hume, Rapin, Henry, Smollet, Tindal, Belsham, Bisset, Adolphus, Holinshed, Froissart's Chronicles (belonging properly to France).

Scotland.—Buchanan, Hector Boethius, both in the Latin.

Ireland.—Gordon.

Rome.—Hooke, Decline and Fall by Gibbon, Ancient History by Rollin (including an account of the Carthaginians, &c.), besides Livy, Tacitus, Eutropius, Cornelius Nepos, Julius Caesar, Arrian, Sallust.

Greece.—Mitford's Greece, Leland's Philip, Plutarch, Potter's Antiquities, Xenophon, Thucydides, Herodotus.

France.—Mezeray, Voltaire.

Spain.—I chiefly derived my knowledge of old Spanish History from a book called the Atlas, now obsolete. The modern history, from the intrigues of Alberoni down to the Prince of Peace, I learned from its connection with European politics.

Portugal.—From Vertot; as also his account of the Siege of Rhodes,—though the last is his own invention, the real facts being totally different.—So much for his Knights of Malta.

Turkey.—I have read Knolles, Sir Paul Rycaut, and Prince Cantemir, besides a more modern history, anonymous. Of the Ottoman History I know every event, from Tangralopi, and afterwards Othman I., to the peace of Passarowitz, in 1718,—the battle of Cutzka, in 1739, and the treaty between Russia and Turkey in 1790.

Russia.—Tooke's Life of Catherine II., Voltaire's Czar Peter.

Sweden.—Voltaire's Charles XII, also Norberg's Charles XII. —in my opinion the best of the two—A translation of Schiller's Thirty Years' War, which contains the exploits of Gustavus Adolphus, besides Harte's Life of the same Prince. I have somewhere, too, read an account of Gustavus Vasa, the deliverer of Sweden, but do not remember the author's name.

Prussia.—I have seen, at least, twenty Lives of Frederick II., the only prince worth recording in Prussian annals. Gillies,

his own Works, and Thiebault,—none very amusing. The last
is paltry, but circumstantial.

Denmark.—I know little of. Of Norway I understand the
natural history, but not the chronological.

Germany.—I have read long histories of the house of Suabia,
Wenceslaus, and, at length, Rodolph of Hapsburgh and his
thick-lipped Austrian descendants.

Switzerland.—Ah! William Tell, and the battle of Morgarten,
where Burgundy was slain.

Italy.—Davila, Guicciardini, the Guelphs and Ghibellines,
the battle of Pavia, Massaniello, the revolutions of Naples, &c. &c.

Hindostan.—Orme and Cambridge.

America.—Robertson, Andrews' American War.

Africa.—merely from travels, as Mungo Park, Bruce.

BIOGRAPHY.

Robertson's Charles V.—Caesar, Sallust (Catiline and Jugurtha),
Lives of Marlborough and Eugene, Tekeli, Bonnard, Buonaparte,
all the British Poets, both by Johnson and Anderson, Rousseau's
Confessions, Life of Cromwell, British Plutarch, British Nepos,
Campbell's Lives of the Admirals, Charles XII., Czar Peter,
Catherine II., Henry Lord Kaimes, Marmontel, Teignmouth's
Sir William Jones, Life of Newton, Belisaire, with thousands
not to be detailed.

LAW.

Blackstone, Montesquieu.

PHILOSOPHY.

Paley, Locke, Bacon, Hume, Berkeley, Drummond, Beattie,
and Bolingbroke. Hobbes I detest.

GEOGRAPHY.

Strabo, Cellarius, Adams, Pinkerton, and Guthrie.

POETRY.

All the British Classics as before detailed, with most of the
living poets, Scott, Southey, &c.—Some French, in the original,

of which the Cid is my favourite.—Little Italian.—Greek and Latin without number ,—these last I shall give up in future.— I have translated a good deal from both languages verse as well as prose.

ELOQUENCE

Demosthenes, Cicero, Quintilian, Sheridan, Austin's Chironomia, and Parliamentary Debates from the Revolution to the year 1742.

DIVINITY

Blair, Porteus, Tillotson, Hooker,—all very tiresome. I abhor books of religion, though I reverence and love my God, without the blasphemous notions of sectaries, or belief in their absurd and damnable heresies, mysteries, and Thirty-nine Articles.

MISCELLANIES

Spectator, Rambler, World, &c. &c.—Novels by the thousand.[1]

He adds, casually, " I have also read (to my regret at present) above four thousand novels, including the works of Cervantes, Fielding, Smollet, Richardson, Mackenzie, Sterne, Rabelais, and Rousseau, &c. &c."

The only adequate commentary indeed at such an array of reading matter is *mirabile dictu*!—at the impossible amount, except for genius, if true; at the poet's presumptuous imagination, if not.[2]

---

[1] Moore, *Life* I, 140 f. Byron explains in a paragraph following:— " 'All the books here enumerated I have taken down from memory. I recollect reading them, and can quote passages from any mentioned. I have, of course, omitted several in my catalogue; but the greater part of the above I perused before the age of fifteen.' "

[2] Moore says:—" The list, indeed . . . is such as almost to startle belief,—comprising, as it does, a range and variety of study, which might make much older ' helluones librorum ' hide their heads."— *Life* I, 89 f.

Lescure very properly employs such terms as " la montagne d'érudition," " ces prodigieuses lectures, cosmopolites et encyclopédiques," " colossale nourriture d'une insatiable imagination," and concludes:— " Dans cette vaste ruche, toutes les poésies du monde avaient déposé

Apparently his reading at the University was not so voluminous, possibly from his having acquired an interest in other pursuits not altogether so happy for criticism.[1] But it is not necessary to suppose that there was any very marked cessation of the practice. The time of the " Paphian girls " at the Abbey,[2] when he would least be expected to have followed the habit, was really remarkable for it.[3] More than his poetry even, which he continually

leur miel. La partie consacrée aux écrivains anglais eût fait plier sous son poids toute autre mémoire que cette mémoire héroïque."—*Lord Byron histoire d'un Homme*, 59.

In 1821 Byron reverts to his reading in the Harrow period in a way that corroborates the claim :—" Till I was eighteen years old (odd as it may seem), I had never read a review. But, while at Harrow, my general information was so great on modern topics, as to induce a suspicion that I could only collect so much information from *reviews*, because I was never *seen* reading, but always idle and in mischief, or at play. The truth is that I read eating, read in bed, read when no one else reads ; and had read all sorts of reading since I was five years old, and yet never *met* with a review, which is the only reason that I know of why I should not have read them."—" Detached Thoughts," *L. & J.* V. 452 f.

The only adverse opinion to be met with, among those in position to know, of the almost impossible extent of Byron's reading knowledge, by the time at which most men are only beginning their general reading, is Sir Walter Scott's, in his account of his first meeting with the younger poet :—" Lord Byron's reading did not seem to me to have been very extensive either in poetry or history."—*Recollections of Byron, L. & J.* III, Appendix IV, 412. But Byron was always reticent toward strangers, and Scott he held to be the greatest man of letters of the age. Sir Walter's impression, only a " seeming " at best, is easily explained in the diffidence of the pupil in the presence of the master. The opinion, which Scott used to his own advantage, did not survive closer acquaintance.

[1] " Since I left Harrow, I have become idle and conceited, from scribbling rhyme and making love to women."—Moore, *Life* I, 144. At the close of his Cambridge career, he says :—"As to my reading, I believe I may aver, without hyperbole, it has been tolerably extensive in the historical department ; so that few nations exist, or have existed, with whose records I am not in some degree acquainted, from Herodotus down to Gibbon."—*L. & J.* I, 172.

[2] See *L. & J.* II, 46.

[3] "A great portion of Byron's time used to be spent on the sofa, reading."—Nancy Smith, an old servant at the Abbey, reported by Brecknock, *The Pilgrim Poet*, 60, and the Countess Guiccioli, *My Recollections*, 109. Cf. *L. & J.* I, 205 and 312.

threatened to abandon, reading was the most constant and serious occupation of his life.[1]

While he was not fastidious in subjects or forms, his preference, as manifested early, was history and poetry.[2] The formidable Harrow list is entitled " Historical Writers," though history is only the main division.[3] Of the special departments of the subject, the greater clashes between the civilizations of the East and the West seemed to occupy his interest most. Gibbon was his model, if any individual author among historical writers can be called so.[4] To the end of his life he never lost his liking for history, its great personages and events, but he professed to have changed his taste for poetry.[5] Fiction of the new type developed within his own day, to wit, the historical novel, particularly in the hands of Scott, delighted him all his life.

He was attracted to the Bible very early, as well, through the same partiality for history,[6] and early became familiar

---

[1] " Redde away the time," or some equivalent phrase, is an expression that occurs frequently in his private memoranda. Cf. *L. & J.* II, 389, 410, etc.

[2] " The moment I could read, my grand passion was *history*."— *L. & J.* V, 406. " His reading in history and poetry was far beyond the usual standard of his age."—Dr. Glennie, reported by Moore, *Life* I, 46.

[3] " His list of books, drawn up in 1807, includes more history and biography than most men of education read during a long life."— Nichol, *Byron*, 26.

[4] The tribute to Gibbon, *Childe Harold* III, 105 f., is at the high-water mark of his criticism.

[5] " Her preference of *prose* (strange as it may seem) *was* and indeed *is* mine (for I hate *reading* verse, and always did)."—*L. & J.* VI, 332. The reference is to his daughter. The fond father is too evident in the remark. His requests to Murray to send him such poetical works— if only such—as were deemed worthy, while he was in Italy, proves the contrary. Cf.,

" I hate your poets, so read none of those."—*Don Juan* II, 165.

[6] " He showed at this age an intimate acquaintance with the historical parts of the Holy Scriptures."—Dr. Glennie, reported by Moore, *Life* I, 46.

" Send . . . . A common Bible, of a good legible print (bound in Russia). I *have* one; but as it was the last gift of my Sister (whom

with its literary contents. His knowledge of it at every period of his life is noted by all his biographers. It was a part of his reputation in his last residence in Greece, when the martial spirit was the dominant one.[1] The fact signifies that he had ever before him for critical stimulus and guidance the greatest prose composition that English literature has to offer.[2]

His vast reading, the reader will note, applied particularly and significantly to the two great subjects of history and poetry, the direct sources, according to Bacon, of the great possessions of wisdom and wit, without either of which, whatever his other capital, a man could hardly become even a tolerable critic.[3]

Languages　The best critic is never he whose knowledge of literature and language is confined to one medium. Byron's reading was not restricted to English, notwithstanding his well-known aversion to the usual method of acquiring foreign tongues.[4] In his schooling,[5] and in the associations of his travel, in some way congenial

I shall probably never see again), I can only use it carefully, and less frequently, because I like to keep it in good order. Don't forget this, for I am a great reader and admirer of those books, and had read them through and through before I was eight years old,—that is to say, the *Old* Testament, for the New struck me as a task, but the other as a pleasure. I speak as a *boy*, from the recollected impression of that period at Aberdeen in 1796."—*L. & J.* V, 391.

[1] Dr. Kennedy, the religious controversialist, acknowledged as much, and he was slow to grant Byron any excellence which implied comparison with himself. See his *Conversations*.

[2] See *Byron und die Bibel*, by Arthur Pönitz, for a full account of the subject.

[3] " No man can so ill afford to be ignorant of history as the critic."— C. T. Winchester, *Some Principles of Literary Criticism*, 312.

[4] " I never could learn anything by *study*, not even a language it was all by rote and ear and memory."—" Detached Thoughts," *L. & J.* V, 409.

[5] Notably the formidable Harrow list of readings was " in different languages "—Latin, Greek, French, and a " Little Italian "—other than his own tongue.

to his tastes,[1] he obtained not indeed a scientific mastery, but a practical use of a number of languages other than his own, of their virtues and vices of expression, their capacities and contents, in all that a critic can reasonably require to enrich his equipment and perfect his powers.

Latin and Greek were the prescribed languages of his schooling, and for this reason more than any other they incurred his dislike. But the present day enquirer is apt to overemphasize his " small " of the one and his " less " of the other, from the changes that have taken place since Byron's day, and from Byron's own outcries against them. It is true that he was not a good classical scholar, according to the reckonings of his time, but his training in the classical languages was much longer and fuller than is given in American colleges today. What he could hardly have avoided getting from such long and intimate association with them, would seem pretty large in the modern Bachelor of Art's equipment. In one he attained at least a degree of conversational proficiency,[2] and in the other, even before he left Harrow, a writing command that would not disgrace many a better critic than himself before and since.[3]

---

[1] His " I have taught me other tongues " was not an idle boast. Cf. *Don Juan* II, 164-5.

[2] " I am very happy here, because I loves oranges, and talks bad Latin to the monks, who understand it, as it is like their own."— *L. & J.* I, 233. " There is a convent annexed ; the monks, who possess large revenues, are courteous enough, and understand Latin, so that we had a long conversation."—*L. & J.* I, 237. " I have a Greek interpreter for general use, but a physician of Ali's named Femlario, who understands Latin, acted for me on this occasion."—*L. & J.* I, 250.

[3] "At School, I was . . . . capable of great sudden exertions (such as thirty or forty Greek Hexameters—of course with such prosody as it pleased God)."—" Detached Thoughts," *L. & J.* V, 453. Leigh Hunt, writing spitefully of him at the time, contrary to his own purpose commends him to the present day student of Greek:—" With the ancient language he was so little conversant, that I doubt whether he could read ' Anacreon ' without the help of a dictionary."—*Lord Byron*, 196. For his appreciation of Homer, see *L. & J.* V, 166. Cf. *L. & J.* IV, 174.

The several editors of the 1845 edition of Byron's poems,
whose words ought to be trustworthy in the matter, accord
him an acquaintance with literary Spanish early in his
career.[1] He came into contact with Portuguese at about
the same time, and evidently responded with all the live-
liness of genius to its qualities as a language, but there is
no evidence that his associations with it were literary at all.
Merely the spoken forms, and these, because of his brief
residence, only to a slight extent, were all that was known
to him of it.   But, not to press a point too far, that little
was something to a nature so sensitive and faculties so
receptive as Byron's, in giving him means of comparison,
if only in the single quality of linguistic vehemence.[2]

While in residence in Greece on the famous pilgrimage,
he made a serious effort to attain a mastery of Romaic
or modern Greek, stimulated and assisted by his knowledge
of the ancient language, and was rewarded with more than

---

[1] " Lord Byron seems to have thus early acquired enough of Spanish
to understand and appreciate the great body of ancient popular poetry—
unequalled in Europe—which must ever form the pride of that magnificent language."—Moore, Scott, Jeffrey, Lockhart, Wilson, Campbell,
et al., note to *Childe Harold* I. He seems to have been able to read
Cervantes in the original with appreciation.

> " To read Don Quixote in the original,
> A pleasure before which all others vanish."
> —*Don Juan* XIV, 98.

Compare also his appreciative references to Cervantes elsewhere in the
poem.

The " Modern Languages," constituting his preference at Harrow,
comprised French certainly and perhaps a little Italian, only conceivably
Spanish. His depreciatory " something of two languages " to his sister,
immediately upon his return from the grand tour, included Romaic
and Italian. Cf. *L. & J.* I, 101, 308, *ibid.* IV, 14, 19, 50, and *Correspondence* I, 16, 23, 26, 29.

[2] " When the Portuguese are pertinacious, I say *Carracho* !—the
great oath of the grandees, that very well supplies the place of ' Damme,'
—and, when dissatisfied with my neighbour, I pronounce him *Ambra
di merdo*. With these two phrases, and a third, *Avra bouro*, which
signifieth ' Get an ass,' I am universally understood to be a person
of degree and a master of languages."—*L. & J.* I, 233.

indifferent success.[1]   The same travels included an excursion through Albania, and in part comprised a tour about the Troad in Asia Minor and a trip to and brief residence in Turkey. The experience—something unusual for an Englishman at the time—was novel from a linguistic point of view, as it took him outside the boundaries of the great Western family, or families, of languages, and gave him a taste of the Oriental tongues. But his knowledge of Turkish was slight, and its consequent effect on him was negligible.[2]

Byron's interest in these various languages was greater than his mere temporary residence in the countries in which they were spoken would indicate. He purposed to return

---

[1] " I am going to Athens, to study modern Greek, which differs much from the ancient, though radically similar."—*L. & J.* I, 256. Early in May, 1810, he writes back :—" I speak the Romaic, or Modern Greek, tolerably. It does not differ from the ancient dialects so much as you would conceive ; but the pronounciation is diametrically opposite."—*L. & J.* I, 266. Two days later, with still a year ahead of intimate contact with the language, he says :—" I have lived a good deal with the Greeks, whose modern dialect I can converse in enough for my purposes."—*L. & J.* I. 271.   More than a dozen years later, in reference to an important war document, he says :—" When I left Greece in 1811, I could gabble Romaic pretty fluently ; but have been long out of the habit, and would rather not trust to what I may recollect of it, in a matter of this kind, where it is requisite to make as few mistakes as possible."—*L. & J.* VI, 225. Cf. *ibid.*, 206.
    It is interesting to note that Byron's solicitations for Greece, to visit and know the country in 1809 and to defend it fifteen years later, were actuated first and last by his ideas of ancient Greece derived from the period of his schooling. In 1824 he was fighting more with Alcibiades than with Prince Mavrocordatos. Cf. *L. & J.* I, 266, VI, 283, *The Isles of Greece* 3, *Giaour* 91 f., *Correspondence* II, 285, etc.
    [2] " I can swear in Turkish ; but, except one horrible oath, and ' pimp,' and ' bread,' and ' water,' I have got no great vocabulary in that language."—*L. & J.* I, 266.
    Cf., " Amidst his excursions and amusements, the noble lord devoted much of his time to the attainment of the Romaic or modern language of Greece, and also of the Turkish, which is infinitely more difficult. Of the former he became complete master ; and the notes to his principal poems evince the diligence of his application, and the extent of his acquirements in philological erudition."— John Watkins, *Memoirs*, 125. Hardly less extravagant is Stendhal's account from personal acquaintance at Venice later :—" He can speak the ancient Greek, the modern Greek, and the Arabic."—*L. & J.* IV, 451.

and continue his studies and researches in them until he
mastered them and their contents.[1] But partly from the
shortness of his life, partly from his somewhat weak
submission to circumstances, but mainly from the large
demands made upon him elsewhere in other things, he
was able to accomplish only a portion of so laudable an
ambition.

A further departure into the realm of the unusual in
linguistic study was his attempt at Armenian in 1816, when
he needed " something craggy to break his mind upon,"
although a cultural aim, and consequently a critical reaction, was thus perhaps minimized.[2] But his appreciation
of linguistic and literary values was neither dulled nor
deadened by the unfavorable circumstance. His efforts at
the task were more with the written products, than was the
case in the other languages of his peregrinations, and the
results were a little more permanent.[3]

[1] " I shall return to Spain before I see England, for I am enamoured
of the country."—*L. & J*. I, 236. " I shall find employment in making
myself a good Oriental scholar."—*L. & J*. II, 100. " My hopes are
limited to the arrangement of my affairs, and settling either in Italy
or the East (rather the last), and drinking deep of the languages and
literature of both."—*L. & J*. II, 336.

[2] " By way of divertisement, I am studying daily, at an Armenian
monastery, the Armenian language. I found that my mind wanted
something craggy to break upon; and this—as the most difficult thing
I could discover here for an amusement—I have chosen, to torture
me into attention. It is a rich language, however, and would amply
repay any one the trouble of learning it. I try, and shall go on;—but
I answer for nothing, least of all for my intentions or my success."—
L. & J. IV, 9 f. " I have begun, and am proceeding in, a study of the
Armenian language, which I acquire, as well as I can, at the Armenian
convent, where I go every day to take lessons of a learned Friar, and
have gained some singular and not useless information with regard
to the literature and customs of that oriental people. . . . I find the
language (which is *twin*, the *literal* and ,the *vulgar*) difficult, but not
invincible (at least I hope not). I shall go on. I found it necessary
to twist my mind round some severer study; and this, as being the
hardest I could devise here, will be a file for the serpent."—*L. & J*. IV, 18.

[3] An Armenian-English and an English-Armenian grammar, in
which Byron coöperated, translations of some New Testament epistles
from the Armenian Version of the Bible, and of one or two secular

Of the three great modern languages—German, French and Italian—most closely associated with his own, Byron had a familiar knowledge of but two. He seems never to have spent a serious moment in an effort to learn German. He had very properly a great critical admiration for Goethe, and at times he expressed an admiration for the German people, but for the most part he was apathetic to all things German. He resided only a short while where German was spoken, the time for an interest in the language was not propitious, no real need for its use ever came to him, hence his less than even a meagre acquaintance all his life with this great modern tongue.[1]

Byron's taste for the classics, displayed in his very early schooling, had changed completely to the modern languages by his Harrow period. This preference remained with him through life,[2] thus evincing him, to that extent, not the complete classicist that a superficial knowledge of his critical system would seem to indicate. Unorthodox as his choice may have appeared at the time, it was not because of a simple obstinacy and a purposed hostility to anything that was prescribed or required, but because of the living qualities of the newer languages, and consequently of their great potentialities and possibilities. He took to French at Harrow quite as eagerly, apparently, as to history and

works, were the main results of his studies of the kind. Cf., " I compiled the major part of two Armenian and English Grammars."— " Detached Thoughts," *L. & J.* V, 436. Cf. *ibid.* IV, 26, 41 f, 44, 65, 90, 221, and *Correspondence* II, 26.

[1] " Dined at Interlaken. Girl gave me some flowers, and made me a speech in German, of which I know nothing."—*L. & J.* III, 362. " Of the *real* language I know absolutely nothing,—except oaths learned from postillions and officers in a squabble ! I can *swear* in German potently, when I like—' Sacrament—*Verfluchter—Hundsfott* '— and so forth ; but I have little less of their energetic conversation."— *L. & J.* V, 172. Cf. *L. & J.* V, 33, *Don Juan* X, 71, and *Correspondence* II, 197.

[2] " The pink of all hexameters " (*Don Juan* VI, 18) was the kindest thing he ever said of Horace.

poetry, perhaps for its history and poetry.[1] He seems to have learned it for its literary content only, and for reading he knew it nearly as well as his own tongue. He was sometimes embarrassed at his inability to speak French,[2] but since his residence never required its use, he remained without a conversational command the whole of his life.[3]

It was reserved for Italian, the language of his exile, to attract him most strongly.[4] Its tonal beauty appealed to him more than any, and its great master poets and prose writers he came to know better than those of his own

---

[1] " Comparatively slight stress was then laid on modern languages. Byron learnt to read French with fluency."—Nichol, *Byron*, 26.

The opinion held by some, notably Armstrong and Kennedy, that Byron cherished a dislike for the French nation, language and literature, is ill-founded. The notion is due, if not to excessive John Bull-ism on their own parts, to too slight a knowledge of Byron's character in his habit of scoffing at certain notable individuals of the French nation, Madame de Staël, occasionally, for instance. Napoleon was his idol till his fall, and even then he could not willingly and completely give him up. Byron himself was never remarkable for national prejudices, and after 1816 he could not be said certainly to have had any that favored England. Cf. *L. & J.* IV, 443.

[2] See *L. & J.* III, 101.

[3] " The *Cosmopolite* was an acquisition abroad. I do not believe it is to be found in England. It is an amusing little volume, and full of French flippancy. I read though I do not speak the language."—*L. & J.* II, 44 f. " I can read French with great pleasure and facility, though I neither speak nor write it."—*L. & J.* IV, 209. Cf. *L. & J.* VI, 230. " No one ever heard him utter a word of French, although he was perfectly conversant with that language."—Armstrong, *Life of Byron*, 171. Cf. *Correspondence* II, 167. Byron no more than touched France in any of his travels. Cf. *Correspondence* II, 166.

[4] " He was induced to make the experiment partly by his love for, and partial intercourse with, the Italian language, of which it is so easy to acquire a slight knowledge, and with which it is so nearly impossible for a foreigner to become accurately conversant. The Italian language is like a capricious beauty, who accords her smiles to all, her favours to few, and sometimes least to those who have courted her longest."—Advertisement to *The Morgante Maggiore*.

> " I love the language, that soft bastard Latin,
> Which melts like kisses from a female mouth,
> And sounds as if it should be writ on satin,
> With syllables that breathe of the sweet South,
> And gentle liquids gliding all so pat in,

country, save for the modern period, and his admiration of them was greater. He attained some skill in the use of the tongue during his first pilgrimage,[1] and in his long residence in Italy later he came to prefer it to his native English for reading.[2] From an aggravated sense of his wrongs at his country's hands, he entertained the thought for a while of trusting his immortality to Italian by adopting it as the medium for his great poetry, but he abandoned the idea.[3] His mastery extended to the oral and written uses as well.[4] He resorted to English in conversation and correspondence only for the sake of those who preferred or required it. Indeed Byron's acquaintance with

> That not a single accent seems uncouth,
> Like our harsh northern whistling, grunting guttural,
> Which we are obliged to hiss, and spit, and sputter all."
> —*Beppo*, 44.

"Their own beautiful language," or a like expression, often accompanies any comment on the people or their literature.

[1] "Luckily they speak Italian which I once spoke fluently and have not quite forgotten."—*L. & J.* III, 101. "I read a little, and luckily could speak Italian (more fluently though than accurately) long ago."—*L. & J.* IV, 14. "As for Italian, I am fluent enough, even in its Venetian modification, which is something like the Somersetshire version of English; and as for the more classical dialects, I had not forgot my former practice during my voyage."—*L. & J.* IV, 19.

[2] "You could not oblige me more than by obtaining me the perusal I request, in French or English,—all's one for that, though I prefer Italian to either."—*L. & J.* IV, 209.

[3] Cf. *L. & J.* IV, 284, and,
> "I twine
> My hopes of being remembered in my line
> With my land's language."—*Childe Harold* IV, 9.

[4] In 1818 he says, "Italian I *can* speak with some fluency, and write sufficiently for my purposes."—*L. & J.* IV, 209. Cf. *L. & J.* V, 381, and, "He spoke Italian with great correctness and purity, and with a pronunciation which differed little from that of a native."—Kennedy, *Conversations*, 244.

Moore says of his letters to the Countess Guiccioli, that they were "written with a degree of ease and correctness attained rarely by foreigners" (*Life* IV, 174 f). Both the Countess and her brother, Pietro Gamba, who were in position to know, if perchance their accounts are somewhat colored, testify to the absolute perfection of his letters in Italian. Cf. *L. & J.* IV, 391 f.

Italian was as great as his familiarity with the society and life where it was spoken. He knew the secrets of the government and was familiar with the privacies of Italian homes.[1] In brief, his all but complete Italianation, as it speaks most convincingly of his versatility, was one of the proudest attainments of his life.

It would be untrue to say that Byron was a great polyglot in the technical sense. Those who cherish his memory most would be the first to deny the assertion. His method of approach was always impressionistic,[2] which, from its implied unsoundness, it is the fashion to decry. But in attempting an estimate of his acquisitions in other tongues, several important cautions must be observed. His

---

[1] "What do Englishmen know of Italians beyond their museums and saloons—and some hack * *, *en passant* ? Now, I have lived in the heart of their houses, in parts of Italy freshest and least influenced by strangers,—have seen and become (*pars magna fui*) a portion of their hopes, and fears, and passions, and am almost inoculated into a family. This is to see men and things as they are."—*L. & J.* V, 70 f. Almost half of his Italian residence was still ahead of him at the time.

One writer speaks with some point, if with unpardonable error in conclusion :—" Of the four English poets whose lives are almost as closely associated with Italy as with England—Browning, Shelley, Byron, Landor—the one whose absorption into this land of their adoption is most obvious and most complete is Byron . . . Byron more than any of the others became Italianized in habits and ideas, entered at once and completely into the associations, the history, the thoughts of the Italian people. He . . . spoke and wrote the language fluently, was well versed in their great literature, planned to write his own masterpiece in Italian, and so often made Italy the subject of his work that it is hardly saying too much to declare that it was through Byron that Englishmen first became interested in Italy."—Anna B. McMahan, *With Byron in Italy*, Introduction, 1.

[2] " I sometimes wish that I had studied languages with more attention : those which I know, even the classical (Greek and Latin, in the usual proportion of a sixth form boy), and a smattering of Modern Greek, the Armenian and Arabic alphabets, a few Turkish and Albanian phrases, oaths or requests, Italian tolerably, Spanish less than tolerably, French to read with ease but speak with difficulty—or rather not at all—all have been acquired by ear or eye, and never by anything like study. Like ' Edie Ochiltree,' ' I never dowed to bide a hard turn o' wark in my life.' "—" Detached Thoughts," *L. & J.* V, 436. He is generally depreciatory, as is often the case with him in matters of the kind.

classical acquirements, while technically inferior to those of the university wits of his own day and before, with whom he is always compared, would do honor to a student of arts to-day. His quick perception and retentive memory were the capacities of genius, and with his exquisitely impressionable nature he did not require the long and grilling routine in languages, that ordinary mortals find necessary, even for the mere cultural effects. And the leisure which he had at his command, joined with some really faithful and arduous exertions at times, his own aristocratic *sang froid* to the contrary notwithstanding, and his great desire to know, if after his own manner and fashion, all combined to make available to him as great a body and variety of foreign literatures as to any English man of his day with half his claims to a literary magistracy.

CHAPTER III

EQUIPMENT

TRAVEL

I cannot quite agree with a remark which I heard made, that " La route vaut mieux que les souvenirs."—Note 21, *Childe Harold* III.

Byron was the most traveled man of letters of his time,[1] and of all those who enjoyed the privilege of journeying abroad he profited most by it. Furthermore, of all the poets of England who improved themselves by travel, and the list is long, none showed in his works immediately or subsequently such extensive and powerful reaction to the scenes and events amid which he sojourned, as did Byron. With his ready adaptability, and his spirit that could not be confined within provincial or even national boundaries,[2] he became a citizen not of one country but of many, with a just claim indeed to a real Weltanschauung.[3]

The First Pilgrimage Both the habit of travel and the artistic expression of its effects were life-long with him. But the time at which such things were potent forces in his development was the period of his first pilgrimage. To a nature so responsive, and a spirit so

---

[1] The Pilgrim Poet is a synonym for his name. It forms the title of one well-known work on his life, *The Pilgrim Poet*, by A. Brecknock, 1911.

[2] " Byron had far more than an average share of the *émigré* spirit."— Nichol, *Byron*, 55.

[3] " He was a citizen of the world; because he not only painted the environs, but reflected the passions and aspirations of every scene amid which he dwelt."—Nichol, *Byron*, 212.

capable of inevitably becoming 'a part of all it met,' [1] such
a period must have counted immensely in shaping his ideals
and standards of life. Inasmuch as the associations were
noble, affording the best examples of nature and art for
exciting the loftiest feelings and reflections, the benefit in
a refinement of taste and enlargement of the critical apper-
ceptions could not but have been great. [2]

The practical value of travel, common to all men of
alert observation, was acknowledged in Byron at once upon
his return to England. When he made his first speech in
Parliament, it was not the weight of his argument, or the
effect of his rhetoric, or the dignity of his name, but his
simple declaration, " I have traversed the seat of war in
the Peninsula," [3] etc. which caused his peers to give more
than customary attention to a maiden speech before their
body. And yet the education which he derived from the
pilgrimage was as far above its mere practical advantage,
as his great poetry was superior to his slight exertions in
the House of Lords.

One of the most important causes of his malcontent and
dissatisfaction with his academic life was his eagerness for
travel, acquired by his custom of reveling in history and
encouraged by his shaping imagination. He early wished
to visit and see for himself the scenes of the celebrated

[1] Cf., " I live not in myself, but I become
    Portion of that around me."—*Childe Harold* III, 72.

[2] " Byron war entzückt und gehoben durch die großen historischen
Erinnerungen ; er war an Ithaka und dem Felsen von Leucadia (Santa
Maura) vorbeigefahren, von dem sich Sappho ins Meer gestürzt; er
sah die Schlachtfelder von Actium und Lepanto, betrat den klassischen
Boden, wo der Pindus ragt und der vom Acheron und Achelous durch-
strömt wird, blickte in die Flut des Acherusischen Sees und sah, wo
die heiligen Eichen von Dodona gerauscht hatten. Konnte sein Geist
von erhabenern und geweihtern Erinnerungen erfüllt, seinem Brüten
über die Vergänglichkeit des Irdischen reichere Nahrung geboten wer-
den ? "—Elze, *Byron*, 94-5.

[3] Debate on the Frame-work Bill, House of Lords, Feb. 27, 1812.

events with which his classical training and omnivorous
reading had made him familiar. He rightly regarded travel
as an essential part of every well-rounded man's education.
He even preferred it to the college career itself, in all except
perhaps the name. In accordance with this belief he sought
the opportunity of travel, by which to improve his education, before a year of his university career was over.[1] His
ideas on the subject thus early formed became his constant
convictions after he had had the chance to apply them in
practice.[2]

[1] " I sincerely desire to finish my education and, having been some-
time at Cambridge, the Credit of the University is as much attached
to my Name, as if I had pursued my Studies *there* for a Century ; but,
believe me, it is nothing more than a Name, which is already acquired.
I can now leave it with Honour, as I have paid everything, & wish to
pass a couple of years abroad, where I am certain of employing my time
to far more advantage and at much less expense, than at our English
Seminaries. ' Tis true I cannot enter France ; but Germany and the
Courts of Berlin, Vienna & Petersburg are still open, I shall lay the
plan before Hanson & Lord C.   I presume you will all agree, and if
you do not, I will, if possible, get away without your Consent, though I
should admire it more in the regular manner & with a Tutor of your
furnishing."—*L. & J.* I, 95 f.   Cf. *L. & J.* I, 143, 146, 176.   After
graduation he writes :—" If I do not travel now, I never shall, and all
men should one day or other . . . If we see no nation but our own,
we do not give mankind a fair chance ;—it is from *experience*, not books,
we ought to judge of them.   There is nothing like inspection, and
trusting to our own senses."—*L. & J.* I, 195.

[2] " I am so convinced of the advantages of looking at mankind
instead of reading about them, and the bitter effects of staying at home
with all the narrow prejudices of an islander, that I think there should
be a law amongst us, to set our young men abroad, for a term, among
the few allies our wars have left us."—*L. & J.* I, 309.
A few weeks after his return he writes to Dallas, proposing as a
motto for *Childe Harold*, then projected for publication, the opening
paragraph of the *Cosmopolite*, a little volume which he had picked
up in the Grecian Archipelago and with which he had been delighted :—
" L'univers est une espèce de livre, dont on n'a lu que la première
page quand on n'a vu que son pays.   J'en ai feuilleté un assez grand
nombre, que j'ai trouvé également mauvaises.   Cet examen ne m'a
point été infructueux.   Je haïssais ma patrie.   Toutes les impertinences
des peuples divers, parmi lesquels j'ai vécu, m'ont réconcilié avec elle.
Quand je n'aurais tiré d'autre bénéfice de mes voyages que celui-là,
je n'en regretterais ni les frais, ni les fatigues."

His early travels were more extensive than is usually supposed.[1] Often it is taken for granted that, after his university career, he, like scores of other Englishmen before and since, made only the regulation grand tour of a few weeks or months across the Continent to Italy, while waiting for some turn of fortune to provide him with a "place in life." As a matter of fact, his travels then did not include Italy. Intimate as his Italian associations are, they are all of later date. The countries which he visited and in which he resided during that first pilgrimage were Portugal, Spain, Albania, Greece, and Turkey in Europe and in Asia. The whole tour included a good deal of cruising in Mediterranean waters, some sojourning among the Greek islands, and an expedition as far as to the Black Sea. His original purpose was to continue to Persia and India,[2] and he made preparations for a trip to Egypt,[3] but his intentions were unfulfilled when, to his regret, he was recalled to England.

He was abroad a few weeks more than two years, enjoying or enduring many and varying modes of life.[4] The ex-

---

[1] " I have left my home, and seen part of Africa and Asia, and a tolerable portion of Europe."—*L. & J.* I, 264.

[2] See *L. & J.* I, 194-5, 258.

[3] See *L. & J.* I, 310, and VI, 455.

In his second pilgrimage he seriously planned a migration to " one of the Americas," preferably South. Postponement of the project was due mainly to his relation with Countess Guiccioli. Finally, his trip to Greece put an end to all plans and travel. See *L. & J.* IV, 355 f., 360, V, 451, and VI, 90, 110, and *Correspondence* II, 128, 131, etc.

[4] Cf., " The simple olives, best allies of wine,
    Must I pass over in my bill of fare ?
    I must, although a favorite *plat* of mine
    In Spain, and Lucca, Athens, everywhere:
    On them and bread 'twas oft my luck to dine—
    The grass my table-cloth, in open air,
    On Sunium or Hymettus, like Diogenes,
    Of whom half my philosophy the progeny is."
                                        —*Don Juan* XV, 73.

Cf. *L. & J.* I, 238, 281, 295, and *Correspondence* I, 176.

perience was not merely a matter of amusement or pastime with him,[1] but a serious occupation. No enterprise of his life, not even his expedition in behalf of Greece in his last days, engaged his undivided attention more than did the business of travel in the years 1809–11. He entered upon the undertaking with the highest anticipations,[2] and with a nature that was singularly fitted to profit from the cultivating influences of the scenes through which he was to wander. And, as rarely happens in cases of such lively expectation, there is nothing to show that his high imaginings were not fulfilled, and others loftier still awakened.[3]

In Byron's own writings, prose and poetry, we find the best evidence of the influence of travel on his literary character. No other author has left in artistic form such a record of the effect of travel on his genius as *Childe Harold*.[4] It is not a mere product of the fancy, but a record of fact and a history that is remarkable in its fidelity. It is a transcript of impressions of real objects upon a mind peculiarly receptive and a nature acutely susceptible to refining influences.[5] His notes and private letters, composed

---

[1] Cf., " Young men should travel, if but to amuse Themselves."—*Don Juan* II, 16.

[2] " Thence shall I stray through Beauty's native clime," he could write at the close of his satire with the journey in anticipation.

[3] " Every resting-place in the pilgrimage is made interesting by association with illustrious memories."—Nichol, *Byron*, 116.

[4] " Jamás el génio del hombre ha escrito paginas tan bellas como las que Byron consagra á su peregrinacion por Crecia."—Castelar, *Vida de Lord Byron*, 58.

[5] It " was written, for the most part, amidst the scenes which it attempts to describe. . . . Thus much it may be necessary to state for the correctness of the descriptions."—Preface to Cantos I & II *Childe Harold*.

" The minute details in the pilgrimage of *Childe Harold* are the observations of an actual traveller. Had they been given in prose, they could not have been less imbued with fiction. From this fidelity they possess a value equal to the excellence of the poetry, and ensure for themselves an interest as lasting as it is intense."—John Galt, *The Life of Byron*, 82. Galt was a fellow traveller with Byron over a part of the journey.

during the course of the journey,[1] contain substantially the same material as the poem, thus confirming the lifelike character of the observations.

The high esthetic plane [2] of the Pilgrim's anticipations is indicated in his delighted comment upon the first place touched at on the long voyage, though intimate contact with the place proved disillusioning.[3] But his unpleasant sensations, arising from a near view of Lisbon, were happily reversed at sight of the neighboring village of Cintra [4]—

"*Childe Harold* contains a lofty and impassioned review of the great events of history, of the mighty objects left as wrecks of time."— Wm. Hazlitt, *The Spirit of the Age*, Collected Works IV, 257. Hazlitt was inimical to Byron.

[1] He kept no journal at the time. " I keep no journal, but my friend Hobhouse scribbles incessantly."—*L. & J.* I, 258. " I keep no journal, nor have I any intention of scribbling my travels."— *L. & J.* I, 309. Cf. *Correspondence* I, 26.

[2] "He takes the highest points in the history of the world, and comments on them from a more commanding eminence. He shows us the crumbling monuments of time; he invokes the great names, the mighty spirits of antiquity."—Wm. Hazlitt, *The Spirit of the Age*.

[3] Cf., " What beauties doth Lisboa first unfold!
Her image floating on that noble tide.

. . . .

But whoso entereth within this town,
That, sheening far, celestial seems to be,
Disconsolate will wander up and down,
'Mid many things unsightly to strange ee;
For hut and palace show like filthily."—*Childe Harold* I, 16 f.

"It has been often described without being worthy of description; for, except the view from the Tagus, which is beautiful, and some fine churches and convents, it contains little but filthy streets, and more filthy inhabitants."—*L. & J.* I, 237. Moore writes of this connection: —" By comparing this and the thirteen following stanzas with the account of his progress which Lord Byron sent home to his mother, the reader will see that they are the exact echoes of the thoughts which occurred to his mind as he went over the spots described."—*Life* VIII, 22, footnote.

[4] Cf., " Lo! Cintra's glorious Eden intervenes
In variegated maze of mount and glen."
—*Childe Harold* I, 18.

"I must just observe, that the village of Cintra in Estremadura is the most beautiful, perhaps, in the world."—*L. & J.* I, 232. "The village of Cintra, about fifteen miles from the capital, is, perhaps,

where was situated the famous Alhambra—and its memorable surroundings.[1] Meanwhile his interest in opinions and estimates of " the critical art," for which these experiences were so much excellent preparation, was maintained.[2]

The associations of Cadiz, after a four-hundred mile ride on horseback across country, were likewise delightful.[3] Acquaintance with some of the grandees of this historic city was just ripening into intimacy, when the Pilgrim felt impelled to set sail " through Calpe's straits " for "Calypso's isles,"

> The sister tenants of the middle deep,

in every respect, the most delightful in Europe; it contains beauties of every description, natural and artificial. Palaces and gardens rising in the midst of rocks, cataracts and precipices; convents on stupendous heights—a distant view of the sea and the Tagus; and, besides (though that is a secondary consideration), is remarkable as the scene of Sir Hew Dalrymple's convention. It unites in itself all the wildness of the western highlands, with the verdure of the south of France."—*L. & J.* I, 237.

The impression was not obliterated by other celebrated scenes. Of Zita, a " small but favored spot of holy ground " in the vicinity of the sacred grove of Dodona and the head waters of Acheron, he could write later:—"A village with a Greek monastery (where I slept on my return), in the most beautiful situation (always excepting Cintra, in Portugal) I ever beheld."—*L. & J.* I, 249.

[1] " Near this place, about ten miles to the right, is the palace of Mafra, the boast of Portugal, as it might be of any other country, in point of magnificence without elegance."—*L. & J.* I, 237.

Cf.,   " Yet Mafra shall one moment claim delay,
    Where dwelt of yore the Lusians' luckless queen," etc.
                    —*Childe Harold* I, 29.

Three miles from Cintra was the famous mansion of William Beckford, author of *Vathek*,—" the most desolate mansion in the most beautiful spot I ever beheld."—*L. & J.* II, 48. Cf. *Childe Harold* I, 22 f.

[2] " Let us hear of literary matters, and the controversies and the criticisms."—*L. & J.* I, 233. Several months later:—" The Mediterranean and the Atlantic roll between me and criticism; and the thunders of the Hyperborean Review are deafened by the roar of the Hellespont."—*L. & J.* I, 267.

[3] " Fair Cadiz, rising o'er the dark blue sea!," " Cadiz, sweet Cadiz !—it is the fairest spot in the creation," " a complete Cythera," and " the most delightful town I ever beheld," are some of the descriptive terms, poetical and epistolary, that he uses of the place at the time and afterwards.

the very names of which excited his keenest expectancy. In Malta he passed a three weeks' sojourn, imagining at the time a second enchantress in Mrs. Spencer Smith (" Florence "). Thence he embarked for ancient Epirus, passing by the way such immortal spots as Ithaca,[1] the Leucadian promontory,[2] where Sappho met a violent death, and Actium,[3] the scene of Antony's defeat at the hands of Octavius Caesar.

The fine prospects of Albania, though less distinguished in their assocations than the great classic lands, stimulated the traveler's fancy in the same way in which beautiful natural scenery had affected him in childhood.[4] Even after his inspiring acquaintance with the immortal relics

---

[1]　" Childe Harold sailed, and passed the barren spot,
Where sad Penelope o'erlooked the wave."
　　　　　　　　　　　—*Childe Harold* II, 39.

" I have some idea of purchasing the Island of Ithaca."—*L. & J.* I, 305.

[2] Cf., " But when he saw the Evening star above
Leucadia's far-projecting rock of woe,
And hailed the last resort of fruitless love,
He felt, or deemed he felt, no common glow."
　　　　　　　　　　　—*Childe Harold* II, 41.

[3] " Today I saw the remains of the town of Actium, near which Antony lost the world, in a small bay, where two frigates could hardly manoeuvre : a broken wall is the sole remnant. On another part of the gulf stand the ruins of Nicopolis, built by Augustus in honour of his victory."—*L. & J.* I, 251 f. Cf. *Childe Harold* II, 45, and *L. & J.* VI, 444. He celebrated the event of his visit in a separate poem to " Florence," " Through cloudless skies," etc.

[4] Cf., " From the dark barriers of that rugged clime,
Ev'n to the center of Illyria's vales,
Childe Harold passed o'er many a mount sublime,
Through lands scarce noticed in historic tales :
Yet in famed Attica such lovely dales
Are rarely seen ; nor can fair Tempe boast
A charm they know not ; loved Parnassus fails,
Though classic ground and consecrated most,
To match some spots that lurk within this lowering coast."
　　　　　　　　　　　—*Childe Harold* II, 46.

of Greece, he could still speak glowingly, in terms of art, of the picturesque wilds of Albania.[1]

Where illustrious traditions were associated with great natural beauty, the appeal was strongest. The sight of Parnassus, as was to be expected, excited an ecstasy akin to that which the proverbial primitive nature-worshipper feels.[2] Everywhere on the sacred soil of Greece, and in adjacent lands where the great memories were, the scenes satisfied all the poet's expectations. The whole second

---

[1] "Albania, indeed, I have seen more of than any Englishman (except a Mr. Leake), for it is a country rarely visited, from the savage character of the natives, though abounding in more natural beauties than the classical regions of Greece, —which, however, are still eminently beautiful, particularly Delphi and Cape Colonna in Attica. Yet these are nothing to parts of Illyria and Epirus, where places without a name, and rivers not laid down in maps, may, one day, when more known, be justly esteemed superior subjects, for the pencil and the pen, to the dry ditch of the Illissus and the bogs of Boeotia."— *L. & J.* I, 264. See *L. & J.* I, 249, for the haunting memories of a Tepaleen sunset.

[2]   " Oh, thou Parnassus! whom I now survey,
         Not in the phrensy of a dreamer's eye,
         Not in the fabled landscape of a lay,
         But soaring snow-clad through thy native sky
         In the wild pomp of mountain-majesty!
         What marvel if I thus essay to sing ?
         The humblest of thy pilgrims passing by
         Would gladly woo thine Echoes with his string,
         Though from thy heights no more one Muse will wave his wing.

         Oft have I dreamed of thee! whose glorious name
         Who knows not, knows not man's divinest lore;
         And now I view thee—'tis, alas! with shame
         That I in feeblest accents must adore.
         When I recount thy worshippers of yore
         I tremble, and can only bend the knee;
         Nor raise my voice, nor vainly dare to soar,
         But gaze beneath thy cloudy canopy
         In silent joy to think at last I look on thee! "
                                        —*Childe Harold* I, 60-1.

This celebrated apostrophe to the home of the Muses, it is customary to note, was written at the foot of the mountain, of whose "snow-clad majesty" Byron had caught his first sight from the Gulf of Corinth nearly a fortnight before.

canto is but an apostrophe, with narrative and recapitu-
latory passages, to the grandeur of ancient Hellas in ruins.[1]

He spent more than half the time of his residence abroad
in Greece, chiefly in Athens with short excursions away,
satisfying his cravings with the sights and suggestions which
this most heroic of all lands had to offer. The sublime
fragments of her departed grandeur were affecting to him
only in their native setting.[2] When transplanted they
no longer retained in his esteem their exalted meanings.
Consequently, when he saw the desecration wrought by
Lord Elgin in lifting the Athenian marbles and transporting
them to England, his indignation was aroused. The sincerest
poem he ever wrote, *The Curse of Minerva*, a true fulmination, was the artistic result.[3]

To attempt an enumeration of the separate objects that
appealed to his interest in Greece would be but to multiply
instances to one effect. At Thebes, at Athens, at Corinth,
his spirit wrought among the ruins as among so many
wrecks in an earthly paradise. Everywhere was consecrated ground,[4] which to behold was to admire, and to

---

[1] " Le second chant est une peinture de la Grèce et de l'Asie Mineure,
où Lord Byron avait fait un premier voyage en 1808 (*sic*). Il salue
tour à tour leurs mers, leurs montagnes, leurs tombeaux, leurs ruines;
et chaque lieu lui inspire des impressions et des vers dignes de ses
immortels souvenirs."—Lamartine, *Le dernier Chant*, etc.

Those who insist on Byron's imperviousness to the classical regime
in his schooling may do well to contemplate his life, with its rich
associations, in Greece on this first pilgrimage.

[2] Cf. *L. & J.* I, 290, footnote.

[3] Cf. also, *Childe Harold* II, 11 f. Cp. Letter to Murray, *L. & J.* V, 547.

[4] Cf., "Where'er we tread 'tis haunted, holy ground;
No earth of thine is lost in vulgar mould,
But one vast realm of Wonder spreads around,
And all the Muse's tales seem truly told,
Till the sense aches with gazing to behold
The scenes our earliest dreams have dwelt upon;
Each hill and dale, each deepening glen and wold
Defies the power which crushed thy temples gone:
Age shakes Athena's tower, but spares gray Marathon."
—*Childe Harold* II, 88. Cf. *Giaour*, 90 f.

admire was to submit the senses to the exquisite pain which
only a genius can feel.

From Athens he made a tour of more than four months
through the Greek islands, over a part of Asia Minor, in
and about Constantinople, and to the entrance waters of
the Black Sea. But his cantos were completed before
he left ancient Greek territory,[1] hence his reactions to this
part of the celebrated pilgrimage remain without artistic
record.[2] The great legendary and historical places visited
on this expedition were the ruins of Ephesus, the plains
of Troy, Sestos and Abydos (where Leander performed his
famous feat, which Byron repeated), Constantinople, and
the Cyanean Symplegades of Argonautic memory. Unfortunately his letters are almost as silent as his poetry on
his impressions of these memorable places.[3]

[1] The second canto was finished at Smyrna, March 28, 1810, when
only the first stage of this trip had been accomplished.

[2] He contemplated a canto of this portion of his journey:—" The
scenes attempted to be sketched are in Spain, Portugal, Epirus,
Acarnania and Greece. There, for the present, the poem stops : its
reception will determine whether the author may venture to conduct
his readers to the capital of the East, through Ionia and Phrygia."—
Preface to *Childe Harold* I & II.

[3] " I smoke, and stare at mountains, and twirl my mustachios very
independently."—*L. & J.* I, 268. " Hobhouse rhymes and journalizes ;
I stare and do nothing."—*L. & J.* I, 271.

Of Ephesus he has nothing worthier to say than, " The Temple
has almost perished, and St. Paul need not trouble himself to epistolise
the present brood of Ephesians."—*L. & J.* I, 268. It may be remembered that his interest in Scripture was in the Old Testament.

The Trojan site received no inspired mention :—"All the remains
of Troy are the tombs of her destroyers, amongst which I saw that
of Antilochus from my cabin window."—*L. & J.* I, 262. " I also
passed a forthnight on the Troad. The tombs of Achilles and Aesyetes
still exist in large barrows, similar to those you have doubtless seen in
the North."—*L. & J.* I, 280. Cf. *Don Juan* IV, 101. For the suggestion it contains in regard to his classical attainments, may be cited his
remark :—" It is one thing to read the *Iliad* at Sigaeum and on the
tumuli, or by the springs with Mount Ida above, and the plain and
rivers and Archipelago around you ; and another to trim your taper
over it in a snug library—*this* I know."—*Childe Harold* III, note 19.

" My only notable exploit lately has been swimming from Sestos
to Abydos in humble imitation of *Leander*, of amorous memory ;

One view of Constantinople he was much impressed with, temporarily esteeming it above all others of his travels.[1] Otherwise ancient Byzantium was not so much a subject for literary commemoration as an inspiration for romantic "dark imaginings" and a source of later richly colored tales. In general, none of the scenes appealed to him as did those of Greece proper.[2] Even the noble prospect from the " Seven Towers to the end of the Golden Horn " was superseded by the familiar and greater scenes about Athens.[3]

though I had no *Hero* to receive me on the other shore of the Hellespont."—*L. & J.* I, 275.

He was impelled by the historic spirit to the farthest point he reached, a spot associated with the mythical ship Argo:—" I am just come from an expedition through the Bosphorus to the Black Sea and the Cyanean Symplegades, up which last I scrambled with as great risk as ever the Argonauts escaped in their hoy."—*L. & J.* I, 275. " The beginning of the nurse's dole in the *Medea* " was ringing in his head as he made his risky scramble, and he made a *jeux d'esprit* translation of the passage on the summit of the rocks. " Had not this sublime passage been in my head, I should never have dreamed of ascending the said rocks, and bruising my carcass in honour of the ancients."—*L. & J.* I, 277.

[1] " The walls of the Seraglio are like the walls of Newstead gardens, only higher, and much in the same *order*; but the ride by the walls of the city, on the land side, is beautiful. Imagine four miles of immense triple battlements, covered with ivy, surmounted with 218 towers, and, on the other side of the road, Turkish burying-grounds (the loveliest spots on earth), full of enormous cypresses. I have seen the ruins of Athens, of Ephesus, and Delphi. I have traversed great part of Turkey, and many other parts of Europe, and some of Asia; but I never beheld a work of nature or art which yielded an impression like the prospect on each side from the Seven Towers to the end of the Golden Horn."—*L. & J.* I, 282.

[2] " You see, by my date, that I am at Athens again, a place which I think I prefer, upon the whole, to any I have seen."—*L. & J.* I, 289.

In 1816 he writes of famous battle plains:—" I have viewed with attention those of Platea, Troy, Mantinea, Leuctra, Chaeronea, and Marathon; and the field around Mount St. Jean and Hougoumont appears to want little but a better cause, and that indefinable but impressive halo which the lapse of ages throws around a celebrated spot, to vie in interest with any or all of these, except, perhaps, the last mentioned."—*Childe Harold* III, note 6.

[3] "At Constantinople I visited the Mosques, plains, and grandees of that place, which, in my opinion, cannot be compared with Athens and its neighbourhood; indeed I know of no Turkish scenery to equal this."—*L. & J.* I, 292.

The several months after his return from Constantinople and preceding his return to England are the most obscure period of Byron's life. Little is known definitely of his pursuits at the time.[1] He was adding little creative work to the already rich store of his impressions, except occasional short poems, notable among which was *The Curse of Minerva*, and annotations to the two cantos of the *Pilgrimage*.[2] Doubtless he was revolving in mind outlines of the remarkable succession of tales with which he was to bewitch the world on his return.   Early in 1811 he was planning a trip to Egypt when financial complications, which had been developing since his minority, reached a crisis, and he was compelled to return " *home* without a hope, and almost without a desire."[3]

Before he again set foot on foreign soil, from intense living and excessive mental and emotional strain, few as were the intervening years, he was a mature man, and the moulding influences upon his character were thus virtually over.

These first years of travel in historical and classical lands cannot be too strongly emphasized in a study of the sources from which Byron drew the elements of his artistic equipment. For a critical rôle, with a nature like his, the experience was all but indispensable.   The narrow range of

---

[1] Byron's fellow traveler, Hobhouse, returned to England from Constantinople, leaving Byron with a year of the Pilgrimage still ahead. His letters in 1811, before his return ro England in July of that year, are far too infrequent to offer any kind of connected account. Cf., " I am still in Athens making little tours to Marathon, Sunium, the top of Hymettus, and the Morea occasionally to diversify the season," and, " I am living in the Capuchin Convent, Hymettus before me, the Acropolis behind, the Temple of Jove to my right, the Stadium in front, the town to the left; eh, Sir, there's a situation, there's your picturesque ! "—*Correspondence* I, 29 f.

[2] The *Hints from Horace*, being an academic exercise, needs hardly be mentioned in this connection. Byron completed the *Hints* at a Franciscan convent in Athens, March 12, 1811.

[3] *L. & J.* I, 316.

studies and the tedious processes at school and college of
acquiring a knowledge of the great universal body of history and literature he openly neglected and despised. But
with a capacious memory and an insatiable appetite for all
reading, he was able, under his own guidance, to gain a store
of knowledge, which few even of the best scholars could
hope to equal. Consequently, when he visited the scenes
of the many events with which his wide reading had made
him acquainted, he felt a stimulus and inspiration, and
derived a profit and uplift, in a hundred ways that are
denied to ordinary travelers.

The setting of the oldest legend and of the latest martial
exploit, and every literary shrine, were familiar to him.
Nothing escaped his eye and attention, or the more scholarly notice of his fellow traveler, Hobhouse.   And every
object that afforded him pleasure to contemplate contributed
to his culture, sharpened and invigorated his wits, and
elevated his character. From this secure vantage he was
prepared to approve or condemn artistic merits or faults
with the authority of a connoisseur. In brief, he was a
traveler of taste inherited from distinguished blood and
improved by study and experience, who saw truly what
travel had to offer, and who profited enormously from the
truths that came under his observation.

Intellectuality In concluding this survey of Byron's
equipment for criticism—what he in-
herited, what the schools imparted, what his associations and
friendships inspired, and what he acquired by reading and
travel—it is desirable to correct a popular misconception,
from which his memory has suffered greatly. The error
is traceable to Goethe's famous saying, "Sobald er reflektiert, ist er ein Kind," which has been wrongly interpreted to mean that Byron was unintellectual. "No in-

spired fool ever wrote a great poem,"[1] and to deny Byron
intellectuality is to deny all his great poetry, much less any
critical ability he might possess. Goethe has elsewhere
referred to him as "Dieser seltsame geistreiche Dichter."[2]
Manifestly what Goethe meant in his much-quoted utterance is not that Byron's powers of thought were inferior
or unmatured, but that he was not constituted for habits of
constructive meditation. A writer in *Blackwood's Magazine*
for August, 1819, attacking the first cantos of *Don Juan*,
calls him " one of the most powerful intellects our island
has ever produced." Captain Parry, who knew him intimately in his last days, says : " He was more a mental
being, if I may use the phrase, than any man I ever saw.
He lived on thought more than on food."[3] And Nichol
asserts, " Byron's life was passed under the fierce light that
beats upon an intellectual throne."[4] Byron's emotional
nature was as strong as any in literature, but it must not
be overlooked that it had adequate intellectual accompani-
ment and support. In short, he had, as he stood upon
the threshold of life, the sensibilities to appreciate artistic
things and the mental power to weigh and estimate them.
What use he would make of his great possessions remained
to be seen.

[1] William Gerard, *Byron Re-studied in His Dramas*, 191.
[2] Review of *Manfred* in *Kunst und Alterthum*.
[3] *Last Days of Lord Byron*, 78.
[4] *Byron*, 1.

CHAPTER IV

THE FIRST VENTURE—FORMAL SATIRE

If I sneer sometimes,
It is because I cannot well do less,
And now and then it also suits my rhymes.
—*Don Juan* XIII, 8.

Byron's taste for satire was evident early,[1] and before his training was complete[2] he had been provoked to a satirical performance that proved one of his greatest triumphs[3] and has been of no small importance in the history of English satire. *English Bards and Scotch Reviewers* was his first sustained effort of any kind. Because it concerned itself so largely with literary matters,[4] and because of its justifiable *raison d'être*, its total critical import is perhaps greater than is customarily granted it.

Its Critical Inception Byron began the poem in a spirit of criticism weeks before the special article appeared which gave him his real satiric motive.[5] The sallies of this fragment are feeble as compared

---

[1] See "On a Change of Masters at a Great Public School," "Damoetas," "To a Knot of Ungenerous Critics," etc., among his early poems.

[2] See Chapter III.

[3] Cf., "I tell you that the two most successful things ever written by me, viz., the *English Bards* and *Childe Harold*," etc.— *L. & J.* VI, 149.

[4] "*English Bards, and Scotch Reviewers* . . . . . is, like the *Dunciad* and the *Baviad*, a satire principally on literary people."—Fuess, *Byron as a Satirist in Verse*, 48.

[5] The first mention of such a poem is in a letter to Miss Pigot in October, 1807 (*L. & J.* I, 147). At the time it was 380 lines in length. The final (Fifth) edition contains 1069 lines.

with the manly assaults of the finished product.[1] The
secret of the difference is that in the first form Byron had
no real satiric incentive. Literary affairs of the time were
showing a spirit of change, which did not conform with
the ideas of literature he had acquired in his schooling.[2]
He had not stopped to analyze the change, but it had
awakened his suspicions and he wished to discourage it.
In such an attitude his remonstrance could hardly have
been more than is expected in legitimate criticism. Without the Edinburgh attack there is hardly a chance that
he would have been regarded as other than a wholesome
conservator of the older literary traditions. He always
required the personal wound to write good satire, and before the Edinburgh critique he had none.[3]

---

[1]   " Time was, ere yet in these degenerate days
Ignoble themes obtained mistaken praise,
When Sense and Wit with Poesy allied,
No fabled Graces, flourish'd side by side;
From the same fount their inspiration drew,
And reared by Taste, bloomed fairer as they grew,
Then, in this happy Isle a Pope's pure strain
Sought the rapt soul to charm, nor sought in vain;
A polish'd nation's praise aspired to claim,
And raised the people's as the poet's fame."

Compare this gentle strain with the reckless vigor of the following
lines, which were not added till Byron affixed his name to the poem : —

" Still must I hear ?—Shall hoarse Fitzgerald bawl
His creaking couplets in a tavern hall,
And I not sing, lest, haply, Scotch Reviews
Should dub me scribbler, and denounce my *Muse* ?
Prepare for rhyme —I'll publish, right or wrong :
Fools are my theme, let Satire be my song."

See Dr. Karl König, " Byrons *English Bards and Scotch Reviewers*,"
20 f., for the portions in the satire constituting the *British Bards*.
[2] Cf. " To the Earl of Clare," stanza 7, *Hours of Idleness*.
[3] " The groundwork of the satire was laid weeks before he received
his ' early intelligence ' of the rod that had been pickled for his back.
Left to himself, Lord Byron of Trinity would have produced a satire,
something stronger than the satirical stuff of the ' Hours of Idleness,'
something weaker than the satire of the ' Hints from Horace,' that

Critical Character of the Expanded Poem

It is noteworthy that the *British Bards* was retained and that its growth into the satire was by addition and revision not by total reconstruction.

The purpose of the poem, as stated in the first edition acknowledged by Byron, is truly critical,[1] although the purpose of satire, as formally declared,[2] is often the same. The distinction in Byron's case is that his original intention was but to protest against the changing literary spirit, and with all the rancor of his preface in general, in the moment of avowing his object, it was but natural for him to hearken back to the motive which impelled him to begin the poem and which directed him in the composition of a considerable part of it.

The reader does not proceed far before he is aware of a striking departure from the common practice of satire. Byron uses real names with almost unbroken regularity. For the sake of variety only does he change to pen names, which is but a help to identification. In the case of only one or two minor figures is the pseudonym alone in the text, and then the real name is carefully supplied in a prose note. In his earlier slight satires he follows, doubtless consciously, classic models—Magnus, Damoetas, Pomposus, Probus. In his later ones he is much less free in his citation of persons by name.

Such usage is critical, rather than satirical. Byron believed at least that he was " arm'd in proof," by reason of which he could fearlessly " speak the truth." And his

might have caught the public attention for an hour, on its way to the oblivion that claims all satire that does not rise to a high standard of excellence."—Jeaffreson, *The Real Lord Byron*, 115.

[1] " My object is not to prove that I can write well, but, *if possible,* to make others write better."

[2] " Nor is it possible to insist upon the reformatory purpose behind the satiric spirit . . . . the common practice has too often been at variance with it."—Fuess, *Byron as a Satirist in Verse*, 3.

belief must have been heartily seconded by opinion of the
time, else the libel laws might have been invoked, or in
their impotency the author's code of honor made to conform with the gentleman's. Byron was easily accessible
for some time after the appearance of the satire.[1] In a
postscript to the second edition he aggravated his offence
by the challenge, " The age of Chivalry is dead, or, in the
vulgar tongue, there is no spirit now-a-days."[2] But only
one of the men attacked felt cause to demand satisfaction,
Thomas Moore, who had formerly engaged in a duel with
Jeffrey over an article that was purely critical.[3] There was
not even verbal remonstrance, so far as we know, by the
persons satirized. The quiet acceptance of the individual
judgments, and the public applause of the whole performance, argue a recognition of the critical nature of the work.
     Various excuses have been offered for the objectionable
judgments expressed in the poem.[4] In all such well-meant
efforts there is an unconscious acknowledgment of the
critical character of the poem. It is a virtue of satire to
deal in extravagance, hence it is a waste of time to try to
equate its judgments with fairness and truth.[5] The present
day critics sometimes forget, as well, that they are trying
to reconcile Byron with the critical practices of the present

---

[1] Cf. " My Satire must be kept secret for a *month*; after that you
may say what you please on the subject."—*L. & J*. I, 217. Cf. also,
Correspondence I, 20, 21.
[2] " Since the publication of this thing, my name has not been
concealed; I have been mostly in London, ready to answer for my
transgressions, and in daily expectation of sundry cartels; but alas!
' the age of Chivalry is over,' " etc. Cf. *L. & J*. II, 62.
[3] Cf. " To the Earl of Clare," stanzas 8-9, and prose notes, in
allusion to this incident. See *Correspondence* I, 52 f.
[4] Gribble's opinion is typical:— " One does not expect sound
criticism from a poet "—we should like to cite such as Dryden,
Coleridge, Arnold, and Swinburne—and " least of all does one expect
it from poets of one and twenty."—*Love Affairs of Lord Byron*, 59.
[5] " Most satire is, of course, biassed and unjust."—Fuess, *Byron
as a Satirist in Verse*, 72.

time, which is an impossible task, in view of the changes that have been wrought since Byron's day. Wholesome advice to all such persons is, to acknowledge the satirical preeminence of the opinions advanced and leave them undefended, or if a critical quality is to be insisted upon, to adopt the criteria of Byron's age.

Contemporary It is fairly certain that the judgments
Opinion in the represent the current conservative
Poem opinion before 1810.[1] Byron himself, much as he depended on the opinion of others through life and little as he liked to be thought to borrow, half confessed an adoption of current opinion in the satire.[2] It seems amusing now that such harsh judgments as are passed upon men like Wordsworth and Coleridge[3] could ever have represented the popular estimate. But " Southey and Co.," as Byron later dubbed them, were as yet pioneers in the literature of the time, and while their popular following

---

[1] " It is not detrimental to Byron to state that he had been anticipated in many of his criticisms to such an extent that his views could have offered little of novelty to his readers."—Fuess, *Byron as a Satirist in Verse*, 51. " Having studied the satirical poets as models, and collected every available bit of gossip floating at the time, he, in 1809, poured forth his wrath."—Alexander Leighton, *Life of Lord Byron*, ix. Dallas's opinion in the matter should carry sufficient weight for all, for the poem came to publication through his hands. He criticized it and suggested freely, while the manuscript was in his possession, until by his careful godfathering it came to light. " I think in general with you of the literary merit of the writers introduced. I am particularly pleased with your distinction in Scott's character."— *Recollections*, 13.

[2] " With regard to the real talents of many of the poetical persons whose performances are mentioned or alluded to in the following pages, it is presumed by the Author that there can be little difference of opinion in the Public at large."—Preface to Second Edition.

[3] " Who, both by precept and example, shows
That prose is verse, and verse is merely prose."
And
" The bard who soars to elegize an ass
So well the subject suits his noble mind,
He brays, the Laureate of the long-eared kind."

was becoming strong, the " combined usurpers of the throne of taste," whence emanated all authoritative criticism, belonged to the opposite school.[1]

In his characterization of the great romantic leaders and others, then, Byron may well have represented but a happy crystallization of orthodox opinion. This robs him of strict originality, but it proves the work the more largely critical. When the critic to-day condemns the findings of the work, let him remember that they are the expressions of an age upon its literature, only phrased by the poet. Such judgments are as apt to be wrong as right, but they are never satirical.

Present Attitude toward the Judgments   The present day is not averse to a partially critical interpretation.[2] Some of the judgments represent as sound criticism as has been uttered of the men they commemorate. Of all the criticism that has been written upon Wordsworth, few phrases are so well known as,

> That mild apostate from poetic rule.

The line on Southey,

> A bard may chant too often and too long,

is simple enough, but there is hardly a parallel to it anywhere in point and aptness as to the primary cause of Southey's decline. And yet it is in the cases of such poets as these that the judgments are supposed to be most unjust.

Byron's apt criticism has preserved the memory of some of the names longer than they deserve.

> The paralytic puling of Carlisle,

---

[1] Jeffrey had praised Wordsworth, but the case was exceptional.
[2] " Many of the judgments, though extravagant in expression as befits the Muse of Juvenal, are shrewdly penetrating."—P. E. Moore, prefatory note to the *English Bards and Scotch Reviewers* in the Cambridge *Byron*.

said of the verse of the poet's guardian is better known to-day than any of that nobleman's works or than Dr. Johnson's or Horace Walpole's favorable opinions of them.[1]

> Oh, Amos Cottle!—Phoebus! What a name!
> To fill the speaking-trump of future fame!

Time has kindly erased from public memory the works of this poetaster. His name and pretensions are preserved only in Byron's couplet. Maurice's "granite weight of leaves" on the beauties of Richmond Hill are fittingly pronounced to be

> Smooth, solid monuments of mental pain.

The work is justly unknown to-day and its memory lives only in Byron's lines.

The criticisms are not confined to individual characteristics, which reviews might supply, or to broad generalizations, which might come from common report. Often the critic turns his attention to single works where only a careful and close reading could suffice for his compact but comprehensive criticism. "Harmonious Bowles," singing,

> With equal ease, and grief,
> The fall of empires, or a yellow leaf,

"whimpering through three-score of years" and coaxing his "whining powers" to

> Whine and whimper to the fourteenth line,

is triumphantly dubbed

> The maudlin prince of mournful sonneteers.

By these suggestive phrases the sentimental quality of Bowles's sonnets, which had influenced so strongly the

---

[1] The accidental identity of names suggests, too, that the judgment is not harsher than many criticisms the wizard of Ecclefechan passed upon his contemporaries in a more enlightened day.

f

tender heart of the greatest man of letters of the age, is
effectively set forth.   The best example of this specialized
criticism is the famous passage on Scott's Marmion,[1] which
is as celebrated as any characterization of any figure from
Scott's numerous progeny.

But all such references are from passages where the adverse judgments are supposed to be least worthily applied.
In addition, there is a formal section wholly devoted to
appreciation.[2] Campbell, Rogers, Cowper, Burns, Gifford,
White, Crabbe, and others, are given the " tribute due " to
" neglected genius."   Needless to say, the noblest passage
of the poem is the eulogy of White,[3] which first recommended
Byron in America.[4]   It is a lofty critical estimate of great
but unfortunate poetical genius.   The praise of the living
is as unstinted, wherever, in the opinion of the critic, the
man deserved it.[5]   In such instances as the comment on
Crabbe the popular notion, that Byron deigned to commend
only the adherents of the classical school,[6] breaks down.
Crabbe was an integral part of the romantic movement,

[1]   " Next view in state, proud prancing on his roan,
       The golden-crested haughty Marmion,
       Now forging scrolls, now foremost in the fight,
       Not quite a Felon, yet but half a Knight,
       The gibbet or the field prepared to grace—
       A mighty mixture of the great and base."—165-70.

[2] Beginning, " To the famed throng now paid the tribute due."—
798 f.
[3]   " Unhappy White ! while life was in its spring,
       And thy young Muse· just waved her joyous wing," etc.
—830 f.   Cf. Byron's own account of White of the same year, *L. & J.*
I, 336 f.
[4] " Very high praise is given to Byron, both as a man and a poet,
for the now famous passage on Henry Kirk White."—Leonard, *Byron
and Byronism in America*, 23.
[5]   " Yet Truth sometimes will lend her noblest fires,
       And decorate the verse herself inspires :
       This fact in Virtue's name let Crabbe attest :
       Though Nature's sternest Painter, yet the best."—854-7.

[6] Fuess, *et al.*

despite his correctness and common sense. Byron at the time could not have been a conscious follower of any school.

Byron's Own Opinion of the Poem Byron always regarded the poem as criticism rather than as satire. He *felt* this distinction between the two types rather than expressed it. A confusion of the two was natural in an age when a differentiation between them was far less clearly made than is done at the present time. A further reason for their confusion in Byron's case is to be found in the source from which he drew his inspiration for the task, the writings of Pope.[1] In such a source, where the body of criticism is dogmatic and magisterial, like the satire, the tone of the poem had its origin.

Immediately before the appearance of the work, when the question of a title arose, Byron showed clearly that classifying the poem as satire was a nominal convenience only.[2] The preface to the second edition declared : " An author's works are public property : he who purchases may judge, and publish his opinions, if he pleases." To this edition he affixed his name, assuming thereby full responsibility for the truth and justice of the assertions made. The conclusion of the poem has the couplet :

> Learned to deride the critic's starch decree,
> And break him on the wheel he meant for me.

Apparently he regarded his work as critical by the proper canons and practices of the day.

----

[1] "Among the preparatives by which he disciplined his talent to the task was a deep study of the writings of Pope; and I have no doubt that from this period may be dated the enthusiastic admiration which he ever after cherished for this great poet."—Moore, *Life* I, 226.

[2] " I am sorry to differ with you with regard to the title, but I mean to retain it with this addition : *The English Bards and Scotch Reviewers* ; and if we call it a *Satire*, it will obviate the objection, as the Bards also were Welch."—*L. & J.* I, 212.

His attitude toward the satire in later life reflects a critical estimate.   In his aroused state of mind at the time of the composition obviously he thought he was inflicting nothing but the justest punishment.   When his anger had subsided his attitude everywhere toward the work, as if he thought of it only as a critical record, and hence of justice, was one of condemnation and regret.[1]   From the day on which he suppressed the carefully prepared Fifth edition to the time of his death, his condemnation of the work is one of the too infrequent consistencies of his life.

His disapprobation was not confined to mere expressions of regret.   He took what steps he could to revoke the whole performance.   Former editions were beyond recall, but the fifth, which was just issuing from the press in March, 1812, he suppressed at no little expense to himself, after the appearance of only a very few copies without title pages. He secured an injunction against republication and never afterward consented to have this legal protection withdrawn.[2]

[1] I " wish I had not been in such a hurry with that confounded satire, of which I would suppress even the memory."—" Journal," Nov. 17, 1813, *L. & J.* II, 322. " The first thing a young writer must expect, and yet can least of all suffer, is *criticism*.   I did not bear it—a few years, and many changes have since passed over my head, and my reflections on that subject are attended with regret.   I find, on dispassionate comparison, my own revenge more than the provocation warranted.   It is true, I was very young,—that might be an excuse to those I attacked—but to *me* it is none."—*L. & J.* III, 47. " My ' Satire,' lampoon, or whatever you or others please to call it . . . was written when I was very young and very angry, and has been a thorn in my side ever since."—*L. & J.* III. 192.   " I regret having published ' English Bards and Scotch Reviewers.' "—Moore, *Life* VII, 246.   Cf. *L. & J.* I, 314, II, 133, etc.

[2] "A new edition of that lampoon was preparing for the press, when Mr. Rogers represented to me, that ' I was *now* acquainted with many of the persons mentioned in it, and with some on terms of intimacy '; and that he knew ' one family in particular to whom its suppression would give pleasure.'   I did not hesitate one moment,— it was cancelled instantly; and it is no fault of mine that it has ever been republished.   When I left England, in April 1816, with no very violent intentions of troubling that country again, and amid scenes

On casually meeting in 1816 with a copy of the suppressed edition, then belonging to a friend, Byron reperused the whole poem, and made with his own hand some annotations of his more mature views.[1] Naturally from the circumstances by which they came to be recorded, the new opinions are mere jottings, but they are sufficient as indications.

On the fly-leaf appears a condemnation of the whole work, which is quite as severe as any of the judgments contained in it.[2] Twice in the poem he had called Wordsworth " simple." By each he writes " *unjust.*" In the same emphatic way he retracts his characterization of Coleridge. " Too savage all this on Bowles," he asserts of his later antagonist in the controversy.[3] " Bad enough, and on mistaken grounds too," he says of his thrust at Lord Holland, believing that his " cause of enmity proceeded from Holland House." An unemphatic " unjust " appears by the criticism of his guardian, Lord Carlisle, and " wrong

of various kinds to distract my attention,—almost my last act, I believe, was to sign a power of attorney, to yourself, to prevent or suppress any attempts (of which several had been made) at a republication."—Letter to Murray, etc., *L & J.* V. 538. Cf. *L. & J.* III, 227. " With regard to the *English Bards, and Scotch Reviewers,* I have no concealments, nor desire to have any from you or yours; the suppression occured (I am as sure as I can be of anything) in the manner stated : I have never regretted that, but very often the composition, that is, the *humeur* of a great deal in it."—*L. & J.* III, 247. " With regard to a future large edition, you may print all, or anything, except *English Bards,* to the republication of which at *no* time will I consent."—*L. & J.* IV, 177.

[1] This copy is preserved in the British Museum. Moore has printed the references, VII, 219 f. For some minor amendments further, see *L. & J.* II, 218.

[2] " The *binding* of this volume is considerably too valuable for the contents; and nothing but the consideration of its being the property of another, prevents me from consigning this miserable record of misplaced anger and indiscriminate acrimony to the flames."

[3] In connection with the controversy in 1821, he says:—" The part which I regret the least is that which regards Mr. Bowles, with reference to Pope."—Moore, *Life* VII, 246.

also " by the passage on his " recreant lines." His early
prose note on that nobleman is pronounced " much too
savage." His reproaches of Jeffrey's qualities of heart
are " unjust," and the famous passage on that great " anthropophagus," who " seems to have been the inspiring
object of the Satire," [1] is " Too ferocious—this is mere
insanity."

The high opinion he entertained of Rogers he found it
necessary to modify. " Rogers has not fulfilled the promise
of his first powers, but has still very great merit." Crabbe
he esteemed still as highly as that poet deserves, and it is
to his critical credit that he could exalt Coleridge to the
same position. " I consider Crabbe and Coleridge as the
first of these times, in point of power and genius."

Some of his severest judgments he regarded as deserved
and therefore, as sound criticism, found it unnecessary to
change them. The " creaking couplets " of Fitzgerald
are " right enough," but it was not worth while to " notice
such a mountebank " at all. Cottle had further justified
his distasteful name by some critical abuses of a defense-
less woman's work, hence the arraignment of him is " all
right." Even the harsh sentence passed on Hewson Clarke
is " Right enough : this was well deserved and well laid on." [2]

When did a poet ever feel such prolonged regret for a
successful satire ? [3] Byron's fame really dates from this
poem. It gave him, as well, his belief and confidence in

---

[1] Dallas, *Recollections*, 25.

[2] Clarke meanwhile by his actions had subjected himself to pro-
ceedings by Byron for libel. See *L. & J.* I, 321 f., and *Correspondence*
I, 42-3.

[3] " The greater part of this satire I most sincerely wish had never
been written—not only on account of the injustice of much of the
critical, and some of the personal part of it—but the tone and temper
are such as I cannot approve."—Written on a copy of the satire in
Murray's possession, dated Diodati, Geneva, July 14, 1816,—Charles
Webb Le Bas, *A Review of the Life and Character of Lord Byron*, 22.

the satirical power of his genius. But the thing was a
thorn in his flesh for the remainder of his life. Whenever
he thought of the poem, it seemed to be in terms of posterity,
consciously or not, and of the misconceptions that might
arise from some of his judgments, or more probably still,
of what the world might think of him as a literary critic,
and it behooved him to change and correct.

An Estimate by Its Time From the abusive character of much of
the criticism of the time, as befitting the
spirit of Juvenal rather than of good criticism, any attempt to judge the critical
element of the *English Bards and Scotch Reviewers* by standards of the present must be accompanied by a good deal
of embarrassment. Moreover, it is but an act of elemental
justice to restore any piece of literature to its own time for
a correct and full estimate of it. At the mere suggestion
of the use of such method with the poem in which Byron
" took the palm from all our Poets," the critical value of
the work increases greatly.

Inasmuch as the age was one of rapid change in the
character of criticism, the condition must be sought in
the immediate decade of the poem. It is desirable, as well,
to have the study apply to the prominent branch of criticism,
which called the poem forth and which it was Byron's
purpose to answer, to wit, reviewing.

Periodical criticism at the time was but a form of reviewing. In fact, the reviewer and the critic in periodical
literature are to be reckoned as one and the same person.
" Is it criticism to rave against a poet's faults, and ignore
his beauties ? " asks Noel, and then answers his own question
by saying, " If so, then every reviewer would be a critic—
which is absurd."[1] But Noel's proposition is made for a

---

[1] *Byron*, 132.

specific purpose, a denunciation of the article on the *Hours
of Idleness*. The distinction he makes places the critical
practice of the time on a higher plane than it deserves,
except in a few instances of criticism of the newer kind.
To Byron the critic and the reviewer were identical, members indistinguishably of the same " heartless crew " and
" censorious throng." [1] And, as has been noted, Byron
was in agreement with his age in the conception and execution of his poem.

The *Edinburgh* and *Quarterly* reviews, edited by Jeffrey
and Gifford, were the chief critical periodicals of the day.
The two publications, differing only in politics, are synony-
mous with harsh and inconsiderate criticism.[2] But only
the elder of the two, and founder of their method, can have
affected materially Byron's production. And so nearly
typical of the *Edinburgh's* practice was the special article,
which provoked Byron's rejoinder, that an analysis of it,
for the purposes of comparison, is sufficient.

[1] As late as 1821 Byron says of Southy,

" He had called
Reviewing ' the ungentle craft,' and then
Became as base a critic as e'er crawled."
—*Vision of Judgment*, 98.

[2] Carlyle says of Jeffrey:—" He may be said to have begun the
rash reckless style of criticising everything in heaven and earth by
appeal to *Molière's maid*; ' Do *you* like it ? ' ' *Don't* you like it ? ' "—
Reminiscences, 319. And Professor Courthope, in the present age
when the tendency is to modify the earlier harsh jugments of Jeffrey
and his manner, acknowledges, " The tone of contemptuous depreciation
which had now become characteristic of that periodical."—*History
of English Poetry* VI, 237.

Ethel Colburne Mayne quotes Henley as saying of Gifford:—" His
literary temper is atrocious; his criticisms, whether aggressive or
corrective, seem the effect of downright malignity; in the long run
you are tempted to side with his victims."—*Byron* I, 122. Saintsbury
writing recently adds:—" Gifford is little read nowadays, and a name
which was not a very popular one even on his own side during his
life-time has, since the triumph of the politics and of some of the
literary styles which he opposed, become almost a byword for savage
and unfair criticism."—*A History of Nineteenth Century Literature*, 24.

The *Edinburgh* had for its motto a sentence from Publius Syrus, "*Judex damnatur cum nocens absolvitur.*" It stands to reason that the *Review* did not condemn everything. But its praise was given sparingly, and rarely without disparaging qualifications. In any case of doubt, true to its policy, it reserved the benefit to itself. The literary world had come to regard the publication [1] as exercising an ill-humored and partisan censorship over literary matters, so Byron was justified in expecting no mercy when he learned that a critique was being prepared for its pages on his boyish volume. [2]

Upon its appearance the article confirmed his anticipations. It fully justified the reputation which the magazine had built up. Indeed its unexceptional character is to be recognized by the manner, adopted from Pope, in which Byron's volume was chosen, from a number of others, for review. [3]

The first two or three sentences of the article are scurrilous. [4] Thereafter the critic abandons himself to a contemptuous persiflage, without an approach to being either forceful or convincing. Only one passage resembles real wit. [5]

[1] The editors of the 1845 edition (Appleton) of Byron's poems say of the *Edinburgh* at the time, that it " possessed nearly undivided influence and authority."

[2] " You know the system of the Edinburgh gentlemen is universal attack. They praise none; and neither the public nor the author expects praise from them."—*L. & J.* I, 183.

[3] Among a score of others, " this one bore a noble name on the title-page."—E. C. Mayne, *Byron* I, 118. " In truth, it is this consideration only that induces us to give Lord Byron's poems a place in our review." —The Article, *L. & J.* I, 345.

[4] " The poesy of this young lord belongs to the class which neither gods nor men are said to permit. Indeed, we do not recollect to have seen a quantity of verse with so few deviations in either direction from that exact standard. His effusions are spread over a dead flat, and can no more get above or below the level, than if they were so much stagnant water."

[5] " So far from hearing, with any degree of surprise, that very poor verses were written by a youth from his leaving school to his leaving college, inclusive, we really believe this to be the most common

The paragraph on the essentials of poetry is exasperating
in its pettiness. The insinuation that Byron in some
poems but grafted upon " what the greatest poets have
done before him " is misleading and, as applies to literary
conduct, insulting. The translations are only " school
exercises," except two which are but " things." The not
unworthy imitations of Ossian " look very like McPherson ;
and we are positive they are pretty nearly as stupid and
tiresome." The poems on habits of life at school and in
college are only so many " ingenious effusions," too many
indeed by their precise number. The final paragraph, in its
mock disappointment at the author's purpose to abandon
writing, is irritating enough of itself to warrant Byron's
reply in kind. Some of the figures and phrases in the
critique, such as the legal terms in the minority plea, the
gift horse, and the like, are foreign to a critical vocabulary.[1]

The whole composition is void of any positive power.
Its spirit is prevailingly listless and apathetic, as if the
critic were too contemptuous of his author to waste a vigorous word on him. In this fact lies the only force, negative
certainly, the piece possesses, to wit, an ire-raising power
in its attitude of indolent, and insolent, superiority over the
poet. The attack was indeed not worth a rejoinder, but
only a poet with a patience like Job's could have suffered
to pass unnoticed so haughty a detraction.

Byron's sensitiveness suffered pretty keenly for a while
from the attack.[2] The infliction was recognized at the time

of all occurrences; that it happens in the life of nine men in ten who
are educated in England; and that the tenth man writes better verse
than Lord Byron."

[1] Byron says in 1821, " That critique was a master-piece of low
wit, a tissue of scurrilous abuse."—Moore, *Life* VII, 223. John
C. Roe, *Some Obscure and Disputed Points in Byron's Biography*,
says Brougham wrote the article and reports him as saying, " There
is not one word in that review of which I am ashamed."

[2] See " Journal," Nov. 22, 1813, *L. & J.* II, 330 f., III, 52, V,
267, etc.

as unmerited. Furthermore, the reputation of the magazine and public sympathy were against the reviewers.[1] Everywhere the justice of Byron's cause was asserted and his counter-attack applauded.[2] It is as nearly universally conceded, too, that he employed the same methods that were used against him.[3] And Byron was assured that all this was criticism, not only the practices of the reviewers but his own poem as well.[4]

The poem was more than an exposure of a system of unjust criticism by its own methods.[5] The part dealing with

[1] " The Edinburgh Reviewers, Chief and subalterns, were proper game, for they were become *ferae naturae*, and of course had put themselves out of the privilege of legal protection as writers. They had in fact made war upon the literary world, and consequently were brigands and pirates, who by their outrages justified every honest trader, in hanging them up to public odium, as robbers and outlaws. Lord Byron merited therefore, the thanks of the commonwealth of letters, for laying open the practices and holding up the names of the persons of these marauders who were known to hold their meetings for the selection of victims under the roof of a British Peer."—John Watkins, *Byron*, 81. Watkins is usually a Byron detractor.

[2] " I had drunk in with youthful avidity, not only his poems but his stinging satire, which appeared to me the grandest piece of poetical justice ever inflicted on the critics, not excepting the ' Dunciad ' itself."—Mary Howitt, *An Autobiography* I, 141 f. " There was, after all, more in the boldness of the enterprise, in the fearlessness of the attack, than in its intrinsic force. But the moral effect of the gallantry of the assault, and of the justice of the cause, made it victorious and triumphant."—Brydges, *Letters*, 35.

[3] " Jeffrey and Brougham were seethed in their own milk."— Nichol, *Byron*, 53. "Assuredly he had turned the weapons of his critics against themselves."—Fuess, *Byron as a Satirist in Verse*, 68. And the poem was " calculated to produce a salutary revolution in literary criticism."—Watkins, *Byron*, 82.

[4] Kennedy reports Byron as saying of Jeffrey much later, " He has been uniform in a more fair and honourable mode of criticism than some who profess to be more decidedly my admirers."—*Conservations*, 158. Cf., " He is the best of men and the ablest of critics." —*L. & J.* III, 124. Cf. *L. & J.* II, 403, IV, 54, *Correspondence* I, 248, *Don Juan* X, 16.

[5] " There is much more in *English Bards* than the outburst against critics."—Fuess, *Byron as a Satirist in Verse*, 58.

the reviewers is only a fragment of the expanded portion. Before the celebrated critique the poem was only the *British Bards*. Nor need the idea prevail that the retaliatory portion was done in an excess of passion. The critique appeared in January, 1808. The satire was published March 1 the following year. The intervening time was spent in addition and revision,[1] under Dallas's careful oversight. Anger at white heat cannot last so long. By continuing his original plan Byron broadened his field so as to include every claimant for literary notice. By the zest given him by the unfavorable review, what would have been little more than meddlesome pastime became a serious pursuit.[2] More than half a hundred names are included in his roster, all contemporary or immediately antecedent. His judgments in the majority of cases were fundamentally sound for his age. Some of his phrases have become proverbs of criticism.

Before another generation had passed, criticism had become much what it is to-day. The type succumbed to a worthier by the same law that makes progress possible. When the right count is taken the *English Bards and Scotch Reviewers* will be recognized as contributing as much to the change as any other single critical work of the century.

The *English Bards and Scotch Reviewers*, from long tenure if nothing else, must remain a part of the permanent possessions of satire. There is no need to insist upon any pressing claims which the poem might possess to permanent worth as an individual critical record. Masterpieces of criticism do not usually come at so early an age. It must suffice that the purpose was critical, that the author *felt*

---

[1] " Dexterously Byron proceeded himself to don the garb of judge and to pass sentence on men older and better known than he."— Fuess, *Byron as a Satirist in Verse*, 58.

[2] " I too can hunt a Poetaster down."—1063.

the work to be critical, that it had a very large critical effect, and by a recent definition of the art[1] it has a right to take rank as criticism.

---

[1] " Literary criticism, in the first instance, is simply any opinion about any writing, or, perhaps a little more definitely, opinion about books and writers of them, or about parts and aspects of books or particular books, or about groups of books and writings, or about all books and writings. That is to say, criticism, regarded as an extant record, not as a theory, is any and all opinion on particular and general matters connected with literature."—W. T. Brewster, *The Logic of Literary Criticism.*

CHAPTER V

CRITICAL PRINCIPLES

If ever I should condescend to prose,
I'll write poetical commandments, which
Shall supersede beyond all doubt all those
That went before; in these I shall enrich
My text with many things that no one knows,
And carry precept to the highest pitch:
I'll call the work " Longinus o'er a Bottle
Or, Every Poet his *own* Aristotle."—*Don Juan* I, 204.

Byron thought too concretely,[1] and wrote too rapidly to formulate a definite code of literary principles.[2] But scattered here and there in his works—in the body of his poetry, where he was compelled to " keep tune "; in *Don Juan* in particular, where the personal interest was not so pronounced as in his other satirical poems on literary subjects; in a portion of his controversial writings, with the usual excesses of the kind; and very largely and more trustworthily in his letters and journals—in all these there are opinions on the general aspects of literature that are sufficient to indicate his often very decided convictions in

---

[1] To what extent he characterized himself rightly as a thinker, from his handwriting, the reader may judge:—" It is that of one who thinks much, rapidly, perhaps deeply, but rarely with pleasure."— *L. & J.* VI, 249.

[2] His nearest approach to anything of the kind is his *Hints from Horace*, done at the outset of his career, before he had found himself. Its generalizations are adapted from Horace, and its original parts are but weak satire. Perhaps no uninitiated reader ever came away from it without a feeling of disappointment.

literary matters. These opinions represent him at every stage of his career, and impress the reader, upon a review of them, as being remarkably consistent, for what has been understood of Byron's character.

Poetry In Byron's diary for 1821 occurs this significant passage:

Memoranda

What is Poetry ?—The feeling of a Former world and Future.[1]

This is his only attempt at a definition of poetry.[2] Perhaps he expected it to become as famous as some of the definitions by great masters of the art. It deserves as much, and yet it is never seen quoted or referred to apart from the connection in which it was written. Apparently it has not been subjected to the right analysis, if indeed to any analysis at all.

The passage is not to be taken simply as a bit of literary musing, or as the fancy of a moment as fancifully expressed. It contains, as nearly as anything can, the essence of Byron's inspired and acquired knowledge of his art. It represents his deliberate and mature judgment. He had been " the sultan of English literature " for a decade, his powers were at their full, and apparently the record was made in as nearly an Aristotelean calm as he ever attained— the privacy of his diary. His ideas on the subject elsewhere are an analytical part of this definition. In fact, they are necessary to explain it. Poetry, to wit, is twofold in its essence.[3] It arises in experience, which is its

---

[1] *L. & J.* V, 189.

[2] " This prose poem of a sentence " should be the starting point of any intelligent study of Byron's poetry.

[3] The idea of the *dream*, the *un*-literal reality of poetry, is a part of his terminology elsewhere, e. g., " Now to dreams of another genus —Poesies."—*L. & J.* II, 37.

former-world character, and it apprehends the future, which is the gift of prophecy.[1]   Its cosmos, be it noted, is *feeling* not intellect.

Byron's conception of poetry comprehends the traditional idea of the divine afflatus, although he identifies the inspired impulse with but some normal human instincts in excess.   Whatever may have been his conscious sympathies, and they have been exaggerated as classical, in this notion he is, at every point in his career, romantic to an extreme.

It is the lava of the imagination whose eruption prevents an earthquake.[2]

Are not the *passions* the food and fuel of poesy?[3]

I can never get people to understand that poetry is the expression of *excited passion*, and that there is no such thing as a life of passion any more than a continuous earthquake, or an eternal fever.[4]

Poetry is in itself passion, and does not systematize.   It assails, but does not argue; it may be wrong, but it does not assume pretensions to Optimism.[5]

His definitive term for the impulse or specific passion is *estro*,[6] without which the person is powerless to indite poetry.   The spell is not subject to his will.   It transcends his control and is a separate and distinct talent or faculty.

---

[1] Cf., " The best of Prophets of the future is the Past."—*L. & J.* V, 190. Notably, Byron's definition of poetry is closer akin to Aristotle's than many other better known ones,—οὐ τὸ τὰ γενόμενα λέγειν, τοῦτο ποιητοῦ ἔργον ἐστίν, ἀλλ᾿ οἷα ἂν γένοιτο.

[2] *L. & J.* III, 405.

[3] *L. & J.* V, 55.

[4] *L. & J.* V, 318.

[5] *L. & J.* V, 582.   The reader need hardly be reminded that in all cases of the kind Byron is self-defining.   Cf. *Prophecy of Dante*, Canto IV, 10 f., *Don Juan* IV, 106-7, & XIV, 8.

[6] Cf. *L. & J.* IV, 11, 43, V, 336, etc.   The word is of classic origin, Latin *oestrus*, Greek οἶστρος, literally *gadfly*.   It is used by Marston in the sense employed by Byron.   Byron uses the word *estrum* once in the ordinary sense of passion, in one of his Venetian intrigues. See *L. & J.* IV, 195. Cf. *L. & J.* IV, 49.

A man's poetry is a distinct faculty, or soul, and has no more to do with the every-day individual than the Inspiration with the Pythoness when removed from her tripod.[1]

His explanation of his own poetical character is to the same effect.

As for poesy, mine is the *dream* of my sleeping Passions; when they are awake, I cannot speak their language, only in their Somnambulism, and just now they are not dormant.[2]

My poesy is one thing, I am another. I am not such an anthropophagus as they make me. My poetry is a separate faculty. The ideal has no effect on the real character. I can only write when the *estro* is upon me; at all other times I am myself.[3]

I feel exactly as you do about our " art," but it comes over me in a kind of rage every now and then, like * * * * , and then, if I don't write to empty my mind, I go mad. As to that regular, uninterrupted love of writing, which you describe in your friend, I do not understand it. I feel it as a torture, which I must get rid of, but never as a pleasure. On the contrary, I think composition a great pain.[4]

The poetical ecstacy, or *estro*, has its life with the other elemental powers, and subsides with them. Its most sanguine period is approximately from twenty to thirty.[5]

---

[1] *L. & J.* V, 479. He repeats himself to Trelawny:—" Extemporizing verses is only nonsense; poetry is a distinct faculty,—it won't come when called,—you may as well whistle for a wind; a Pythoness was primed when put upon her tripod."—*Records of Byron, Shelley and the Author*, 202. It is amusing to note that despite Byron's tenet of the independence of the poetical gift and his insistence upon this recognition everywhere, he is universally acknowledged as having written less apart from himself and his life than any other poet in the language.

[2] *L. & J.* IV, 43.

[3] Trelawny, *Records*, 22.

[4] *L. & J.* V, 214-15. Cf., " My passions, when once lighted up, raged like so many devils till they got vent in rhyme."—Burns, Letter to Dr. Moore, August 2, 1787.

[5] See *L. & J.* V, 450, VI, 163, " To the Countess of Blessington," and *Don Juan* IV, 3.

g

Correspondingly, the fervor is never at any one time maintained long at full glow. Because of the impossibility of so maintaining it, a poem of any great length or an extensive body of poetry, excellent throughout, is not to be expected.

> After all, what is a work—any—or every work—but a desert with fountains, and, perhaps, a grove or two, every day's journey.[1]

> *Where* is the poetry of which *one half* is good ? is it the *Æneid* ? is it *Milton's* ? is it *Dryden's* ? is it any one's except *Pope's* and Goldsmith's, of which *all* is good ? and yet these two last are the poets your pond poets would explode. But if *one half* of the two new Cantos be good in your opinion, what the devil would you have more ? No—no: no poetry is *generally* good—only by fits and starts—and you are lucky to get a sparkle here and there. You might as well want a Midnight *all stars* as rhyme all perfect.[2]

It is evident that Byron's conception of the essential character of " *the art of magic* " is consistent in every particular with the great movement of which he formed so vital a part. At every point, wherever he took occasion to express himself on the subject, he is found to be romantic in the fullest sense. To him poetry was not an intellectual accomplishment, was not evolved by the will or process of the reasoning faculty. It was a gift born with the man, and had its own distinctive entity in the emotions. His view is wellnigh perfectly phrased by the great leader of the school, Wordsworth, whom he for several years affected to despise, in the well-known definition, " Poetry is the spontaneous overflow of powerful feeling."

---

[1] *L. & J.* II, 326.
[2] *L. & J.* V, 18. In this judgment Byron is at one with Coleridge, the greatest critic of the period if not of all English literature :— "A poem of any length neither can be, nor ought to be, all poetry."— *Biographia Literaria*, XIV. One associates, as well, the American romantic poet, Poe, in his *The Poetic Principle*. Cf. *L. & J.* IV, 165, and I, 122.

The Poet Byron did not entertain a high opinion of the poet *per se*. Apart from any generous self-depreciation that may have been behind his utterances on the subject, the reader will remember his early preference for a life of action, political or military, his repeatedly expressed determination to abandon the literary career, and his final adoption of a course of action which led to his death. There is little reason to doubt the sincerity of his attitude.

In his estimate of the poet he agrees further with the romantic idea of the poetic faculty as inhering in original genius. It possesses the man, as the spell the Ancient Mariner, without his will or consent. Its presence depresses or weakens the other powers, and constitutes in its own excess a trait of unsoundness.[1]

As to defining what a poet *should* be, it is not worth while, for what are they worth ? What have they done ? [2]

I have no great esteem for poetical persons, particularly women ; they have so much of the " ideal " in *practics*, as well as *ethics*.[3]

I by no means rank poetry or poets high in the scale of intellect. This may look like affectation, but it is my real opinion. . . . They say poets never or rarely go *mad*. Cowper and Collins are instances to the contrary (but Cowper was no poet). It is, however, to be remarked that they rarely do, but are generally so near it that I cannot help thinking rhyme is so far useful in anticipating and preventing the disorder. I prefer the talents of action—of war, or the senate, or even of science, —to all the speculations of those mere dreamers of another existence (I don't mean religiously but fancifully) and spectators of this apathy.[4]

[1] It is worth while to note that his view is historical, —διὸ εὐφυοῦς ἡ ποιητική ἐστιν ἢ μανικοῦ.—Aristotle, *Poetics*.
[2] Diary, *L. & J.* V, 196.
[3] *L. & J.* II, 346 f.
[4] *L. & J.* III, 405. Cf.,
                 " Most wretched men
Are cradled into poetry by wrong,
They learn in suffering what they teach in song."
       —Maddalo (Byron) in Shelley's *Julian and Maddalo*.

An addiction to poetry is very generally the result of " an uneasy mind in an uneasy body " ; disease or deformity have been the attendants of many of our best. Collins mad—Chatterton, I think, mad—Cowper mad—Pope crooked—Milton blind—Gray (I have heard that the last was afflicted by an incurable and very grievous distemper, though not generally known) and others—I have somewhere read, however, that poets rarely go mad.[1]

I believe that *prose* is, after all, the most reputable, for certes, if one could foresee—but I won't go on—that is, with this sentence ; but poetry is, I fear, incurable.[2]

Great imagination is seldom accompanied by equal powers of reason, and *vice versâ*, so that we rarely possess superiority in any one point, except at the expense of another. It is surely then unjust to render poets responsible for their want of common sense, since it is only by the excess of imagination they can arrive at being poets, and this excess debars reason ; indeed the very circumstance of a man's yielding to the vocation of a poet ought to serve as a voucher that he is no longer of sound mind.[3]

Byron harbored the notion, with not a little pride, that in the possession of his talent, or accompanying it, he had a strain of insanity in his make-up. Certainly he lived under a partial reputation of the kind for a good portion of his life.[4]

[1] *L. & J.* III, 247.
[2] *L. & J.* III, 372.
[3] Countess of Blessington, *Conversations*, 192.
[4] Lady Caroline Lamb's expression upon her first acquaintance with him is too well known to require repeating. Nor does the reader need to be reminded of the charges made against him at the time of his separation from Lady Byron. Cf. also, " During all this period, when his fame culminated, he is represented as being little better than mad."—Alexander Leighton, *Life of Lord Byron*, XII. " It has been thought by some, that there was madness in his composition. He himself talked sometimes as if he feared it would come upon him."—Leigh Hunt, *Lord Byron*, 146. Schopenhauer, who strikingly resembled Byron in some particulars of his character, regarded Byron as mad.

I feel a something, which makes me think that, if I ever reach near to old age, like Swift, " I shall die at top" first. Only I do not dread idiotism or madness as much as he did. On the contrary, I think some quieter stages of both must be preferable to much of what men think the possession of their senses.[1]

I hope that the Gods have made her anything save *poetical*— it is enough to have one such fool in a family.[2]

The compensation, at least partial, and to Byron more than sufficient, for the taint of insanity in the poet, was the gift of prophecy.[3] The poet was " something of the vates or prophet." This gives to poetry its future-world character, as indicated in Byron's definition.

The Poetic Life The life given up to poetry, as an integral and useful part of society, Byron deplored wherever occasion offered. The poetic life was reserved for him who was caught in the toils and could not escape.

No one should be a rhymer who could be anything better.[4]

I do think the preference of *writers* to *agents*—the mighty stir made about scribbling and scribes, by themselves and others —a sign of effeminacy, degeneracy, and weakness. Who would write, who had anything better to do ? "Action—action— action"—said Demosthenes : "Actions—actions," I say, and not writing,—least of all, rhyme. Look at the querulous and

---

[1] *L. & J.* V, 156. Cf. *Correspondence* II, 123.

[2] *L. & J.* VI, 264. The reference is to his daughter. Cf. *L. & J.* II, 54, 222, 390, IV, 4, *Correspondence* I, 259. The Countess Guiccioli gives an account of Byron's having composed some verses while in a delirium from a fever, and concludes, " The rhythm of these verses was quite correct, and the poetry itself had no appearance of being the work of a delirious mind. He preserved the verses for some·time afterwards and then burned them."

[3] See *L. & J.* III, 95, 274, IV, 368, V, 19-20, and " Ode to Napoleon Buonaparte," " The Prophecy of Dante," and *Correspondence* II, 158, 164.

[4] *L. & J.* II, 338.

monotonous lives of the " genus ";—except Cervantes, Tasso,
Dante, Ariosto, Kleist (who were brave and active citizens),
Æschylus, Sophocles, and some others of the antiques also—
what a worthless, idle brood it is![1]

If one's years can't be better employed than in sweating
poesy, a man had better be a ditcher.[2]

Poetry should only occupy the idle.   In more serious affairs
it would be ridiculous.[3]

Obviously in all this there is an implied acknowledgment
of the romantic idea of the moral aloofness and solitude,
the isolated grandeur of poetical genius, and the special
election of the muse-controlled life.

Poetic Sources   Experience is the true fountain head of
poetry, and a leaven of truth, though
not all truth or fact, an essential.   The end and aim of
writing is to stimulate in the reader the sensations the
author has experienced.   If the author's production is pure
invention it cannot have this effect.

To write so as to bring home to the heart, the heart must
have been tried,—but, perhaps, ceased to be so.[4]

A man cannot paint a storm with the vessel under bare
poles on a lee-shore.[5]

I could not write upon anything, without some personal
experience and foundation.[6]

There was no expectation, of course, that composition
should be coincidental with the experience.   It was sufficient that there had been experience.   Memory could be
trusted to select and organize for the best effect.

---

[1] *L. & J.* II, 345.
[2] *L. & J.* IV, 284.
[3] Count Gamba, *Expedition to Greece*, 48. Cf. *L. & J.* II, 18, 402,
and *Beppo*, stanza 75.
[4] *L. & J.* II, 387 f.
[5] *L. & J.* III, 126.
[6] *L. & J.* III, 254. Cf. *L. & J.* V, 70, *Don Juan* III, 87.

While you are under the influence of passions, you only feel, but cannot describe them,—any more than, when in action, you could turn round and tell the story to your next neighbour! When all is over,—all, all, and irrevocable,—trust to memory— she is then but too faithful.[1]

My first impressions are always strong and confused, and my Memory *selects* and reduces them to order, like distance in the landscape, and blends them better, although they may be less distinct.[2]

In his insistence upon experience Byron has nothing critically new to offer. It is in his requirement of truth that he is more individual. He equates truth with fact, although he is a little confused in his usage,[3] and allows all the liberty of a potter with his clay. His one condition is that there shall be a foundation of fact in any attempt at a work of art.

I hate things *all fiction*; and therefore the *Merchant* and *Othello* have no great associations to me: but *Pierre* has. There should always be some foundation of fact for the most airy fabric, and pure invention is but the talent of a liar.[4]

I detest all fiction even in song.[5]

And fact is Truth, the grand desideratum!
Of which, howe'er the Muse describes each act,
There should be ne'ertheless a slight substratum.[6]

'Tis the part
Of a true poet to escape from fiction
Whene'er he can; for there is little art
In leaving verse more free from the restriction
Of Truth than prose.[7]

---

[1] *L. & J.* II, 388.
[2] *L. & J.* IV, 119. Cf. Wordsworth's ," Poetry . . . takes its origin from emotion recollected in tranquillity."—Preface to *Lyrical Ballads.*
[3] Cf. *Don Juan* XI, 37.
[4] *L. & J.* IV, 93.
[5] *Don Juan* VI, 8.
[6] *Don Juan* VII, 81.
[7] *Don Juan* VIII, 86. Cf., " If the essence of poetry must be a *lie*, throw it to the dogs."—Letter to Murray on Bowles.

Even the novel, the most fictional of all types, is not exempt from the general requirement.

> For Truth is always strange—
> Stranger than fiction: if it could be told,
> How much would novels gain by the exchange![1]

But he is not realist enough to admit all truths.

> Some truths are better kept behind a screen,
> Especially when they would look like lies.[2]

The analytical method, or scientific search for primary causes or truths, is discouraged.

> 'Tis sad to hack into the roots of things,
> They are so much intertwisted with the earth;
> So that the branch a goodly verdure flings,
> I reck not if an acorn gave it birth.
> To trace all actions to their secret springs
> Would make indeed some melancholy mirth.[3]

And he was classic enough to allow, with proper caution, the use of second-hand material.

> As to originality, all pretensions are ludicrous,—" there is nothing new under the sun." [4]

How difficult it is to say anything new! Who was that voluptuary of antiquity, who offered a reward for a new pleasure? Perhaps all nature and art could not supply a new idea.[5]

Of abstract subjects, as materials for literary treatment, he has next to nothing to say.

> I hate all mystery, and that air
> Of clap-trap, which your recent poets prize,[6]

---

[1] *Don Juan* XIV, 101.
[2] *Don Juan* XIV, 80. Cf. Aristotle, *Poetics* XXIV, 9&10.
[3] *Don Juan* XIV, 59.
[4] *L. & J.* II, 373.
[5] Medwin, *Conversations of Lord Byron at Pisa*, 244. Cf. *Hints from Horace*, 183 f.
[6] *Don Juan* II, 124.

is hardly true, coming from a mystery-shrouded romantic like Byron. Of the sources of the sublime he says tritely, perhaps lightly, enough:

> The sad's a source of the sublime.[1]

But he seems to have been in earnest in his notion of the possibilities of a treatment of fear.

We have had " Pleasures of Hope," " Pleasures of Memory," " Pleasures of Imagination," and " Pleasures of Love." I wonder that no one has thought of writing " Pleasures of Fear." It surely is a poetical subject, and much might be made of it in good hands. . . . it has more of the true sublime than any of the other passions.[2]

Poetic Diction Byron has not much to say of the diction of poetry. In his letters to his publishers and literary advisers, there is frequent commentary on epithets, or choice between words or expressions, showing that he studied his own phrasing carefully, or rather restudied questionable passages carefully.[3] Occasionally, too, there is a discussion of some individual quality or effect of words.

"Adorn " and " mourn " are lawful rhymes in Pope's *Death of the Unfortunate Lady*.—Gray has " forlorn " and " mourn "— and " torn " and " mourn " are in Smollett's famous *Tears of Scotland*.[4]

He is known to have preferred the Italian as a poetical language to any other,[5] but he made no analysis of his preference. And of the qualities of special vocabularies, or of groups and classes of words, he is only too reticent.

---

[1] *Don Juan* XIII, 1.
[2] Countess of Blessington, *Conversations*, 185 f. Cf. *L. & J.* V, 190.
[3] Cf., " I believe this is the third scrawl since yesterday—all about epithets."—*L. & J.* II, 152.
[4] *L. & J.* II, 155.
[5] See Chapter II, 46 f. Cf., " That most poetical of all languages." —Review of W. R. Spenser's Poems. Cf. *Correspondence* I, 84, 87.

In regard to the use of new and old words he but voices the common opinion.[1] He condemns compound terms as a principle, but employs them himself at times in lieu of better.

I hate compounds, for the present I will try (*col' permesso*) the word " genius gifted patriots of our line " instead. Johnson has " many-coloured life," a compound—but they are always best avoided.[2]

In dialogue the speech must be natural to the character using it.[3] The character is an individual, separate and apart from the author. He may have his creator's acumen and power behind him, but his speech and processes of thought must be his own.

My ideas of a character may run away with me: like ·all imaginative men, I, of course, embody myself with the character while I *draw* it, but not a moment after the pen is from off the paper.[4]

Byron doubtless never stopped to argue in his mind any difference between poetic speech and any other literary or practical medium.[5] What he used in his own compositions was natural to him, and he would have denounced artificiality of expression in others. In this respect he was consistently romantic.

The Literary Spirit Classic and Romantic Byron did not attempt to analyze general poetical content, or interest himself in a distinction between the two conventional extremes, romantic and classic, of the literary spirit. His early expressions of regard for

---

[1] Cf. *Hints from Horace*, 79 f.
[2] *L. & J.* II, 152. Cf. *L. & J.* III, 27.
[3] Cf. *Hints from Horace*, 127 f.
[4] *L. & J.* VI, 32.
[5] " The language of all nations nearest to a state of nature is said to be Poetry."—Reported by Hobhouse as being just about what Byron wrote to Lady Byron on sending her his " Fare Thee Well."—*Recollections* II, 316.

Pope became later vehement protestations, but he did not
have a very clear idea of any principle involved, and he
was not aware that he was professing himself an adherent
of any school. His sympathies were personal more than
anything else. Earlier, as might be divined from his distaste for classical studies in his school life, his inclinations
were romantic. If the *Hints from Horace*, as classical a
work as he ever did, is interesting for anything, it is for
its tendency away from what is commonly understood as
classicism in the direction of romanticism.[1] The terms
classic and *romantic* are not unknown in his writings as
referring to literary manner and spirit.[2] But he seems
never to have formed an opinion of the elements of the
movement in which he was so large a figure.

An " Epicurean system," carried on by men of the most opposite habits, tastes, and opinions in life and poetry (I believe),
that ever had their names in the same volume—Moore, Byron,
Shelley, Hazlitt, Haydon, Leigh Hunt, Lamb—what resemblance do ye find among all or any of these men ? and how
could any sort of system or plan be carried on, or attempted
amongst them ? [3]

I perceive that in Germany, as well as in Italy, there is a
great struggle about what they call " *Classical* " and " *Romantic*,"
—terms which were not subjects of classification in England,
at least when I left if four or five years ago. Some of the English
Scribblers, it is true, abused Pope and Swift, but the reason
was that they themselves did not know how to write either
prose or verse ; but nobody thought them worth making a sect
of. Perhaps there may be something of the kind sprung up

---

[1] Cf. lines 423-432, 505-508, 697-701, etc., and, " I have adapted
it entirely to our new school of poetry, though always keeping pretty
close to the original."—*Correspondence* I, 31.

[2] Cf. *L. & J.* II, 407, V, 554, note, " To Romance," *Don Juan*
IV, 18, and Preface to *The Prophecy of Dante*.

[3] *L. & J.* IV, 273.

lately, but I have not heard much about it, and it would be such bad taste that I shall be very sorry to believe it.[1]

Types and Forms As of the more pervasive elements of spirit and style, so of the more general types or forms he has not said much. His utterances, as might be supposed, are confined almost wholly to poetry.[2] For one form of discourse, Description,[3] common to both prose and poetry, he expressed dislike at times, despite his own superb descriptive powers. This was doubtless because to him the descriptive element more than any other distinguished the age from the one preceding.

He has more to say of the epic genre than of any other, except drama. His contribution to the type is *Don Juan*.[4] It is the only poem of his that could make any pretensions, in his judgment, to epic proportions. It occupied his last years and was unfinished at his death. His declarations on the type, in the poem itself and in his correspondence connected with it, contain something new for criticism.

It was his unshaken conviction that the poem was epic in substance and structure —the *modern* epic.

---

[1] *L. & J.* V, 104. Cf. his *jeux d'esprit* verse:—

" Besides my style is the romantic,
Which some call fine, and some call frantic;
While others are or would seem *as* sick
Of repetitions nicknamed Classic.
For my part all men must allow
Whatever I was, I'm classic now."—*E Nihilo Nihil.*

The Italian police records (*L. & J.* IV, 463), 1819, show that Byron belonged to a society called " Romantici," which "aims at the destruction of our literature, our politics, our country."

[2] "As to *prose*, I don't know Addison's from Johnson's."—*L. & J.* III, 10. Late in life he expressed a preference for prose for reading. See Chapter II, 39. Cf. *L. & J.* IV, 43, and *Correspondence* I, 254.

[3] Cf. *L. & J.* I, 234, 267, *Don Juan* V, 52, *ibid.* X, 28.

[4] Karl Elze asserts :—" Der *Don Juan* ist kein Epos . . . . . . nur ein einziges Element fehlt ihm, das ist das epische."—*Byron*, 415.

My poem's epic, and is meant to be
Divided in twelve books; each book containing,
With Love, and War, a heavy gale at sea,
A list of ships, and captains, and kings reigning,
New characters; the episodes are three:
A panoramic view of Hell's in training,
After the style of Virgil and of Homer,
So that my name of Epic's no misnomer.

All these things will be specified in time,
With strict regard to Aristotle's rules,
The *Vade Mecum* of the true sublime.[1]

                        You have now
Had sketches of Love—Tempest—Travel—War,—
All very accurate, you must allow,
And *Epic*, if plain truth should prove no bar.[2]

It shall have twenty-four books too, the legitimate number.
Episodes it has, and will have, out of number; and my spirits,
good or bad, must serve for the machinery. If that be not
an epic, if it be not strictly according to Aristotle, I don't
know what an epic poem means.[3]

Except in little departures in method from " the heroic
turn-pike road," which he regarded as but a matter of
individual privilege, the poem from the start, in its consistency of design, was epic in his mind. That its " design "
was in having no design at all, was no detriment to it in
such ordering. The old classic epics were never noted for
their regularity or consecutiveness of plot.

I *have* no plan—I *had* no plan; but I had or have materials. . . .
Why, Man, the Soul of such writing is its license; at least the
liberty of that *license*, if one likes—*not* that one should abuse it.[4]

----

[1] *Don Juan* I, 200 f.

[2] *Don Juan* VIII, 138.

[3] Medwin, *Conversations*, 202 f. He later declared, because of the
attacks upon the poem, he would make the number of cantos ' a
hundred at least.' See *L. & J.* VI, 429, V, 242, etc.

[4] *L. & J.* IV, 343.

If you must have an epic, there's " Don Juan " for you. I call that an epic: it is an epic as much in the spirit of our day as the Iliad was in Homer's. Love, religion, and politics form the argument, and are as much the cause of quarrels now as they were then.[1]

In the sense of *the modern epic*, the only sense in Byron's mind, and the one on which he insisted repeatedly, his interpretation deserves careful weighing. The materials, form, and larger treatment of the poem are legitimately epic, but whether its spirit will come to be recognized as proper for epic remains yet to be seen. In something of the kind lies perhaps the only chance the genre has of permanence. Epics do not come every generation and Byron's is only a century removed. A continuation of or return to the older models cannot be expected.

The sonnet is a rare form in Byron's poetry, notwithstanding its popularity as a romantic product. But its absence is hardly remarkable when his opinion of the form is taken into account. The opinion, however, is somewhat surprising coming as it does from the author of as fine examples as the sonnets on *Chillon* and to *Lake Leman*. •

Redde some Italian, and wrote two Sonnets on * * * . I never wrote but one sonnet before, and that was not in earnest, and many years ago, as an exercise—and I will never write another. They are the most puling, petrifying, stupidly platonic compositions. I detest the Petrarch so much, that I would not be the man even to have obtained his Laura, which the metaphysical, whining dotard never could.[2]

His idea of poetry, from his definition, fits the lyrical poet better than the poet of more sustained efforts. But Byron's talent was not conspicuously lyrical. All that he has to say of the whole *singing* genre is merely:

---

[1] Medwin, *Conversations*, 202. Cf., " The *Æneid* was a *political* poem, and written for a *political* purpose."—*L. & J*. II, 26.

[2] *L. & J*. II, 379.

Repetition is only the " soul of Ballad singing." [1]

He is essentially romantic in approving and practicing many verse forms.[2]

Metrical Forms He has spoken more fully on metrical structures. As an admirer of Pope he naturally commends the heroic couplet.

Not the most difficult, but, perhaps, the best adapted measure to our language, the good old and now neglected heroic couplet.[3]

He employed the couplet here and there throughout his career, and approved it ever, but he abandoned it in attempting his more ambitious efforts.

The couplet is more difficult still, because the last line, or one out of two, must be good.[4]

I can weave a nine-line stanza faster than a couplet, for which measure I have not the cunning.[5]

The Spenserian stanza—or the kindred octave—was, on the whole, his preference,[6] in accordance with the romantic trend. Its freedom, next to blank verse, suited his talent best, he understood its uses and possibilities most, and he employed it to the greatest advantage of all measures.[7]

---

[1] *L. & J*. IV, 218.

[2] He purposely varied the metrical forms of his tales and received some severe criticism for it. See *L. & J*. III, 263 f.

[3] Dedication to the *Corsair*.

[4] Captain Medwin, *Conversations*, 291.

[5] *L. & J*. II, 150.

[6] He disapproved wide liberties with the measure. Appropos to Hodgson's *Friends*, he says:—"As to the poetry of his Newfangled Stanza, I wish they would write the octave or the Spenser; we have no other legitimate measure of that kind."—*L. & J*. IV, 304. And of Herbert's *Hedin* :—"What does Helga Herbert mean by his *Stanza* ? which is octave got drunk or gone mad. He ought to have his ears boxed with Thor's hammer for rhyming so fantastically."—*L. & J*. V, 39 f. Cf. *L. & J*. IV, 164.

[7] Saintsbury says that interest in Byron's prosody lies in his Spenserians, but he denies him excellence therein.—*History of English Prosody* III, 97 f.

The stanza of Spenser is perhaps too slow and dignified for narrative; though, I confess, it is the measure most after my own heart.[1]

The stanza of Spenser, according to one of our most successful poets, admits of every variety. Dr. Beattie makes the following observation:—"Not long ago, I began a poem in the style and stanza of Spenser, in which I propose to give full scope to my inclination, and be either droll or pathetic, descriptive or sentimental, tender or satirical, as the humour strikes me; for, if I mistake not, the measure which I have adopted admits equally of all these kinds of composition." Strengthened in my opinion by such authority, and by the example of some in the highest order of Italian poets, I shall make no apology for attempts at similar variations in the following composition; satisfied that, if they are unsuccessful, their failure must be in the execution, rather than in the design sanctioned by the practice of Ariosto, Thomson, and Beattie.[2]

The Spenser stanza is difficult, because it is like a sonnet, and the finishing line must be good.[3]

Octosyllabic measure he shrewdly characterized as possessing a "fatal facility," which rendered its use hazardous and required caution.

Scott alone, of the present generation, has hitherto completely triumphed over the fatal facility of the octosyllabic verse.[4]

Terza rima, admirable in the language of its origin, is suited to English, apparently, only in short poems of the nature and dignity of the ode.

Terza Rima does not seem to suit the genius of English poetry—it is certainly uncalculated for a work of any length.

---

[1] Dedication to the *Corsair*.
[2] Preface to *Childe Harold* I & II.
[3] Captain Medwin, *Conversations*, 291.
[4] *Corsair*, Letter of Dedication to Moore. Byron's criticism of the measure was doubtless from its use by such poets as Dyer, Collins, and Prior. He could hardly have had in mind Milton's masterful employment. Cf. *Hints from Horace*, 400 f.

In our language, however, it may do for a short ode. The public at least thought my attempt a failure, and the public is in the main right.[1]

He recognized the greatness of blank verse in his native language.

Blank-verse is the most difficult of all, because every line must be good.[2]

In blank verse, Milton, Thomson, and our dramatists, are the beacons that shine along the deep, but warn us from the rough and barren rock on which they are kindled.[3]

But he associated its use mainly with drama.[4] It was ill adapted to use in shorter poems.[5]

[1] Captain Medwin, *Conversations*, 194 f. Byron had reference to *The Prophecy of Dante*. He thought his use an innovation and but tried the experiment in the poem.

[2] *Ibid.*, 292.

[3] Dedication to the *Corsair*.

[4] Cf., " Blank verse is now, with one consent, allied
        To Tragedy, and rarely quits her side."
                                —*Hints from Horace* , 117 f.

[5] He says, 1812, of a poem by the future Lady Byron:—" Though I have an abhorrence of Blank Verse, I like the lines on Dermody so much that I wish they were in rhyme."—*L. & J.* II, 119-20. In 1819, he writes in some heat:—" Blank verse, which, unless in the drama, no one except Milton ever wrote who could rhyme, became the order of the day,—or else such rhyme as looked still blanker than the verse without it. I am aware that Johnson has said, after some hesitation, that he could not ' prevail upon himself to wish that Milton had been a rhymer.' The opinions of that truly great man, whom it is also the present fashion to decry, will ever be received by me with that deference which time will restore to him from all; but, with all humility, I am not persuaded that the *Paradise Lost* would not have been more nobly conveyed to posterity, not perhaps in heroic couplets, although even *they* could sustain the subject if well balanced, but in the stanza of Spenser or of Tasso, or in the terza rima of Dante, which the powers of Milton could easily have grafted on our language. The *Seasons* of Thomson would have been better in rhyme, although still inferior to his *Castle of Indolence*; and Mr. Southey's *Joan of Arc* no worse, although it might have taken up six months instead of weeks in the composition."—Reply to *Blackwood's, L. & J.* IV, 490-1.

h

Translations Byron believed the individual qualities of language to be great, every language, so to speak, having its own genius, to such an extent as to preclude the setting of a production from its native medium into another without serious impairment of its worth.

Translations almost always disappoint me; I must, however, except Pope's " Homer," which has more of the spirit of Homer than all the other translations put together, and the Teian bard himself might have been proud of the beautiful odes which the Irish Anacreon has given us.[1]

His translation of Persius is not only very literal, but preserves much of the spirit of the original . . . . he has escaped all the defects of translators, and his Persius resembles the original as nearly in feeling and sentiment as two languages so dissimilar in idiom will admit.[2]

But despite his low estimate of the art of translating, he became a translator himself, and regarded highly his works of the kind. Chief among these was his rendition of a part of Pulci's *Morgante Maggiore* into English, in the verse and stanza of the original. Its claim to merit lay, as he insisted, in its " wonderful *verbum pro verbo* " closeness to the Italian. He urged the publication of the original lines along with his translation side by side, in order to show the singular merit of his performance [3]—a model, as he esteemed it, of the translator's art.

Pulci is my favorite, that is, my translation: I think it the *acme* of putting one language into another.[4]

---

[1] Lady Blessington, *Conversations*, 240. He himself suffered a good deal from translation, and he resented always liberties of the kind with his works. But singularly enough he maintained a high regard for his own translations as such. See Chapter IX, 282 f.

[2] *Ibid.*, 239 f. The translator was Sir Wm. Drummond.

[3] " You must print it side by side with the original Italian, because I wish the reader to judge of the fidelity."—*L. & J.* IV, 407.

[4] *L. & J.* V, 64.

Pulci I am proud of : it is superb ; you have no such translation. It is the best thing I ever did in my life.[1]

The *Morgante* is the *best* translation that ever was or will be made ; and the rest are—whatever you please to think them.[2]

But there is a greater interest to us in Byron's relation to Pulci than his opinion of translations or his private estimate of his own achievement. His critical inter- pretation of Pulci is significant in literary history, because it modified existing opinion of Pulci's spirit and style, and of the quality and influence of his work. Against the popular notion Byron held that Pulci's spirit and manner was one of levity and wholesome fun-making, that his good humor was a leaven for a more serious compound, and that he was the forerunner of similar styles of writing in both Italy and England.

The Morgante Maggiore, of the first canto of which this translation is offered, divides with the Orlando Inamorato the honour of having formed and suggested the style and story of Ariosto. The great defects of Boiardo were his treating too seriously the narratives of chivalry, and his harsh style. Ariosto, in his continuation, by a judicious mixture of the gaiety of Pulci, has avoided the one ; and Berni, in his reformation of Boiardo's poem, has corrected the other. Pulci may be con- sidered as the precursor and model of Berni altogether, as he has partly been to Ariosto, however inferior to both his copyists. He is no less the founder of a new style of poetry very lately sprung up in England. I allude to that of the ingenious Whistle- craft. The serious poems on Roncesvalles in the same language, and more particularly the excellent one of Mr. Merivale, are to be traced to the same source. It has never yet been decided entirely whether Pulci's intention was or was not to deride the religion which is one of his favorite topics. It appears to me, that such an intention would have been no less hazardous to

[1] *L. & J.* V, 83.
[2] *L. & J.* VI, 31.

the poet than to the priest, particularly in that age and country; and the permission to publish the poem, and its reception among the classics of Italy, prove that it neither was nor is so interpreted. That he intended to ridicule the monastic life, and suffered his imagination to play with the simple dulness of his converted giant, seems evident enough; but surely it were as unjust to accuse him of irreligion on this account, as to denounce Fielding for his Parson Adams, Barnabas, Thwackum, Supple, and the Ordinary in Jonathan Wild—or Scott, for the exquisite use of his Covenanters in the " Tales of my Landlord." [1]

At this time there prevailed in England an idea that the " ingenious Whistlecraft " was the originator of the humorous style of poetry which he employed. Byron detected the misconception and corrected it.

I have finished my translation of the first Canto of the "*Morgante Maggiore*" of Pulci, which I will transcribe and send: it is the parent, not only of *Whistlecraft*, but of all jocose Italian poetry.[2]

I have written since about sixty stanzas of a poem, in octave stanzas, (in the Pulci style, which the fools in England think was invented by Whistlecraft—it is as old as the hills in Italy,) called *The Vision of Judgment*, by Quevedo Redivivus.[3]

Drama[4]   Byron was actively interested in drama for the greater part of his life. His interest began with a brief career in amateur dramatics at Southwell.[5] Before his exile he was for a long while a member of the committee of management of Drury Lane Theatre in Lon-

---

[1] Advertisement to *Morgante Maggiore*.
[2] *L. & J.* IV, 407.
[3] *L. & J.* V, 385.
[4] Much of the material in Byron on drama belongs earlier in the chapter, and to later chapters, but the composite character of the subject renders it desirable to treat the whole together here.
[5] See Chapter II, 32.

don.[1] From 1816[2] to the end of his career he was a writer of drama. Except *Don Juan* his plays for that period are his most considerable work. They constitute, as well, his greatest critical undertaking, to wit, an attempt to lead the way to a reformation of English drama.[3]

His interest was confined almost wholly to tragedy. He thought highly of comedy as a form,[4] although in his judgment it had degenerated,[5] just as tragedy had done. But unlike tragedy, the cause of its decline was not in the English conception of the type, or too free a departure from classic models. Its best examples were English, and the reason for its deterioration lay partly in society[6] and partly in the increasingly complicated character of the type. Its complications were a concession to the bad taste of the age, and led to melodrama in its emphasis upon device and change rather than upon matter.[7] The reclamation of the type did not require a reconstruction of the native system,

[1] Byron's connection with Drury Lane gave him an unusual opportunity to know the drama of his time and to speak upon it with authority. Cf. *L. & J.* V, 442: No other great literary figure of the time was so favored, and there is every evidence that he profited fully from his opportunity.

[2] It is creditable to his self-criticism that he distrusted his dramatic powers too much to attempt playmaking for a long while, despite many solicitations to do so. Cf., *L. & J.* II, 387, III, 16, 126, 198, etc.

[3] Cf., " In his heart he longed to see them drive the accepted drama of the day off the boards."—P. E. More, Prefatory note to the dramas, Cambridge *Byron.* See *English Bards and Scotch Reviewers,* 558 f., for an account of the drama of his day.

[4] "A comedy I take to be the most difficult of compositions, more so than tragedy."—*L. & J.* II, 373.

[5] " The days of Comedy are gone, alas!
When Congreve's fool could vie with Molière's *bête.*"—*Don Juan* XIII, 94.

[6] " Congreve and Vanbrugh are your only comedy. Our society is too insipid now for the like copy."—*L. & J.* II, 398.

[7] " Nothing so easy as intricate confusion of plot, and rant. Mrs. Centlivre, in comedy, has *ten times the bustle of Congreve*; but are they to be compared ? and yet she drove Congreve from the theatre."—*L. & J.* V, 218 f. " I also know that Congreve gave up writing because Mrs. Centlivre's balderdash drove his comedies off."—*L. & J.* IV, 426.

as did tragedy, hence he did not attempt its better-ment.[1]

It is not to be assumed that Byron's ideas of what English drama should be were servilely classical. He did not recommend a return in total outline to the Roman and Greek practice. Nor did he condemn unreservedly the great productions of English " irregular " drama. He admired its outstanding figures because they had been able to do well, with little restraint or rule, what he believed could have been done as well in most individual cases and better in general, by a conformity with rule. What he taught in precept and tried to show by example was what may be called a drama that was progressively regular. Such a type was to be realized only by a due observance of the principles which begot the best features of Greek and Roman drama adapted to the higher enlightenment and different temper of the later time.

It appears to me that there is room for a different style of the drama; neither a servile following of the old drama, which is a grossly erroneous one, nor yet *too French*, like those who succeeded the older writers. It appears to me, that good English, and a severer approach to the rules, might combine something not dishonorable to our literature.[2]

I am, however, persuaded, that this is not to be done by following the old dramatists, who are full of gross faults, pardoned only for the beauty of their language; but by writing naturally and *regularly*, and producing *regular* tragedies, like the Greeks; but not in *imitation*,—merely the outline of their conduct,

---

[1] Byron began one or two comedies, but produced none. Cf. *L. & J.* II, 314, 323, etc. From the evidence of his powers in *Don Juan*, it is interesting to speculate what he might have done in the type, if he had given himself up to it seriously as he did to tragedy.

His approval of an older ideal of comedy is further indicated in his suggestion of the close kinship of the type with tragedy:—" ' Sardana-palus ' is, however, almost a comic character; but for that matter so is Richard the third."—*L. & J.* V. 324.

[2] *L. & J.* V, 243.

adapted to our own times and circumstances, and of course *no* chorus.[1]

I want to make a *regular* English drama, no matter whether for the Stage or not, which is not my object,—but a *mental theatre*.[2]

Drama, as he conceived it, was not to be romantic. Romantic drama, preeminently that of his own day, had failed. It had not been able to combine both literary and dramatic qualities in enduring products, and it was therefore to be abandoned. Exceptional genius here and there might be its own excuse to follow its own self-appointed course. But the many who would turn to playmaking could not be trusted to manage romantic license in as technical a form as drama. Such license—and in this respect he was undoubtedly right in his criticism of plays of the time—might produce poetry but never good drama. For the sake of the anticipated reform, the first examples of the new practice should of course be severer in adherence to regularity than would be expected to prevail once the norm was attained.[3]

His first object was to attain the severe simplicity of Alfieri and the Greeks.[4]

If you want to have a notion of what I am trying, take up a *translation* of any of the *Greek* tragedians. If I said the original,

---

[1] *L. & J.* V, 217 f.

[2] *L. & J.* V, 347. Cf., " The irregularity, which is the reproach of the English theatrical compositions."—Preface to *Marino Faliero*.

[3] His idea of the permanent type is pretty concretely given in a sentence to the Countess Guiccioli on *Marino Faliero* :—" Ma non è però romantico il disegno, è piuttosto regolare."—*L. & J.* V, 295.

[4] He says of the *Doge* :—" There are neither rings, nor mistakes, nor starts, nor outrageous ranting villains, nor melodrame in it. All this will prevent it's popularity, but does not persuade me that it is *therefore* faulty. Whatever faults it has will arise from deficiency in the conduct, rather than in the conception, which is simple and severe."—*L. & J.* V, 243 f. Cf. *ibid.*, 167. Again he is indicating a close structural kinship between comedy and tragedy.

it would be an impudent presumption of mine; but the translations are so inferior to the originals, that I think I may risk it. Then judge of the " simplicity of plot, etc.," and do not judge me by your mad old dramatists, which is like drinking Usquebaugh and then proving a fountain : yet after all, I suppose that you do not mean that spirits is a nobler element than a clear spring bubbling in the sun ; and this I take to be the difference between the Greeks and those turbid mountebanks— always excepting B. Jonson, who was a Scholar and Classic. Or, take up a translation of Alfieri, and try the interest, etc., of these my new attempts in the old line, by *him* in *English*. And then tell me fairly your opinion. But don't measure me by YOUR OWN *old* or *new* tailor's yards.[1]

It has been my object to be as simple and severe as Alfieri.[2]

My dramatic simplicity is *studiously* Greek, and must continue so : *no* reform ever succeeded at first. I admire the old English dramatists ; but this is quite another field, and has nothing to do with theirs.[3]

A part of his corrective plan was to turn to history as a source of material.[4] His principle in this regard is but a part of his demand for fact as subject matter for all types of writing, and is again Greek.[5] Useless to say, he did not acknowledge all history, however striking or significant, as fit material for use, any more than he approved any and all fact for use in all writing, whatever its character.

---

[1] *L. & J.* V, 218.

[2] *L. & J.* V, 323.

[3] *L. & J.* V, 347.

[4] P. E. More says his second group of plays was " an attempt to show the playwrights of the day what could be done with mateials of history."—Cambridge *Byron,* 477.

[5] Cf., " The Venetian play, too, is rigidly historical. My object has been to dramatize, like the Greeks (a *modest* phrase!), striking passages of history, as they did of history and mythology. You will find all this very *un*like Shakespeare ; and so much the better in one sense, for I look upon him to be the *worst* of models, though the most extraordinary of writers."—*L. & J.* V, 323.

He is more nearly himself than Greek in this requirement. His restrictions were greatest of all for drama that was intended for the stage.[1]

Without ever understanding very clearly the unities himself,[2] he advised a return to them, more as a disciplinary measure than anything else. His idea was that an artistry which works consciously within certain clearly defined bounds—bounds that nature has fixed for it, as recognized, in its history—is higher and nobler and its influence more wholesome, than a romantic ignorance or wanton disregard of limitations altogether. And his position was strengthened by the fact that practice in this license had ceased to yield artistic products.

I was always a friend to the unities, and believe that subjects are not wanting which may be treated in strict conformity to their rules. No one can be absurd enough to contend, that the preservation of the unities is a defect,—at least a fault. Look at Alfieri's plays, and tell me what is wanting in them. Does

---

[1]   " Yet many deeds preserved in History's page
        Are better told than acted on the stage;
        The ear sustains what shocks the timid eye,
        And Horror thus subsides to Sympathy.
        True Briton all beside, I here am French—
        Bloodshed 'tis surely better to retrench:
        The gladiatorial gore we teach to flow
        In tragic scenes disgusts, though but in show;
        We hate the carnage while we see the trick,
        And find small sympathy in being sick.
        Not on the stage the regicide Macbeth
        Appals an audience with a Monarch's death;
        To gaze when sable Hubert threats to sear
        Young Arthur's eyes, can *ours* or *Nature* bear ?
        A haltered heroine Johnson sought to slay—
        We saved Irene, but half damned the play."
                              —*Hints from Horace* , 267 f.

[2] Samuel C. Chew says that Byron derived his ideas of the unities from Dryden chiefly:—" That he had studied the arguments for and against the unities in the *Essay of Dramatic Poesy* is proved by a close verbal reminiscence."—*The Dramas*, 165.

he ever deviate from the rules prescribed by the ancients, from the classical simplicity of the old models ? [1]

It is well-known that Jeffrey attacked Byron at the time for presuming to maintain that the unities were "essential to the existence of the drama." He denounced Byron as guilty of "mere caprice and contradiction," that having been "*a law unto himself*" he now "wants to do penance within the unities." [2] The charge was over-stated. All that can be said certainly is that Byron held a higher form of tragic drama to be possible by an observance of the ancient laws than was being produced in his day without such observance. He had a more intimate acquaintance with the drama of the time than any of the other great literary figures, and he knew and felt its unworthiness more acutely than any. He but recommended a technique which promised an improvement, the quicker for being somewhat drastic, and which anticipated a permanent high type. To direct the way to reform, he wrote plays that would introduce and illustrate his theory, but he always insisted on their unfitness for the stage.

With a little wavering on the subject, he held that love rarely constitutes the best subject matter for tragedy. He favored rather the epic elements of human action.

I carried Teresa the Italian translation of Grillparzer's *Sappho*, which she promises to read. She quarrelled with me, because I said that love was *not the loftiest* theme for true tragedy ; and, having the advantage of her native language, and natural female eloquence, she overcame my fewer arguments. I believe

---

[1] Captain Medwin, *Conversations*, 108 f. *Sardanapalus* is without doubt his nearest approach to a model of what he thought drama should be. " Mind the *Unities*, which are my great object of research."— *L. & J.* V, 324. " The Author has in one instance attempted to preserve, and in the other to approach, the ' unities '; conceiving that with any very distant departure from them, there may be poetry, but can be no drama."—Advertisement to the play.
[2] *Edinburgh Review* XXXVI.

she was right. I must put more love into *Sardanapalus* than I intended. I speak, of course, *if* the times will allow me leisure. That *if* will hardly be a peace-maker.[1]

As I think that *love* is not the principal passion for tragedy (and yet most of ours turn upon it), you will not find me a popular writer. Unless it is Love, *furious, criminal,* and *hapless,* it ought not to make a tragic subject: when it is melting and maudlin, it *does,* but it ought not to do; it is then for the Gallery and second price boxes.[2]

He is studiously classical in his conception of the tragic hero, derived from Aristotle through Rymer and Johnson.

I must remark from *Aristotle* and *Rymer,* that the *hero* of tragedy and (I add *meo periculo*) a tragic poem must *be guilty,* to excite "*terror and pity,*" the end of tragic poetry. But hear not *me,* but my betters. "The pity which the poet is to labor for is *for* the criminal. The terror is likewise in the punishment of the said criminal, who, if he be represented too great an offender, will *not be pitied*; if altogether *innocent* his punishment will be unjust." In the Greek Tragedy innocence is unhappy often, and the offender escapes. I must also ask you is *Achilles* a *good* character? or is even Æneas anything but a successful run-away? It is for Turnus men feel and not for the Trojan. Who is the hero of *Paradise Lost*? Why Satan, —and Macbeth, and Richard, and Othello, Pierre, and Lothario, and Zanga?[3]

He held that drama should not be a very poetical form. A high poetical quality was the chief merit irregular drama possessed, a degenerate type of which he was trying to reform, and that merit belonged to it as literature not as drama. In a play it was but one defect, and the least

[1] *L. & J.* V, 173.
[2] *L. & J.* V, 218. He says of his *Doge*:—"I have also attempted to make a play without love."—*L. & J.* V, 243. He says, with evident satisfaction, of the same play in his diary:—"No *love*—the grand ingredient of a modern play."—*L. & J.* V, 167.
[3] *L. & J.* V, 284.

regrettable, of many arising from the common fault of romantic license. The language of a play should be a nearer approach to natural speech, to increase the illusion and add to the likeness of truth.[1]

What has poetry to do with a play, or in a play? There is not one passage in Alfieri strictly poetical; hardly one in Racine.[2]

Apparently he wished to have correct drama deprived of all operatic features[3]—a desire naturally arising from his gleanings in the dramatic history and criticism of the century preceding. The verse should not be measured or recitative, and the old Greek chorus was intolerable.[4]

The authorship of tragedy should be left to men. Women as a rule lack experience.

Women (saving Joanna Baillie) cannot write tragedy: they have not seen enough nor felt enough of life for it. I think Semiramis or Catherine II. might have written (could they have been unqueened) a rare play.[5]

---

[1] See the preface to the *Cenci* for a very possible influence by Byron on the play, in this respect.

[2] Captain Medwin, *Conversations*, 108. Byron says of *Sardanapalus,* his model:—" I have broken down the poetry as nearly as I could to common language."—*L. & J.* V, 323. This effort brought against him the charges by Campbell, of writing prose in verse form. Mr. Chew ascribes the quality of his blank verse to inability to write better,— " something of the wealth of imaginative poetry, which was apparently beyond his grasp."—*The Dramas of Byron*, 21. Compare also Roden Noel, *Poets and Poetry of the Century,* and Saintsbury, *A History of Criticism.* Did Byron ever really make a serious effort to write great blank verse? His *Dream* and *Darkness* have had the reputation of great poems.

[3] Cf., *Hints from Horace*, 295 f.

[4] *Manfred, Heaven and Earth, The Deformed Transformed* have choral parts, but they are only dramatic poems or pieces, not plays.

[5] *L. & J.* III, 197. Cf., "Voltaire has asked *why* no woman has ever written even a tolerable tragedy? 'Ah (said the Patriarch) the composition of a tragedy requires * * * (a man).' If this be true, Lord knows what Joanna Baillie does."—*L. & J.* IV, 92.

His disparagement of women as tragic writers, and insistence upon experience, are, of course, but a part of his beliefs respecting all authorship.

The appendages of classical and older native drama, the prologue and epilogue, he seems to have approved, not as essentials but as effective parts when done well, and as offering an opportunity to the good playwright to distinguish himself. The status of these parts in English drama was generally bad.

There are but two decent prologues in our tongue—Pope's to *Cato*—Johnson's to Drury-Lane. These, with the epilogue to the *Distrest Mother*, and, I think, one of Goldsmith's, and a prologue of old Colman's to Beaumont and Fletcher's *Philaster*, are the best things of the kind we have[1].

There is no cause to question Byron's good faith with himself and the public in his "dramatic system" and in his efforts to set it forth practically. He well knew the bad condition of drama in his time. He did not have any great confidence, be it said to his critical credit, in his own dramatic powers, but he had been solicited to write drama by men whose judgment he trusted more than his own. He knew that in attempting a change he was antagonizing well established opinion, but for the sake of the far-reaching results he was willing to engage in the enterprise. He did so with all the force of his nature, and with not a little of its recklessness. And there is some evidence of a sanguine hope on his part of ultimate success, not in the use of his own plays on the stage but in the triumph of

[1] *L. & J.* II, 151 f. Byron attached neither prologue nor epilogue to his dramatic compositions, but he wrote and delivered a prologue (See *Hours of Idleness*) for the performances given at the Leacrofts in Southwell, 1806. His address (prologue) at the opening of Drury Lane theatre is well known. He suffered more nervous excitement over it apparently than over any other poem he ever wrote. See *L. & J.* II, Chapter VI.

the system he was fostering, through its adoption by future playwrights.[1]

It is highly creditable to him that he denied repeatedly the fitness of his productions for the stage.[2] He was but trying to create a " mental theatre " as the initial step necessary to the reform which he hoped to accomplish.[3] His own plays might remain merely dramatic literature.[4]

English drama received a new impulse, a new inspiration, a new lease of life, and withal a new idea of what was possi-

---

[1] Cf., " My object is not *immediate* popularity in my present productions, which are written on a different system from the rage of the day. But, *mark what I say*; that the time will come when these will be preferred to any I have before written :—it is not from the cry or hubbub of a month that these things are to be decided upon. In the meantime I intend to be as a Calderon, or Lope de Vega."—*L. & J.* VI, 25.

[2] Good self-judgment is recognized in his almost nervous activities in Italy, against the opinion of actors and managers, to prevent through his friends, his publisher, his attorney, and the Lord Chancellor, the production of *Marino Faliero.* It would *not* succeed, he protested. The play was produced straightway but failed. None of the others succeeded. Byron has been charged too much with vehemently protesting one thing while believing in and secretly hoping for another. A strange and sinister fate to overtake any man !

[3] Gerard is a little extravagant :—"A ' new kind of drama ' with ' Humanity ' for its theme !   The man who, with whatever confusions and hesitations, could grasp such a conception as this was not far from being a dramatic poet; and something more even than this—the forerunner of a genuine reform, reaching back to Shakespeare on the one hand, reaching forward on the other to new times, which need ever new methods of expression. That Byron can lay claim to such a position is as undoubted as that his success was unconscious."— *Byron Restudied in His Dramas* 50 f.

[4] The impracticability of his dramatic scheme Byron seems later to have recognized :—"Ah that is a subject in which I have failed ; I shall write no more tragedies I think."—Dr. Kennedy, *Conversations,* 158. " Speaking one day of a manuscript tragedy of mine, which in our dearth of books he had asked to read, he said he thought it the next best thing I had written, to the ' Story of Rimini.' I said, I wished I could think anything favourable of it, even by courtesy ; but I could not. I was quite sure that I had no faculty for the drama. He reflected upon this ; and observed in an under-tone between question and no-question,—' Perhaps I have not succeeded in the drama myself.' " —Leigh Hunt, *Lord Byron,* 202 f. But there is no evidence to indicate that his faith was dead in the influence which he hoped to exert.

ble for it, almost immediately after Byron. The ripe products were half a century in coming, but the seeds of reform were sown and the growth begun before Byron ended his career. Some of the honors of an innovator should be accorded him in this the largest critical undertaking he ever conceived or tried to execute.[1]

Material Considerations The critical consideration at Byron's hands, of the purposes, opportunities, and conduct of authorship, is mainly the reflection of his own habits.

The pursuit of literature should not be regarded as a profession. It is not therefore subject to the common conditions. There is nothing absolute or final in it.

There is no sovereign in the republic of letters.[2]

What does it signify who is before or behind in a race where there is no *goal* ?[3]

As we have seen, literature was only for him who could essay no other, for the elect—or derelict, as Byron perhaps would have said.

Above all, a writer's mind should be free from every external consideration,[4] for the treatment of his subject

---

[1] It is not just to a good cause and an honest motive to assert as, " an undeniable truth that Lord Byron's attempts to compose dramas on the very model of the ancients, as they are characterized by their few personages, their uniform gravity and stiffness, arose from a certain jealousy or envy which Lord Byron bore to Shakespeare."—Köhler, *A Glance at Lord Byron as Dramatist.* Byron was not interested in challenging Elizabethan drama or committed to the task of proving it wrong. He but purposed to correct the unworthy product of his own time, and the purpose was worthy of " so vigorous and sublime a genius as Lord Byron was."

[2] *L. & J.* VI, 231.

[3] Journal, *L. & J.* II, 366.

[4] He says of his own practice :—" To withdraw *myself* from *myself* (oh that cursed selfishness !) has ever been my sole, my entire, my sincere motive, in scribbling at all ; and publishing is only the continuance of the same object, by the action it affords to the mind, which else recoils upon itself. If I valued fame, I should flatter received opinions,

solely, untrammeled by a thought of any effect to be produced and without fear of the public estimate.[1]   Publication
should be only a remote contingency.

Periodical writing is unworthy because it carries with
it a certain quantum of regard for popular taste and is
really begot on demand by it. There is meanness and
servility in its method.

Reviews and Magazines are at the best but ephemeral and
superficial reading : *who thinks* of the *grand article* of *last year*
in any *given review* ? [2]

I think the periodical style of writing hurtful to the habits of
mind, by presenting the superficies of too many things at once.[3]

which have gathered strenght by time, and will yet wear longer than
any living works to the contrary."—*L. & J.* II, 351. " I write only
for the *reader*, and care for nothing but the *silent* approbation of those
who close one's book with good humour and quiet contentment."—
L. & J. V, 231. " I have never written but for the solitary *reader*,
and require no experiments for applause beyond his silent approbation."—
L. & J. V, 257. " I follow the bias of my own mind, without considering
whether women or men are or are not to be pleased."—*L. & J.* VI, 41.
Compare his long itemized letter to Murray, 1821, forbidding the latter's
sending magazines containing criticism, etc., because, " these do not
interrupt, but they *soil* the *current* of my *Mind* . . . . . to keep my
mind *free and unbiassed* by all paltry and personal irritabilities of praise
or censure ;—to let my Genius take its natural direction, while my
feelings are like the dead, who know nothing and feel nothing of all
or aught that is said or done in their regard."—*L. & J.* V, 375.

[1] " I do not think publishing at all creditable either to men or
women, and (though you will not believe me) very often feel ashamed
of it myself."—*L.· & J.* II, 121. " I once wrote from the fullness of
my mind and the love of fame, (not as an *end*, but a *means*, to obtain
that influence over men's minds which is power in itself and in its
consequences,) and now from habit and from avarice ; so that the effect
may probably be as different as the inspiration."—*L. & J.* IV, 248.
" Writing and composition are habits of my mind, with which Success
and Publication are objects of remoter reference—*not causes* but *effects*,
like those of any other pursuit."—*L. & J.* VI, 173. His own evolution is interesting. First, he was the old " courtly maker." He often
purposed to abandon the art. Then as the addiction became stronger,
he preserved his honor by refusing to receive money for his writings.
Finally, as the habit became fixed he published for pay from the good
" old gentlemanly vice of avarice."

[2] *L. & J.* V, 374.
[3] *L. & J.* VI, 143.

A review may and will direct or " turn awry " the Currents of opinion, but it must not directly oppose them.[1]

But while the literary genius should refrain from periodical writing, he cannot expect to be independent of it in every way. His salvation depends upon his maintaining a position above such compositions.

The first thing a young writer must expect, and yet can least of all suffer, is *criticism*. . . . The best reply to all objections is to write better, and if your enemies will not then do you justice, the world will. On the other hand, you should not be discouraged; to be opposed is not to be vanquished, though a timid mind is apt to mistake every scratch for a mortal wound. There is a saying of Dr. Johnson's, which it is as well to remember that " no man was ever written down except by himself." [2]

The praise or blame of Reviewers does not last long now-a-days. It is like straw thrown up in the air[3].

If they crush an author, it must be in the shell, as they tried to do with me: if the book has life enough to outlive the year, it defies their malice—for who reads a last year's review ? . . . Where are the great poets and writers the Reviewers predicted were to be the leviathans of our literature ? Extinct: their bones hereafter may be grubbed up in a fossil state with those of the reptiles that puffed them into life.[4]

At the same time Byron recognized the worth and dignity of the true critic—Gifford was his supreme example—but the general class of writers of the kind he despised. The creator of literature ought to endure them but never to be overcome by them. At best their writings are but hasty and ephemeral.

Literature is to be produced with a degree of spontaneity, but no manner of haste should be excused in appearing

[1] *L. & J.* VI, 155.
[2] *L. & J.* III, 47.
[3] Captain Medwin, *Conversations*, 147.
[4] Trelawny, *Records*, 214.

i

before the public with a work. Byron indeed shows a classic reserve in this particular, although he takes a liberty with the Horatian figure.

I think a *year* a very fair allotment of time to a composition which is not to be Epic; and even Horace's "*Nonum prematur*" must have been intended for the Millenium, or some longer-lived generation than ours.[1]

Don't let it cool in the composition! You can always delay as long as you like revising, though I am not sure, in the very face of Horace, that the *nonum*, etc., is attended with advantage, unless we read "months" for "years."[2]

A fair interim between creation and publication should be spent in revising, though not in re-making. It is but wisdom to exercise a strict surveillance and review of one's work—in brief, to subject one's productions to a rigid self-criticism.

Second thoughts in everything are best, but, in rhyme, third and fourth don't come amiss.[3]

In composition I do not think *second* thoughts, though *second* expressions may improve the first ideas.[4]

With regard to what you say of retouching the *Juans* and the *Hints*, it is all very well; but I can't *furbish*. I am like the tyger (in poesy), if I miss my first Spring, I go growling back to my Jungle. There is no second. I can't correct; I can't, and I won't. Nobody ever succeeds in it, great or small. Tasso remade the whole of his Jerusalem; but who ever reads that

---

[1] *L. & J.* III, 56.

[2] *L. & J.* III, 257. Byron's own practice was at variance with his recommendations. The *Giaour* grew from less than 700 lines in the first edition to double the number in the seventh in half a year. The *Bride of Abydos* was written "*stans pede in uno*" and published as recklessly. His best works were published in parts, as he wrote them. He frequently urged his publisher to make haste, "for I am bitten again." His own composition of classical character, *Hints from Horace*, waited more than twenty years before seeing light. Cf. *L. & J.* II, 8.

[3] *L. & J.* II, 150.

[4] *L. & J.* II, 305.

version ? All the world goes to the first. Pope *added* to the
" *Rape of the Lock*," but did not reduce it. You must take
my things as they happen to be : if they are not likely to suit,
reduce their *estimate* then accordingly. I would rather give
them away than hack and hew them. I don't say that you
are not right : I merely assert that I cannot better them.
I must either " make a spoon, or spoil a horn."[1]

Finally he says of the character of all writing, whatever
the circumstances, or conduct of the author, in bringing
it forth: .

There is a *fortune* in *fame* as in everything else in this world.
Much, too, depends upon a publisher, and much upon luck ;
and the number of writers is such, that as the mind of a reader
can only contain a certain quantum of poetry and poet's glories,
he is sometimes saturated, and allows many good dishes to
go away untouched (as happens at great dinners), and this
not from fastidiousness but fulness.[2]

There is a certain fatality then in a life of letters. And
literature itself is subject to the same chance in life as the
individual in any craft, profession, art, or field of endeavor.[3]

[1] *L. & J.* V, 120. The many verbal changes made in his own works
while they were going through the press indicate his belief in a careful
revision of the minor elements of composition.
[2] *L. & J.* V, 282. Cf., " There is a fortune in fame as in all other
things."—Reply to *Blackwood's Edinburgh Magazine.*
[3] " I have met with most poetry upon trunks; so that I am apt
to consider the trunk-maker as the sexton of authorship," he says
with fine epigrammatic effect toward the end of his career.—*L. & J.*
V, 149.

Chapter VI

FORMAL CRITICISM

This is true criticism, and you may kiss—
Exactly as you please, or not,—the rod;
But if you don't, I'll lay it on, by G-d!
                                —*Don Juan* I, 206.

Such reputation as Byron has as critic has rested upon his formal criticism, which therefore, unworthy as it is in general, cannot be ignored. And to treat it at all, one must treat it mort or less exhaustively, hence the unusual length of the present chapter.

Byron's occasional assumptions of the rôle of professional critic at various periods of his life cannot be called mere acts of caprice. They represent a real ambition in him, developing early and engrossing his attention now and then in his career as seriously as did any of his writings. He held the age to be a critical one,[1] and he was too much a part of it not to wish instinctively to excel in any form of writing that was in popular favor.

The critical art he held in very high regard.[2] Its possibilities allured him, if its common practices repelled. In his declarations, at least, he exalted the critic above the poet.[3]

---

[1] " This is the age of criticism."—*L. & J.* II, 253.

[2] " We will now, *paulo majora*, prattle a little of literature in all its branches; and first of the first—criticism."—*L. & J.* II, 245.

[3] " If I had my choice, I would rather be the Earl of Warwick than all the *kings* he ever made ! Jeffrey and Gifford I take to be the monarch-makers in poetry and prose."—" Journal," *L. & J.* II, 322.

And even the claims of the mediocre censor, if a true one, he could handsomely acknowledge.[1]

In the course of his life Byron projected a number of critical works, some of which were to be very comprehensive.[2] He was offered space for reviewing at his pleasure in the principal magazines of the day.[3] He himself volunteered several reviews.[4] But his actual critical performances were few.

Nor are they superior in quality. They represent as hasty work as ever he did. They are positive enough, even dogmatic, and in parts they show his great creative genius. All bear the Byron image and superscription. But the

---

[1] Cf., " Still I must yield those worthies merit
      Who chasten, with unsparing spirit,
      Bad rhymes, and those who write them."
                              —" To the Earl of Clare," *Hours of Idleness.*
Cf., *L. & J.* V, 102.

He could recommend a critical career to his best friend, Thomas Moore, the second poet of the age, as he held him :—" Your article on * * * * is perfection itself. You must not leave off reviewing. By Jove, I believe you can do anything. There is wit, and taste, and learning, and good humor (though not a whit less severe for that), in every line of that critique."—*L. & J.* III, 149. " Positively, you must not leave off reviewing. You shine in it—you kill in it : and this article has been taken for Sydney Smith's (as I heard in town), which proves not only your proficiency in parsonology, but that you have all the airs of a veteran critic at your first onset. So, prithee, go on and prosper."—*L. & J.* III, 168 f.

[2] He proposed some work on the literatures of Italy and Greece and apparently accomplished " a short dissertation on the literature of the modern Greeks," which later was cut up and used for notes. Cf. *L. & J.* II, 2, 26. Once he half-heartedly contemplated editing a volume of letters of Lord Hervey, Gray, Lady M. W. Montague, *et al.* from MSS. See *L. & J.* IV, 223 f.

[3] " I have been *offered* more than one review in our principal journals." —" Detached Thoughts," *L. & J.* V, 452. Cf. *L. & J.* II, 188.

[4] " Pray is it fair to ask if the ' *Twopenny Postbag* ' is to be reviewed in this No. ? because, if not, I should be glad to undertake it, and leave it to Chance and the Editor for a reception into your pages."— *L. & J.* II, 209. " I have no objection to review, if it pleases Griffiths to send books, or rather *you*, for you know the sort of things I like to (play) with."—*L. & J.* II, 102. Cf. *ibid.* III, 177, 180.

fault which denies them real greatness is not, at least entirely, in his critical creed,[1] although that was reactionary, but in a vital lack in the man. Byron was not wise. Despite all his fine preparation for a critical career, he was not constituted for habits of reflection, and criticism has only a slight chance of permanent worth unless the critic possesses and exercises fully and freely the reflective powers.[2]

The very first critical work, complete in itself, that came from Byron's pen is an effusion of the *Hours of Idleness* period. Byron himself may hardly have been aware of the genrc to which it belongs. It is in verse form, but in neither poetical nor critical quality is it important. For its historical significance among Byron's works of the kind, it may be given here entire.

>   To the Author of a Sonnet Beginning,
>
>   " Sad is my verse, you say, and yet no tear."
>
> Thy verse is " sad " enough, no doubt :
> A devilish deal more sad than witty !
> Why we should weep I can't find out,
> Unless for *thee* we weep in pity.
>
> Yet there is one I pity more ;
> And much, alas ! I think he needs it
> For he, I'm sure, will suffer sore,
> Who, to his own misfortune, reads it.
>
> Thy rhymes, without the aid of magic,
> May *once* be read — but never after :
> Yet their effect's by no means tragic,
> Although by far too dull for laughter.

---

[1] " He affects to patronize a system of criticism fit for the production of mediocrity."—Shelley, Letter from Ravenna, Aug. 7, 1821.

[2] Goethe's dictum is almost too well known to require repeating— " Sobald er reflektiert, ist er ein Kind."—*Conversations*, Jan. 18, 1825.

But would you make our bosoms bleed,
And of no common pang complain—
If you would make us weep indeed,
Tell us, you'll read them o'er again.[1]

Two facts that are indicative of the future critic appear in the production: (1) it is fairly representative of the methods of contemporary reviewers, and (2) it is significant of the whole tendency of Byron's criticism. It is a part of the older order, and Byron as professional critic stands irreconcilably with his face to the past.

Byron's known critical works, inadequate to his gifts as they are, are as follows:

1. Review of Wordsworth's Poems of 1807.[2]
2. Review of Gell's *Geography and Antiquities of Ithaca* and *Itinerary of Greece*.[3]
3. Two articles, reviewing the poems of W. R. Spencer and *Neglected Genius*, a poem, of W. H. Ireland.[4]
4. Some Observations upon an Article in *Blackwood's Magazine*.[5]
5. Two " Letters " to John Murray on the Reverend Wm. L. Bowles's Strictures on the Life and Writings of Pope.[6]
6. The enterprise of the *Liberal*.[7]

---

[1] Dated March 8, 1807, first published, 1832.
[2] *Monthly Literary Recreations*, July, 1807.
[3] *Monthly Review*, August, 1811.
[4] *Monthly Review*, January, 1812, and February, 1813.
[5] March, 1820, not published till the '45 edition of Byron's Works, edited by Jeffrey, Wilson, Lockhart, *et al.*
[6] Only the first of these was published at the time, March, 1821. The other did not appear in print till 1835.
[7] This amounted to little more than a projection. Only four numbers appeared.

Byron was not sure himself, late in life, what he had done early in the anonymous vein:—" I have been a reviewer. In ' the Monthly Review' I wrote some articles, which were inserted. This was in the latter part of 1811. In 1807, in a Magazine called ' Monthly Literary Recreations,' I reviewed Wordsworth's trash of that time. Excepting

Wordsworth's *Poems* Byron began his public career as critic with a conventional review. Wordsworth's poems, including many of his very finest pieces, were collected and issued in two volumes in May, 1807. Byron reviewed the volumes, in an essay of only a few hundred words length, in the July number of *Monthly Literary Recreations* for the same year.[1] The event was not long after his first acquaintance with the branch of literature to which his article belongs,[2] and antedates by only a few months his own flagellation at critical hands.

His review is a very superficial study made evidently from only a cursory examination of the material. The consciousness of playing a rôle is unmistakable through the whole composition.[3] The idea, too, impresses itself upon the reader of a close parallelism in kind with the celebrated review half a year later of Byron's own volume. Each is the instance of an amateurish critic trying to confound in a few careless phrases great literary genius. The error in each case is the reviewer's complete ignorance and inappreciation of the quality of his subject's talent. Advantage in the justice of the attack, one must confess, lies with the Edinburgh critic, even if his criticism was a little more opprobrious.

these, I cannot accuse myself of anonymous Criticism (that I recollect)."
—"Detached Thoughts," *L. & J.* V, 452 Needless to say, anonymous criticism was the regular method in Byron's day.

[1] See *L. & J.* I, 140.

[2] " Till I was eighteen years old (odd as it may seem), I had never read a review .... The first I ever read was in 1806-7."—" Detached Thoughts," *L. & J.* V, 452 f.

[3] Cf., " It would be difficult to imagine anything more banal. The ready-made phrase glides from his pen without intermission; nor is any kind of penetration displayed in the criticism."—Ethel Colburn Mayne, *Byron* I, 111. " This first attempt of Lord Byron at reviewing is remarkable only as showing how plausibly he could assume the established tone and phraseology of these minor judgment-seats of criticism."—Moore, *Life* VI, 295.

The information in Byron's critique is not exact in all particulars.

The volumes before us are by the author of Lyric Ballads, a collection which has not undeservedly met with a considerable share of public applause.

Structural irregularities occur.

The characteristics of Mr. Wordsworth's muse are simple and flowing, though occasionally inharmonious verse; strong and sometimes irresistible appeals to the feelings, with unexceptionable sentiments.

The critic's judgment is recognized as unsound for declaring the best sonnet in the collection to be the one beginning,

"Another year! another deadly blow,"

when the reader is reminded that such sonnets as "Upon Westminster Bridge," "Milton," and "The world is too much with us," were published in the same volumes.

Byron said a few months later that the way to "*cut up*" in reviewing "is to quote long passages, and make them appear absurd."[1] His formula might well have been derived from his practice in the emphatic portion of this article. In some selections Wordsworth is granted "the force and expression that of a genuine poet." Others show "all the beauties and few of the defects of the writer." But others, "in language not simple but puerile," are only "namby-pamby," imitative of the childish "shrill ditty,"

"Hey de diddle,
The cat and the fiddle," etc.

The general purpose is manifestly condemnatory. Wordsworth is but wasting his time on subjects and sentiments that are unworthy of his "not inferior abilities."

[1] *L. & J.* I, 148.

The best commentary on the whole performance is Byron's own remark on the work of another several years later:

All such expressions are the mere cant of a schoolboy hovering round the Skirts of Criticism.[1]

Gell's *Ithaca* and *Itinèrary of Greece* The review of Sir William Gell's two volumes is concerned chiefly with items of topographical interest, but it treats as well the author's execution of his task and is therefore a real review and critique.[2] Byron had long been familiar with the earlier volume. He had had occasion to refer to it and study it during his travels. The second was intimately associated with his experiences on the journey. His article followed immediately his return, while every memory was fresh. He was admirably equipped for the task, and the resulting critique is the most careful and painstaking attempt at formal criticism that he ever made.

The article is a little more ambitious than would ordinarily be expected of such writing. It covers fifteen or more close pages of large octavo size, and, in addition to showing an accurate knowledge of places from actual observation, it professes a familiarity with Homer and classical scholarship. All the evidence goes to show that it is a thoughtful, carefully prepared work. It is as far removed from the reviewer of Wordsworth's " trash of that time " as four full years of vital experience and growth well can remove a man from his former self. It hardly represents Byron in his customary prose vein at all, being more elevated in its manifest seriousness of aim, freedom from violence, and dignity of tone.

---

[1] Apropos to Hare's *Economy*, August 31, 1811, *L. & J.* II, 15.
[2] *The Geography and Antiquities of Ithaca* was published in 1807. The *Itinerary of Greece* appeared three years later.

The opening paragraph, although a little stilted from the office which it performs, is fairly indicative of the character of the entire work.

That laudable curiosity concerning the remains of classical antiquity, which has of late years increased among our country-men, is in no traveller or author more conspicuous than in Mr. Gell. Whatever difference of opinion may yet exist with regard to the success of the several disputants in the famous Trojan controversy, or, indeed, relating to the present author's merits as an inspector of the Troad, it must universally be acknowledged that any work, which more forcibly impresses on our imaginations the scenes of heroic action, and the subjects of immortal song, possesses claims on the attention of every scholar.

A clear distinction, running throughout the study, between the two works, is made at the very beginning.

We conceive the former to be by far the most interesting to the reader, as the latter is indisputably the most serviceable to the traveller.

Pronouncing then the superior merit of the earlier volume as a literary work, he proceeds to analyze it.

The former of these volumes, we have observed, is the most attractive in the closet. It comprehends a very full survey of the far-famed island which the hero of the *Odyssey* has im-mortalized; for we really are inclined to think that the author has established the identity of the modern *Theaki* with the *Ithaca* of Homer. At all events, if it be an illusion, it is a very agreeable deception, and is effected by an ingenious interpreta-tion of the passages in Homer that are supposed to be descrip-tive of the scenes which our traveller has visited.

The primary object of the book was to identify the modern Theaki with the Ithaca of Ulysses. The critic quotes striking passages pretty freely from the first chapters to illustrate the character of the work. He restates its purpose

and explains the evidence.   He is inclined to accept the
argument and to agree with the author's conclusions.[1]
Incidentally, the reader is impressed with the critic's
command of Homeric Greek.

The traveler's manner and method of treatment of special
topics he elucidates with due point.

Mr. Gell then proceeds to invalidate the authority of previous
writers on the subject of Ithaca.   Sir George Wheeler and M.
le Chevalier fall under his severe animadversion; and, indeed,
according to his account, neither of these gentlemen had visited
the island, and the description of the latter is "absolutely
too absurd for refutation."   In another place, he speaks of M.
le C. "disgracing a work of such merit by the introduction of
such fabrications"; again, of the inaccuracy of the author's
maps; and, lastly, of his inserting an island at the southern
entry of the channel between Cephalonia and Ithaca, which
has no existence.   This observation very nearly approaches to
the use of that monosyllable which Gibbon, without expressing
it, so adroitly applied to some assertion of his antagonist, Mr.
Davies.   In truth, our traveller's words are rather bitter towards
his brother tourist; but we must conclude that their justice
warrants their severity.

The work is subjected to a critical scrutiny in a minor
vein.   The geographer's sentences, their kind and quality,
are commented upon, and the critic is careful to observe
any verbal discrepancies that occur.

We must, however, observe that "demonstration" is a
strong term.—In his description of the Leucadian Promontory
(of which we have a pleasing representation in the plate), the
author remarks that it is "celebrated for the *leap* of Sappho,
and the *death* of Artemisia."   From this variety in the expression, a reader would hardly conceive that both the ladies

---

[1] It may be remembered that Byron was interested enough in
Ithaca on his travels to propose purchasing the whole island.   See
Chapter III, 57, footnote 1.

perished in the same manner; in fact, the sentence is as proper as it would be to talk of the decapitation of Russell, and the death of Sidney.

The review is thorough-going and exhaustive. The spirit is kindly : praise is dispensed rather than blame, and yet the author is not lavish of one or niggard of the other. A sane, helpful tone prevails throughout, and not once is the suspicion raised that justice is spared or the " quality of mercy strained." The impression is given that the reviewer has found a pleasing book, is fully qualified to judge of its contents and manner, and has done so with the intelligence and good will that accompanies constructive criticism. The conclusion is typical.

We can certainly recommend a perusal of this volume to every lover of classical scene and story. If we may indulge the pleasing belief that Homer sang of a real kingdom, and that Ulysses governed it, though we discern many feeble links in Mr. Gell's chain of evidence, we are on the whole induced to fancy that this is the Ithaca of the bard and of the monarch. At all events, Mr. Gell has enabled every future traveller to form a clearer judgment on the question than he could have established without such a "Vade-mecum to Ithaca," or a " Have with you, to the House of Ulysses."

The second volume, the *Itinerary of Greece*, is found to be less commendable, but is reviewed with no less candor and good feeling. The book was written for utility rather than delectation, and therefore offers not such attractive material for the reviewer of taste.

The author is reproached for concealing his identity too closely within his work, for the use of ancient names instead of modern ones for familiar reference, for the inadequacy of his maps, drawings, and " panoramic designs," and for some inaccuracies of data such as might be brought against any ordinary bureau of information. But once the faults are pointed out the critic hastens to approve the general quality of the work.

Though we have made the above exceptions to the accuracy of Mr. Gell's information, we are most ready to do justice to the general utility of his directions, and can certainly concede the praise which he is desirous of obtaining,—namely, " of having facilitated the researches of future travellers, by affording that local information which it was before impossible to obtain." This book, indeed, is absolutely necessary to any person who wishes to explore the Morea advantageously ; and we hope that Mr. Gell will continue his Itinerary over that and over every other part of Greece.

He concludes by acknowledging in the work the scholarly interest, which was the not undeserved ambition of its author.

We shall conclude by an extract from the author's work : which, even if it fails of exciting that general interest which we hope most earnestly it may attract towards its important subject, cannot, as he justly observes, " be entirely uninteresting to the scholar " ; since it is a work " which gives him a faithful description of the remains of cities, the very existence of which was doubtful, as they perished before the æra of authentic history."

The entire critique is in advance of the time, and as such is exceptional among Byron's critical works.

Spencer's *Poems* and Ireland's *Neglected Genius*

Byron's articles on Spencer and Ireland,[1] published separately through the same columns within a few months of each other, do not reflect the credit upon Byron as critic which the reader

---

[1] From the very close association between the two articles in subject matter, time, and treatment, the study of the two together is made here for the sake of space.

Byron remarks in his " Detached Thoughts " :—" In ' the Monthly Review ' I wrote some articles which were inserted. This was in the

has been led to expect from the critique on Gell. In manner they follow more naturally and logically the boyish critique upon Wordsworth, and, like it, echo the spirit of periodical criticism of the time. From the order and emphasis in treatment, obviously his purpose is to flay. At the same time his utterances are not banal. There are signs of critical growth in the four intervening years, within which time his fine training has been completed.

These studies are much more intelligent than the one on Wordsworth. They show more critical penetration and acumen than his maiden essay, and certain shrewd observations in them evince an entirely new power in his criticism. A fundamental difference from the study of Wordsworth is in the talent criticised. Spencer and Ireland are obscure names in literature to-day. The fact, to some extent, justifies Byron's strictures upon them, as he was not justified in his animadversions upon Wordsworth.

The article on Spencer is longer and is a little more considerate in tone than the study of Ireland. The reader at once infers that the former in the critic's opinion is the less unworthy subject. Spencer was favorably known at the time, indeed he was esteemed above his merit, as subsequent events have shown.

The author of this well-printed volume has more than once been introduced to our readers, and is known to rank among that class of poetical persons who have never been highly favored by stern criticism.

With this ominous beginning the critic proceeds to administer the "favor" adjudged merited but too long withheld.

latter part of 1811."—*L. & J.* V, 452. The date corresponds better with the article on Gell and the review of Spencer. The critique of Ireland's *Neglected Genius* did not appear until February, 1813. It is probable that Byron had forgotten this article entirely in his late memorandum. Cf. *Correspondence* I, 69.

It consists chiefly of *"Vers de Société,"* calculated to prove very delightful to a large circle of fashionable acquaintance, and pleasing to a limited number of vulgar purchasers. These last, indeed, may be rude enough to expect something more for their specie during the present scarcity of change, than lines to " Young Poets and Poetesses," " Epitaphs upon Years," Poems " to my Grammatical Niece," " Epistle from Sister Dolly in Cascadia to Sister Tanny in Snowdonia," etc.: but we doubt not that a long list of persons of quality, wit, and honour, " in town and country," who are here addressed, will be highly pleased with themselves and with the poet who has *shewn them off* in a very handsome volume: as will doubtless the " Butterfly at the end of Winter," provided that he is fortunate enough to survive the present inclemencies.

Some of Spencer's most popular poems had been re-published in the new volume, with only slight revisions which the critic generally condemns. In deference to the public praise of these and in anticipation of favor to a very few new pieces like them, the critic grants that " the volume contains poems exquisitely beautiful." The examples he gives are well chosen.

> " Too late I staid, forgive the crime,
> Unheeded flew the hours;
> How noiseless falls the foot of Time,
> That only treads on flow'rs! " etc.

Manifestly the purpose in the judgments is to concur with popular opinion. In acknowledgment of his reputation, the poet is credited with a " well-known taste," and " a most exquisite irony."

The far greater part of the volume, however, contains pieces which can be little gratifying to the public:—some are pretty; and all are besprinkled with " gems," and " roses," and " birds," and " diamonds," and such like cheap poetical adornments, as are always to be obtained at no great expense of thought or of metre.—It is happy for the author that these *bijoux* are presented to persons of high degree; countesses, foreign and domestic; " Maids of Honour to Louisa Landgravine of Hesse D'Armstadt"; Lady Blank, and Lady Asterisk, besides—, and—, and others anonymous; who are exactly the kind of people to be best pleased with these sparkling, shining, fashionable trifles.

Some of his attempts at verbal criticism, although done with greater levity than kindness, are shrewdly penetrating and effective.

" Reviving Friendship" is perhaps less expressive than " Relenting," as it once stood; and the phrase, " ten thousand *furlowed* heroes," throws a new light on the heroic character. It is extremely proper that heroes should have " furlows," since school-boys have holidays, and lawyers have long vacations: but we very much question whether young gentlemen of the scholastic, legal, or heroic calling, would be flattered by any epithet derived from the relaxation of their respectable pursuits. We should feel some hesitation in telling an interesting youth, of any given battalion from Portugal, that he was a " furlowed hero," lest he should prove to us that his " furlow" had by no means impaired his " heroism." The old epithet, " war-worn," was more adapted to heroism and to poetry; and, if we mistake not, it has very recently been superseded by an epithet which precludes " otium cum dignitate" from the soldier, without imparting either ease or dignity to the verse. Why is " horse and horse-man *pant* for breath" changed to " *heave* for breath," unless for the alliteration of the too tempting aspirate ? " Heaving " is appropriate enough to coals and to sighs, but " panting" *belongs* to successful lovers and spirited horses; and why should Mr. S.'s horse and horseman not have panted as heretofore ?

The critic descends in one or two places to a little self-exploitation, though in a semi-disguised way, just as the Edinburgh lawyer had done.

We are sorry to observe that the compliment paid to Mr. Wedgewood by a " late traveller " viz. that " an Englishman

k

in journeying from Calais to Ispahan may have his dinner served every day on Wedgewood's ware," is no longer a matter of fact. It has lately been the good or evil fortune of one of our travelling department to pass near to Calais, and to have journeyed through divers Paynim lands to no very remote distance from Ispahan; and neither in the palace of the Pacha nor in the caravanserai of the traveller, nor in the hut of the peasant, was he so favoured as to masticate his pilaff from that fashionable service. Such is, in this and numerous other instances, the altered state of the continent and of Europe, since the annotation of the " late traveller"; and on the authority of a *later*, we must report that the ware has been all broken since the former passed that way.

The French and Italian poems at the end of the volume are summarily condemned. The latter are adjudged better finished, and with so much praise the poet is told that he may continue to advantage his exercises in foreign languages.[1]

The final paragraph summarizes succinctly the whole performance.

We now take our leave of Mr. Spencer, without being blind to his errors or insensible to his merits. As a poet, he may be placed rather below Mr. Moore and somewhat above Lord Strangford; and if his volume meet with half their number of purchasers, he will have no reason to complain either of our judgment or of his own success.

The second article, less by half than the first, is justly severer in tone. The subject is a poetical medley, *Neglected Genius*, by W. H. Ireland, lamenting the fates of some unfortunate English poets. Ireland, in the last decade of the century, had attempted to impose upon the public his Shakespearian forgeries, after the manner of McPherson

---

[1] " In 1812 he criticised with much intelligence the ' Italian Rhymes of W. R. Spencer."—C. M. Fuess, *Byron as a Satirist in Verse*, 115. Can Mr. Fuess have mistaken the Italian poems for the whole volume?

and Chatterton, but had been speedily exposed. Byron cannot have been ignorant of this event, although he is courteous enough not to allude to it in his critique, or for that matter to refer in any way to Ireland's ignominious life.

Knowing the circumstances, the reader would be content to have a much severer sentence passed upon the volume, for its own mediocrity and for Ireland's baseness, were it done with dignity. But it is not. The air of offended authority is absent from the censure. In its place is a mean littleness that defeats the effect of the adverse criticism otherwise justly applied.

The critic begins:

This volume, professing in a moderately long title-page to be " illustrative of the untimely and unfortunate fate of *many* British Poets," might with great propriety include the author among the number; for if his " imitations of their different styles" resemble the originals, the consequent starvation of " many British poets " is a doom which is calculated to excite pity rather than surprise.

He says of the opening monody:

Lest the Monody should be mistaken for anything but itself, of which there was little danger, it is dressed in marginal mourning, like a dying speech, or an American Gazette after a defeat.

Memories of Chatterton are the subject of petty detraction only.

Chatterton is a great favourite of this imitative gentlemen ; and Bristol, where he appears to have been held in no greater estimation than Mr. Ireland himself deserves, is much vituperated in some sad couplets, seemingly for this reason, " All for love, and a little for the bottle," as Bannister's song runs,—" All for Chatterton, and a little for myself." thinks Mr. Ireland.

k 2

An echo of Byron's affected critical system, fit only " for the production of mediocrity," is given the reader, when a passage like the following is pronounced to be " a very correct imitation of Milton " :

> " To thee, gigantic genius, next I'll sound;
> The clarion string, and fill fame's vasty round:
> 'Tis *Milton* beams upon the wond'ring sight
> Rob'd in the splendor of Apollo's light," etc.

The critic appropriately enquires:

Where did Mr. Ireland learn that *hold fast* and *ballāst*, *stir* and *hungēr*, *please* and *kidnēys*, *plane* and *capstāne*, *expose* and *windōws*, *forgot* and *pilōt*, *sail on* and *Deucālon*! (Lemprière would have saved him a scourging at school by telling him that there was an *i* in the word), were legitimate Hudibrastic rhymes ?

One or two errors in literary history are pointed out—Byron ever had all the historical information at command that any critic could require—and the reviewer concludes in the same manner in which he began.

We must be excused from a more detailed notice of Mr. Ireland for the present; and indeed we hope to hear no more of his lamentations, very sure that none but reviewers ever will peruse them : unless, perhaps, the unfortunate persons of quality whom he may henceforth single out as proper victims of future dedication.

The critique is but evidence that Byron, with his excessively receptive nature, is too much affected by the critical methods of his time. He is not justifying the high claims of his superb equipment; or fulfilling the promise of his fine beginning.

Within the space of a few months after his return from the pilgrimage, Byron had appeared three times as formal critic, twice before he " awoke and found himself famous." In about the same time he had made as many speeches in the House of Lords and had grown tired of the experiment. He had previously left England just after a semi-critical adventure that had brought him his first success. His more serious employment on the voyage had been with a work of larger critical import. He threatened repeatedly at the time to abandon creative work, esteeming the critic higher than the poet. The chances are excellent that, without the raging success of his poetry,[1] he would have developed into a critic.

His critique on Ireland, so far as we know, was his last attempt in criticism, purely and disinterestedly as such. His next appearance in a critical rôle was as controversialist only four years before his death.

Reply to *Blackwood's* Byron's answer to the critic of *Don Juan* in *Blackwood's Edinburgh Magazine* was a more comprehensive effort in what it attempted than any other single critical work he ever performed.[2] Its criticism is of a more general character, its argument is fundamentally sounder and is more logically presented, and the excesses of language common in controversial writings are fewer, than in the much longer compositions to Murray in the quarrel with Bowles. It occupies therefore a large place—indeed too large—among his works as a source of opinion of his critical powers and beliefs. It is a vital part, the first regular onslaught, of his warfare in behalf of Pope, and is an integral part of his long and relentless fight against Southey.

Byron had been openly attacked in both his personal and his literary character. His article was therefore a reply. He writes to Murray on March 25, 1820:

[1] See Chapter I, 2 f., and " Detached Thoughts," *L. & J.* V, 415.
[2] It was inscribed to Disraeli, and was sent to Murray as co-proprietor of *Blackwood's* at the time. The article was inserted for publication but was withdrawn. It did not finally appear in print till 1845.

I am now foaming an answer (in prose) to the Blackwood Article of last August: you shall have it when done; it will set the kiln in a low.[1]

Six days later he says:

I sent you yesterday eight sheets of answer to Jack Wilson and the *Edin. Mag.* of last August. Herewith you will receive a note (enclosed) on Pope, which you will find tally with a part of the text of last Post. I have at last lost all patience with the atrocious cant and nonsense about Pope, with which our present blackguards are overflowing, and am determined to make such head against it as an Individual can, by prose or verse; and I will at least do it with good will. There is no bearing it any longer; and if it goes on, it will destroy what little good writing or taste remains amongst us. I hope there are still a few men of taste to second me; but if not, I'll battle it alone, convinced that it is in the best cause of English literature.[2]

It is true that he was aware of the offensive article three months before. On December 10 of the preceding year he had referred to it in a letter to Murray,[3] but it is evident that his work was executed in great haste. Some new turn of affairs doubtless had furnished him with the *estro*. In no more than a week's time, we may reasonably assume, it was planned, executed, and despatched.

Byron wrote under the oppression of such heavy indictment as the following:

It appears, in short, as if this miserable man, having exhausted every species of sensual gratification—having drained the cup of sin even to its bitterest dregs—were resolved to show us that he is no longer a human being, even in his frailties; but a cool, unconcerned fiend, laughing with a detestable glee over the whole of the better and worse elements of which human life is composed—treating well nigh with equal derision the

[1] *L. & J.* IV, 422.
[2] *L. & J.* IV, 425 f.
[3] See *L. & J.* IV, 384.

most pure of virtues, and the most odious of vices—dead alike
to the beauty of the one, and the deformity of the other—a mere
heartless despiser of that frail but noble humanity, whose type
was never exhibited in a shape of more deplorable degradation
than in his own contemptuously distinct delineation of himself.
To confess to his Maker, and weep over in secret agonies, the
wildest and most fantastic transgressions of heart and mind,
is the part of a conscious sinner, in whom sin has not become
the sole principle of life and action. But, to lay bare to the
eye of man—and of *woman*—all the hidden convulsions of a
wicked spirit—and to do all this without one symptom of
contrition, remorse, or hesitation, with a calm, careless ferocious-
ness of contented and satisfied depravity—this was an insult
which no man of genius had ever before dared to put upon
his Creator or his species. Impiously railing against his God—
madly and meanly disloyal to his Sovereign and his country,—
and brutally outraging all the best feelings of female honor,
affection, and confidence,—how small a part of chivalry is that
remains to the descendant of the Byrons—a gloomy visor and
a deadly weapon!

And yet Byron is not violent, as might have been expected, against the author who could pen such opprobrious
sentences upon him. He supposed his assailant to be John
Wilson, and names him as such in the concluding paragraphs
of his article. On first learning of the attack he remarks
to Murray simply:

I like and admire Wilson, and *he* should not have indulged
himself in such outrageous license.[1]

And at the conclusion of his own article he says :

And although I do not think that Mr. John Wilson has in
this instance treated me with candour or consideration, I trust
that the tone I have used in speaking of him personally will
prove that I bear him as little malice as I really believe at the

[1] *L. & J*. IV, 385.

bottom of his heart he bears toward me; but the duties of an editor, like those of a tax-gatherer, are paramount and peremptory.

There is indeed more than the customary Christian charity in such response.

It was not then the attack on his personal character that Byron most resented, vigorous as his defense was. It was the affront to his literary character, the unfavorable comparison made between him and the " Lakers."[1] Byron was never reticent when the topic was himself, but if the order, the proportion, the details, and the tone of his Reply mean anything, he was most aroused when this comparison was made.[2] It was there his chief cause for offense lay, and thereabout the critical portion of the work turns.[3]

---

[1] Ironically enough, the author of the article, according to Mr. Moorman in the *Cambridge History of English Literature*, was not Wilson but Southey himself. At the complacency of Southey's evident intention of being included himself among the "lofty-minded and virtuous men," "whose virtues few indeed can equal," and the like, Byron's reply becomes all the more justifiable and praiseworthy. Byron's handling of the subject can well be imagined, if he had been aware that his old enemy penned the article.

[2] Miss Mayne calls the passage beginning, " The man who is exiled by a faction," the " true climax " of the Reply. It is doubtful if she has read closely. She adds:—" The letter then degenerates into the too frequent personal attacks on Wordsworth and ' the Lakers,' and ends in the tedious vindication of the ' great little Queen Anne's man,' which was the King Charles's head of his critical writings."—*Byron* II, 168 f.

[3] The only portion of the defense proper that is of the least critical value is the passage explaining Byron's own literary characters:—" In my writings I have rarely described any character under a fictitious name: those of whom I have spoken have had their own—in many cases a stronger satire in itself than any which could be appended to it. But of real circumstances I have availed myself plentifully, both in the serious and the ludicrous—they are to poetry what landscapes are to the painter; but my *figures* are not portraits. It may even have happened, that I have seized on some events that have occurred under my own observation, or in my own family, as I would paint a view from my grounds, did it harmonise with my picture; but I never would introduce the likenesses of its living members, unless their features could be made as favourable to themselves as to the effect; which, in the above instance, would be extremely difficult."

I have now arrived at a passage describing me as having vented my " spleen against the lofty-minded and virtuous men," men " whose virtues few indeed can equal " ; meaning, I humbly presume, the notorious triumvirate known by the name of "Lake Poets" in their aggregate capacity, and by Southey, Wordsworth, and Coleridge, when taken singly. I wish to say a word or two upon the virtues of one of those persons, public and private, for reasons which will soon appear.

With his personal grievance against Southey in mind,[1] he proceeds then to an arraignment of the trio, singly and collectively, and of the system of writing which he deemed them to represent.

His summary of his somewhat personal commentary is characteristic of his method.

I have said more of these people than I intended in this place, being somewhat stirred by the remarks which induced me to commence upon the topic. I see nothing in these men as poets, or as individuals—little in their talents, and less in their characters, to prevent honest men from expressing for them considerable contempt, in prose or rhyme, as it may happen. Mr. Southey has the *Quarterly* for his field of rejoinder, and Mr. Wordsworth his postscripts to *Lyrical Ballads*, where the two great instances of the sublime are taken from himself and Milton. . . . " What divinity doth hedge" these persons, that we should respect them ? Is it Apollo ? Are they not of those who called Dryden's *Ode* " a drunken song" ? who have discovered that Gray's *Elegy* is full of faults. . . and have published what is allowed to be the very worst prose that ever was written, to prove that Pope was no poet, and that William Wordsworth is ? . . . Who is there who esteems those parricides of their own principles ?

As in his early satire, he enlarges his theme and includes

---

[1] Byron's special grievance against Southey began in 1816, during his residence in Switzerland, when the laureate made the charge that the two poets, Byron and Shelley, were living " in a league of incest " with two sisters.

the poets and poetry of the day as opposed to Pope and English classical poetry. This enlargement of the subject fortunately gives to the work its more general character and hence its greater critical worth.

And here I wish to say a few words on the present state of English poetry. That this is the age of the decline of English poetry will be doubted by few who have calmly considered the subject. That there are men of genius among the present poets makes little against the fact, because it has been well said, that " next to him who forms the taste of his country, the greatest genius is he who corrupts it." . . . The great cause of the present deplorable state of English poetry is to be attributed to that absurd and systematic depreciation of Pope, in which, for the last few years, there has been a kind of epidemical concurrence. Men of the most opposite opinions have united upon this topic. Warton and Churchill began it, having borrowed the hint probably from the heroes of the *Dunciad*, and their own internal conviction that their proper reputation can be as nothing till the most perfect and harmonious of poets—he who, having no fault, has had REASON made his reproach— was reduced to what they conceived to be his level; but even *they* dared not degrade him below Dryden.

Byron's failure to understand the essential difference between the main body of English poetry of his age and that of the classical regime has been pointed out.[1] The term

---

[1] See Chapter IV, 96 f. In a note subjoined to some remarks, hardly pertinent to the subject, on Southey and Wordsworth, he reveals a shrewd understanding of one of the vital characteristics of Romantic poetry, in an effort to define " Lake poetry," to its hurt, of course :— " Goldsmith has anticipated the definition of the Lake poetry, as far as such things can be defined. ' Gentlemen, the present piece is not of your *common epic poems*, which come from the press like paper kites in summer; there are none of your Turnuses or Didos in it; *it is an historical description of nature.* I only beg you'll endeavour to make your souls in unison with mine, *and hear with the same enthusiasm with which I have written.'* Would not this have made a proper proem to the *Excursion*, and the poet and his pedler ? It would have answered perfectly for that purpose, had it not unfortunately been written in good English."

" classical " signified to him *form* and little else. Specifically, it meant the ability to write the heroic couplet well. He falls into his customary error in his attempt to name the adherents of the one school or the other.

These three personages, Southey, Wordsworth, and Coleridge, had all of them a very natural antipathy to Pope ; and I respect them for it, as the only original feeling or principle which they have contrived to preserve. But they have been joined in it by those who have joined them in nothing else : by the Edinburgh Reviewers, by the whole heterogeneous mass of living English poets, excepting Crabbe, Rogers, Gifford, and Campbell, who, both by precept and practice, have proved their adherence ; and by me, who have shamefully deviated in practice, but have ever loved and honoured Pope's poetry with my whole soul, and hope to do so till my dying day. All, with the exception of Crabbe, Rogers and Campbell, who may be considered as having taken their station, will, by the blessing of God, survive their own reputation, without attaining any very extraordinary period of longevity. . . . . and of Moore, who as the Burns of Ireland, possesses a fame which cannot be lost.

He is not, of course, so uncritical, the reader has observed, as to ignore his own part in the corruption of taste, which he deplores. He is more voluble than convincing in his palliation of the fault.

It may be asked, why, having this opinion of the present state of poetry in England, and having had it long, as my friends and others well knew—possessing, or having possessed too, as a writer, the ear of the public for the time being—I have not adopted a different plan in my own compositions, and endeavoured to correct rather than encourage the taste of the day. To this I would answer, that it is easier to perceive the wrong than to pursue the right, and that I have never contemplated the prospect " of filling (with *Peter Bell*, see its Preface) permanently a station in the literature of the country."

Those who know me best, know this, and that I have been considerably astonished at the temporary success of my works, having flattered no person and no party, and expressed opinions which are not those of the general reader. Could I have anticipated the degree of attention which has been accorded me, assuredly I would have studied more to deserve it. But I have lived in far countries abroad, or in the agitating world at home, which was not favourable to study or reflection ; so that almost all I have written has been mere passion,—passion, it is true, of different kinds, but always passion : for in me (if it be not an Irishism to say so) my *indifference* was a kind of passion, the result of experience, and not the philosophy of nature. . . . Without being old in years, I am old in days, and do not feel the adequate spirit within me to attempt a work which should show what I think right in poetry, and must content myself with having denounced what is wrong. There are, I trust, younger spirits rising up in England, who escaping the contagion which has swept away poetry from our literature, will recall it to their country, such as it once was and may still be.

The article reaches its climax as criticism in the explicit defense of Pope.

There will be found as comfortable metaphysics, and ten times more poetry in the *Essay on Man*, than in the *Excursion*. If you search for passion, where is it to be found stronger than in the epistle from Eloisa to Abelard, or in *Palamon and Arcite* ? Do you wish for invention, imagination, sublimity, character ? seek them in the *Rape of the Lock*, the *Fables* of Dryden, the *Ode of Saint Cecilia's Day*, and *Absalom and Achitophel* : you will discover in these two poets only, *all* for which you must ransack innumerable metres, and God only knows how many *writers* of the day, without finding a tittle of the same qualities,—with the addition, too, of wit, of which the latter have none. . . . It is this very harmony, particularly in Pope, which has raised the vulgar and atrocious cant against him :—because his versification is perfect, it is assumed that it is his only perfection ; because his truths are so clear, it is asserted that he has no invention; and because he is always intelligible, it is taken for granted that he has no genius. We are sneeringly told that he is the " Poet of Reason," as if this was a reason for his being no poet. Taking passage for passage, I will undertake to cite more lines teeming with *imagination* from Pope than from any *two* living poets, be they who they may. To take an instance at random from a species of composition not very favorable to imagination—Satire: set down the character of Sporus, with all the wonderful play of fancy which is scattered over it, and place by its side an equal number of verses, from any two existing poets, of the same power and the same variety— where will you find them ? [1]

[1] Byron is not so reckless in his challenge, perhaps, as he seems. A year later in a letter to Murray he analyzes the passage with a good deal of effectiveness. He is certainly judicious in his selection of the passage:—" I will show more *imagery* in twenty lines of Pope than in any equal length of quotation in English poesy, and that in places where they least expect it: for instance, in his lines on *Sporus*,—now, do just *read* them over—the subject is of no consequence (whether it be Satire or Epic)—we are talking of *poetry* and *imagery* from *Nature and Art*. Now, mark the images separately and arithmetically:—

1. The thing of *Silk*.
2. The *Curd* of *Ass's* milk.
3. The *Butterfly*.
4. The *Wheel*.
5. Bug with gilded wings.
6. *Painted* Child of dirt.
7. Whose *Buzz*.
8. Well-bred *Spaniels*.
9. *Shallow streams run dimpling*.
10. *Florid impotence*.
11. *Prompter. Puppet squeaks*.
12. *The Ear of Eve*.
13. *Familiar toad*.
14. *Half-froth, half-venom, spits* himself abroad.
15. *Fop* at the *toilet*.
16. *Flatterer* at the *board*.
17. *Amphibious thing*.
18. Now *trips a lady*.
19. Now *struts a Lord*.
20. A *Cherub's face*.
21. A *reptile* all the rest.
22. The *Robbins*.
23. Pride that *licks the dust*.

Argument of the kind would have been regarded as final in the age before Byron's, and it would be applauded in any age, since or yet to come, that was not more romantic than " correct."

In a subsequent reference to the article[1] Byron has given a hint of the spirit in which the work was composed.

Mr. Keats died at Rome about a year after this was written, of a decline produced by his having burst a blood-vessel on reading the article on his *Endymion* in the *Quarterly Review*. I have read the article before and since ; and although it is bitter, I do not think that a man should permit himself to be killed by it. But a young man little dreams what he must inevitably encounter in the course of a life ambitious of public notice. My indignation at Mr. Keats's depreciation of Pope has hardly permitted me to do justice to his own genius, which, malgré all the fantastic fopperies of his style, was undoubtedly of great promise. His fragment of *Hyperion* seems actually inspired by the Titans, and is as sublime as Æschylus.[2]

Less than a year afterwards the matter seems quite to have lapsed from his memory.

Now, is there a line of all the passage without the most *forcible* imagery (for his purpose) ? Look at the *variety*, at the *poetry*, of the passage— at the *imagination* : there is hardly a line from which a *painting* might not be made, and *is*. But this is nothing in comparison with his higher passages in the *Essay on Man*, and many of his other poems, serious and comic."—*L. & J.* V, 259 f.

[1] One or two fragments in Byron's hand-writing, printed for the first time, *L. & J.* VI, Appendix I, are manifestly some rejected portions of the Reply. They are part and parcel with it in manner but add nothing to it of critical value.

[2] A manuscript note, November 12, 1821, *L. & J.* IV, 491. Byron had been incensed with Keats for his attack on Pope in *Sleep and Poetry*, and in his Reply had compared unfavorably some of the " manikin's " poems with some of the early compositions of Pope. But he had made no greater detraction of him than to denominate him the " Tadpole of the Lakes." The year before Keats had written to his brother and sister, " Lord Byron cuts a figure but he is not figurative," but Byron can hardly have known of Keats's depreciation of him. Needless to say, Keats was really an admirer of Byron. Shelley was doubtless responsible for Byron's ultimate favorable opinion of *Hyperion*. See his letters to Byron from Pisa, April 16, May 4, and July 16, 1821.

I must now, however, say a word or two about Pope, of whom you have my opinion more at large in the unpublished letter *on* or *to* (for I forget which) the Editor of *Blackwood's Edinburgh Magazine*.[1]

The Reply, after the personal defense, is as full of positive critical matter as anything of equal length in the language. Its argument is not unsound but superseded and outworn. Were this not the case, it would not suffer greatly in comparison even with Wordsworth's Preface to *Lyrical Ballads* and Arnold's *The Function of Criticism at the Present Time*. It shows a more fertile power of illustration and a more vigorous creative talent than either. Even in its discarded character it evinces Byron's ability and equipment for criticism as of unusually high quality.

The Polemics against Bowles   In the famous war of the pamphlets, precipitated by Bowles, on the moral and literary character of Pope, Byron is again seen in the rôle of " controvertist and critic." His contribution was made in two articles, written within a few weeks of each other and designated as " Letters " to John Murray. Together these compositions cover more than fifty pages of close print, and constitute Byron's longest single work in criticism. Their subject is narrower, however, than that of the shorter Reply to *Blackwood's*, they comprehend less a critical system, but they contain a more elemental enquiry, to wit, the nature and quality of the poetical object.

An account of the controversy sufficient for our purpose is given, in the " House-that-Jack-built " formula, in *Blackwood's* for July, 1821, after Byron's part in the pastime is over.

---

[1] *L. & J.* V, 539.

1. Mr. Bowles wrote a book upon Pope.
2. Mr. Campbell abused Mr. Bowles's book on Pope.
3. Mr. Bowles wrote an answer to Mr. Campbell's abuse of Mr. Bowles's book on Pope.
4. Lord Byron wrote a letter to certain stars in Albemarle-street, in answer to Mr. Bowles's answer to Mr. Campbell's abuse of Mr. Bowles's book on Pope.
5. Jeremy Bentham Esq. wrote a letter to Lord Byron about Lord Byron's letter to certain stars in Albemarle-street, in answer to Mr. Bowles's answer to Mr. Campbell's abuse of Mr. Bowles's book on Pope.
6. Mr. Bowles wrote an answer, not to Jeremy Benthan, but to Lord Byron's Letter to certain stars in Albemarle-street, in answer to Mr. Bowles's answer to Mr. Campbell's abuse of Mr. Bowles's book on Pope. . . . We omit by-battles.[1]

The immediate subject arose out of the much agitated larger topic, the poetry of the day *versus* the poetry of Pope. Byron's main contention then is identical with his Reply, to wit, a defense at all points of the " Nightingale of Twickenham " against the " Cockney-and-Water washing-

---

[1] Mr. Bowles's " book " was an edition of Pope's complete works, ten volumes, in 1806. Byron had protested in the *English Bards and Scotch Reviewers* against the attack on Pope's morals, but the defense was not taken up regularly until Campbell's *Essay on English Poetry*, prefixed to his *Specimens of the British Poets*, seven volumes, in 1819. Bowles replied to Campbell's challenge, other disputants entered, and the pamphlets fell thick and fast until March 25, 1821, when Byron dispatched his second letter to Murray. This did not end the controversy. On the other hand, it continued to rage and increased in bitterness. Byron's final letter really had no part in the actual conflict, inasmuch as it was not made public until several years later. But it was Byron's last word, Bowles's courtesies afterwards disarmed him (Cf. *L. & J.* V, 277, 286, 310, 338), hence it concludes all interest in the subject for the purposes of this study. With reference to the outcome of the whole, suffice that Bowles beat Byron and Campbell " hollow out of the ring," in the opinion of *Blackwood's* at the time. The opinion is acquiesced in generally, but the situation is best explained by Professor Beers:—" The victory remained with Bowles, not because he had won it by argument, but because opinion had changed, and changed probably once and for all."—*A History of English Romanticism of the Nineteenth Century*, 73.

tub Schools." The fire is a little diverted, however, from the Lake group proper and concentrated on the less worthy Cockney subdivision.[1] But while the attack on the "smaller fry" was more becoming, it was not so vehement, nor so virile for that matter, as the Reply, though it was a blast of the same ill wind.

The letters were undoubtedly hastily done, although Byron had entertained impulses to engage in the conflict some time before. In November of the previous year, 1820, he writes to Murray:

I have read part of the *Quarterly* just arrived: Mr. Bowles shall be answered.[3]

Later in the same month he says:

Bowles must be *bowled* down: 'tis a sad match at Cricket, if that fellow can get any Notches at Pope's expence.[3]

And before the year ends:

I mean to plunge thick, too, into the contest upon Pope, and to lay about me like a dragon till I make manure of Bowles for the top of Parnassus.[4]

His spirit at the time is evident. He was but nursing his indignation from the former bout, and because the Reply remained unpublished he was perhaps annoyed by the thought that his effort had been in vain. There is no doubt that he was in the right humor for a fulmination at any time.

They support Pope, I see, in the *Quarterly*. Let them continue to do so: it is a Sin, and a Shame, and a *damnation* to think that *Pope*!! should require it—but he does. Those miserable mountebanks of the day, the poets, disgrace themselves and

---

[1] " This comes of Southey and Wordsworth and such renegado rascals with their systems."—*L. & J.* V, 142.
[2] *L. & J.* V, 108. Cf. *ibid.*, 113.
[3] *L. & J.* V, 121.
[4] *L. & J.* V, 132.

1

deny God, in running down Pope, the most *faultless* of Poets, and almost of men.[1]

But of the actual accomplishment of the task he has little to say. The first letter is under date of February 7. It was probably begun then. In his diary two days before he says :

Read some of Bowles's dispute about Pope, with all the replies and rejoinders. Perceive that my name has been lugged into the controversy, but have not time to state what I know of the subject. On some " piping day of peace " it is probable that I may resume it.[2]

It is to be noted that this was just at the time when Byron was most active with the Carbonari. On February 10 he records briefly :

Rode out between four and six —finished my letter to Murray on Bowles's pamphlets—added postscript.[3]

The letter was not begun on February 5, it was completed by February 10. In all probability it was the labor of three or four days at best, and was done at a time when the chief claim upon Byron's attention was the Italian conspiracy.[4] It is a remarkable piece of work for the time spent on it. From a composition of such length, done in great haste and amid distractions, it is idle to expect a masterpiece of criticism.

Definite occasion was given him to enter the fray by a reference to himself in Bowles's first pamphlet, and then by the use of his name by other disputants of the quarrel.

In the different pamphlets which you have had the goodness to send me, on the Pope and Bowles controversy, I perceive

---

[1] *L. & J.* V, 109.
[2] *L. & J.* V, 199 f.
[3] Diary, *L. & J.* V, 201.
[4] " I wrote the whole off-hand, without copy or correction, and expecting then every day to be called into the field."—*L. & J.* V, 273.

that my name is occasionally introduced by both parties. Mr. Bowles refers more than once to what he is pleased to consider "a remarkable circumstance," not only in his letter to Mr. Campbell, but in his reply to the *Quarterly*. The *Quarterly* also and Mr. Gilchrist have conferred on me the dangerous honor of a quotation ; and Mr. Bowles indirectly makes a kind of appeal to me personally, by saying, "Lord B., *if he remembers the* circumstance, will *witness* "—.

It is no affair of mine ; but having once begun (certainly not by my own wish, but called upon by the frequent recurrence to my name in the pamphlets,) I am like an Irishman in a " row," " anybody's customer."

The first point of attack is the title of Bowles's pamphlet, " The Invariable Principles of Poetry." The objection is well made, as casting doubt upon the soundness of Bowles's premise, but the argument is not conclusive.

I do hate that word "*invariable*." What is there of *human*, be it poetry, philosophy, wit, wisdom, science, power, glory, mind, matter, life, or death, which is "*invariable*" ? Of course I put things divine out of the question. Of all arrogant baptisms of a book, this title to a pamphlet appears the most complacently conceited.

The controversy had developed the qestion of the superiority of natural objects over artificial ones as subjects of poetical contemplation and use.[1] The discussion of such a topic is really futile, inasmuch as nothing final could come from it, yet it is here that Byron's most important critical material is presented. His primary idea is fundamentally right, but he does not adhere to it, and his treatment, from the haste and the immature condition of his thought, is rambling and illogical.

---

[1] " Let us examine a little further this ' Babble of green fields ' and of bare Nature in general as superior to artificial imagery, for the poetical purposes of the fine arts."

Mr. B. Asserts that Campbell's " Ship of the Line " derives all its poetry, not from " *art*," but from " *Nature*." " Take away the waves, the winds, the sun, etc., etc., etc., *one* will become a stripe of blue bunting ; and the other a piece of coarse canvas on three tall poles." Very true ; take away the " waves," " the winds," and there will be no ship at all, not only for poetical, but for any other purpose ; and take away " the sun," and we must read Mr. B.'s pamphlet by candle light. But the " poetry " of the " Ship " does *not* depend on the "waves," etc. ; on the contrary, the " Ship of the line " confers its own poetry upon the waters, and heightens *theirs*. I do not deny, that the " waves and winds," and above all " the sun," are highly poetical ; we know it to our cost, by the many descriptions of them in verse : but if the waves bore only the foam upon their bosoms, if the winds wafted only the seaweed to the shore, if the sun shone neither upon the pyramids, not fleets, nor fortresses, would its beams be equally poetical ? I think not : the poetry is at least reciprocal. Take away " the Ship of the Line " " swinging round " the " calm water," and the calm water becomes a somewhat monotonous thing to look at, particularly if not transparently *clear* ; witness the thousands who pass by without looking on it at all. What was it attracted the thousands to the launch ? They might have seen the poetical " calm water " at Wapping, or in the " London Dock," or in the Paddington Canal, or in a horse-pond, or in a slop-basin, or in any other vase. They might have heard the poetical winds howling through the chinks of the pigstye, or the garret window ; they might have seen the sun shining on a footman's livery, or on a brass warming pan ; but could the " calm water," or the " wind," or the " sun," make all, or any of these " poetical " ? I think not. Mr. B. admits " the Ship " to be poetical, but only from those accessaries : now if they *confer* poetry so as to make one thing poetical, they would make other things poetical ; the more so, as Mr. B. calls a " ship of the line " without them,—that is to say, its " masts and sails and streamers,"—" blue bunting," and " coarse canvas," and " tall poles." So they are ; and porcelain is clay, and man is dust, and flesh is grass, and yet the two latter at least are the subjects of much poesy.

The point he has in mind, that the poetry " is at least reciprocal " in the two classes of objects, is sound, but he does not make an effective use of it or round his principle to a poignant conclusion. When he does summarize, it is in the middle of a paragraph, which almost defeats itself in its conclusion.

The water, etc., undoubtedly HEIGHTENS the poetical associations, but it does not *make* them; and the ship amply repays the obligation: they aid each other; the water is more poetical with the ship—the ship less so without the water. But even a ship laid up in dock is a grand and a poetical sight. Even an old boat, keel upwards, wrecked upon the barren sand, is a " poetical " object . . . whilst a long extent of sand and unbroken water, without the boat, would be as like dull prose at any pamphlet lately published.

Toward the end of his study he displays some keen penetration in an analysis of a passage from Milton, cited by Bowles, for the special application of his theme.

In speaking of artificial objects, I have omitted to touch upon one which I will now mention. Cannon may be presumed to be as highly poetical as art can make her objects. Mr. B. will, perhaps, tell me this is because they resemble that grand natural article of Sound in heaven, and Similie (*sic*) upon earth— thunder. I shall be told triumphantly, that Milton made sad work with his artillery, when he armed his devils therewithal. He did so; and this artificial object must have had much of the Sublime to attract his attention for such a conflict. He *has* made an absurd use of it; but the absurdity consists not in using *cannon* against the angels of God, but any *material* weapon. The thunder of the clouds would have been as ridiculous and vain in the hands of the devils, as the " villainous saltpetre "; the angels were as impervious to the one as to the other. The thunderbolts become sublime in the hands of the

Almighty, not as such, but because *he* deigns to use them as a means of repelling the rebel spirits; but no one can attribute their defeat to this grand piece of natural electricity: the Almighty willed, and they fell; his word would have been enough; and Milton is as absurd, (and, in fact, *blasphemous*,) in putting material lightnings into the hands of the Godhead, as in giving him hands at all.[1]

But the reader is confused by his saying in the same sentence :

The thunderbolts become sublime in the hands of the Almighty,

and,

Milton is absurd, (and, in fact, *blasphemous*,) in putting material lightnings into the hands of the Godhead, as in giving him hands at all.

It is an instance of his not expressing clearly and fully what he had—but vaguely at best—in mind.

He is more argumentative than critical in his *reductio ad absurdum* treatment of his opponent's line of thought.

Mr. B. then proceeds to press Homer into his service, in answer to a remark of Mr. Campbell's, that " Homer was a great describer of works of art." Mr. B. contends that all his great power, even in this, depends upon their connection with nature. The " shield of Achilles derives its poetical interest from the subjects described on it." And from what does the *spear* of Achilles derive its interest ? and the helmet and the mail worn by Patroclus, and the celestial armour, and the very brazen greaves of the well-booted Greeks ? Is it solely from the legs, and the back, and the breast, and the human body, which they enclose ? In that case, it would have been more poetical to have made them fight naked; and Gulley and Gregson, as being nearer to a state of nature, are more poetical boxing in a pair of drawers than Hector and Achilles in radiant armour,

---

[1] Cf., *Vision of Judgment*, stanza 52.

and with heroic weapons. Instead of the clash of helmets, and the rushing of chariots, and the whizzing of spears, and the glancing of swords, and the cleaving of shields, and the piercing of breast-plates, why not represent the Greeks and Trojans like two savage tribes, tugging and tearing, and kicking and biting, and gnashing, foaming, grinning, and gouging, in all the poetry of martial nature, unencumbered with gross, prosaic, artificial arms; an equal superfluity to the natural warrior and his natural poet ? Is there anything unpoetical in Ulysses striking the horses or Rhesus with *his bow* (having forgotten his thong), or would Mr. B. have had him kick them with his foot, or smack them with his hand, as being more unsophisticated ?

And, with the loss of critical dignity :

Mr. Bowles makes the chief part of a ship's poesy depend upon the " *wind* " : then why is a ship under sail more poetical than a hog in a high wind ? The hog is all nature, the ship is all art, " coarse canvas," " blue bunting," and " tall poles " ; both are violently acted upon by the wind, tossed here and there, to and fro, and yet nothing but excess of hunger could make me look upon the pig as the more poetical of the two, and then only in the shape of a griskin.

At times he incurs the suspicion of introducing an opportunity for a little self-celebration.

I look upon myself as entitled to talk of naval matters, at least to poets. . . . I stood upon the Symplegades—I stood by the broken altar still exposed to the winds upon one of them—I felt all the " *poetry* " of the situation, as I repeated the first lines of Medea ; but would not that " poetry " have been heightened by the *Argo* ?

But as often he produces some magnificent effects.

The aspect of a storm in the Archipelago is as poetical as need be, the sea being particularly short, dashing, and dangerous and the navigation intricate and broken by the isles and currents. Cape Sigeum, the tumuli of the Troad, Lemnos, Tenedos, all added to the associations of the time. But what seemed the most " *poetical* " of all at the moment, were the numbers (about two hundred) of Greek and Turkish craft, which were obliged to " cut and run " before the wind, from their unsafe anchorage, some for Tenedos, some for other isles, some for the Main, and some it might be for Eternity. The sight of these little scudding vessels, darting over the foam in the twilight, now appearing and now disappearing between the waves in the cloud of night, with their peculiarly *white* sails, (the Levant sails not being of " *coarse canvas*," but of white cotton,) skimming along as quickly, but less safely than the sea-mew which hovered over them ; their evident distress, their reduction to fluttering specks in the distance, their crowded succession, their *littleness*, as contending with the giant element, which made our stout 44's *teak* timbers (she was built in India) creak again ; their aspect and their motion, all struck me as something far more " poetical " than the mere broad, brawling, shipless sea, and the sullen winds, could possibly have been without them.

His illustrations from his voluminous reading are just as effective.

In the sublime of sacred poetry, "Who is this that cometh from Edom ? with *dyed garments* from Bozrah ? " would " the comer " be poetical without his " dyed garments ? " which strike and startle the spectator, and identify the approaching object.

His combative spirit is shown by his arguing beyond his own proposition. His intention at the outset was not to elevate artificial objects *above* natural ones. But as he warms to the discussion he seems to assert not only the superiority of the former but their complete transcendence over the latter.

Nature, exactly, simply, barely, Nature, will make no great artist of any kind, and least of all a poet—the most artificial, perhaps, of all artists in his very essence.

There are a thousand rocks and capes far more picturesque than those of the Acropolis and Cape Sunium in themselves ;

what are they to a thousand scenes in the wilder parts of Greece, or Asia Minor, Switzerland, or even of Cintra in Portugal, or to many scenes of Italy, and the Sierras of Spain ? But it is the " art," the columns, the temples, the wrecked vessel, which give them their antique and their modern poetry, and not the spots themselves. Without them, the *spots* of earth would be unnoticed and unknown : buried, like Babylon and Nineveh, in indistinct confusion, without poetry, as without existence ; but to whatever spot of earth these ruins were transported, if they were *capable* of transportation, like the obelisk, and the sphinx, and the Memnon's head, *there* they would still exist in the perfection of their beauty, and in the pride of their poetry. I opposed, and will ever oppose, the robbery of ruins from Athens, to instruct the English in sculpture (who are as capable of sculpture as the Egyptians are of skating) ; but why did I do so ? The *ruins* are as poetical in Piccadilly as they were in the Parthenon ; but the Parthenon and its rock are less so without them. Such is the poetry of art.

His appeal to sculpture for proof is a deft stroke, although he is guilty of more than ordinary irrelevancy in presenting his thought.

Of sculpture in general, it may be observed, that it is more poetical than nature itself, inasmuch as it represents and bodies forth that ideal beauty and sublimity which is never to be found in actual Nature. This at least is the general opinion. But, always excepting the Venus di Medicis, I differ from that opinion, at least as far as regards female beauty ; for the head of Lady Charlemont (when I first saw her nine years ago) seemed to possess all that sculpture could require for its ideal. I recollect seeing something of the same kind in the head of an Albanian girl, who was actually employed in mending a road in the mountains, and in some Greek, and one or two Italian, faces. But of *sublimity*, I have never seen anything in human nature at all to approach the expression of sculpture, either in the Apollo, the Moses, or other of the sterner works of ancient or modern art.

One more poetical instance of the power of art, and even its *superiority* over nature, in poetry; and I have done :—the bust of *Antinous*! Is there any thing in nature like this marble, excepting the Venus ? Can there be more *poetry* gathered into existence than in that wonderful creation of perfect beauty ? But the poetry of this bust is in no respect derived from nature, nor from any association of moral exaltedness; for what is there in common with moral nature, and the male minion of Adrian ? The very execution is *not natural*, but *supernatural*, or rather *super-artificial*, for nature has never done so much.[1]

The futility of a discussion of the question, whether or not poetry is inherent in one class of objects more than in another, must have struck Byron in the course of his argument. Before he concludes he approaches the subject from the point of view of the artist, and here his criticism is as sound as could be offered.

To the question, "Whether the description of a game of cards be as poetical, supposing the execution of the artists equal, as a description of a walk in a forest ? " it may be answered, that the *materials* are certainly not equal; but that "the *artist*," who has rendered the " game of cards poetical," is *by far the greater* of the two. But all this " ordering " of poets is purely arbitrary on the part of Mr. B. There may or may not be, in fact, different " orders " of poetry, but the poet is always ranked according to his execution, and not according to his branch of the art.[2]

Poets are classed by the power of their performance, and not according to its rank in a gradus. In the contrary case, the

---

[1] Cp., " I never yet saw the picture—or the statue—which came within a league of my conception or expectation; but I have seen many mountains, and Seas, and Rivers, and views, and two or three women, who went as far beyond it,—besides some horses; and a lion (at Veli Pasha's) in the Morea; and a tiger at supper in Exeter ' Change.' "— *L. & J.* IV, 107.

[2] It is amusing to imagine what Byron's notion would have been, if he had been aware of Wordsworth's description of a game of cards in the first book of *The Prelude*.

forgotten epic poets of all countries would rank above Petrarch, Dante, Ariosto, Burns, Gray, Dryden, and the highest names of various countries.

Were Petrarch to be ranked according to the order of his compositions, where would the best of sonnets place him? with Dante and the other? no; but, as I have said before, the poet who *executes* best is the highest, whatever his department, and will ever be so rated in the world's esteem.

A great artist will make a block of stone as sublime as a mountain, and a good poet can imbue a pack of cards with more poetry than inhabits the forests of America.

In a long note he returns to the title of Bowles's pamphlet, and attacks with great ardor the term " invariable."

Mr. Bowles's title of "*invariable* principles of poetry," is, perhaps, the most arrogant ever prefixed to a volume. So far are the principles of poetry from being "*invariable*," that they never were nor ever will be settled. These "principles" mean nothing more than the predilections of a particular age; and every age has its own, and a different from its predecessor. It is now Homer, and now Virgil; once Dryden, and since Walter Scott; now Corneille, and now Racine; now Crebillon, now Voltaire. The Homerists and Virgilians in France disputed for half a century. Not fifty years ago the Italians neglected Dante—Bettinelli reproved Monti for reading " that barbarian "; at present they adore him. Shakespeare and Milton have had their rise, and they will have their decline. Already they have more than once fluctuated, as must be the case with all the dramatists and poets of a living language. This does not depend upon their merits, but upon the ordinary vicissitudes of human opinions.

The letter ends, except for several lengthy postscripts and notes, with a somewhat servile adulation of Pope.

They have raised a mosque by the side of a Grecian temple of purest architecture; and, more barbarous than the barbarians from whose practice I have borrowed the figure, they are not

contented with their own grotesque edifice, unless they destroy
the prior, and purely beautiful fabric which preceded, and which
shames them and theirs for ever and ever. I shall be told
that amongst those I *have* been (or it may be still *am*) conspicuous—true, and I am ashamed of it. I *have* been amongst
the builders of this Babel, attended by a confusion of tongues,
but never amongst the envious destroyers of the classic temple
of our predecessor. I have loved and honoured the fame and
name of that illustratious and unrivalled man, far more than
my own paltry renown, and the trashy jingle of the crowd of
" Schools " and upstarts, who pretend to rival, or even surpass
him. Sooner than a single leaf should be torn from his laurel,
it were better that all which these men, and that I, as one of
their set, have ever written, should

> " Line trunks, clothe spice, or, fluttering in a row,
> Befringe the rails of Bedlam, or Soho ! "

There can be no worse sign for the taste of the times than
the depreciation of Pope. It would be better to receive for
proof Mr. Cobbett's rough but strong attack upon Shakespeare
and Milton, than to allow this smooth and " candid " under-
mining of the reputation of the most *perfect* of our poets, and
the purest of our moralists. Of his power in the *passions*,
in description, in the mock heroic, I leave others to descant.
I take him on his strong ground as an *ethical* poet : in the
former, none excel ; in the mock heroic and the ethical, none
equal him ; and, in my mind, the latter is the highest of all
poetry, because it does that in *verse*, which the greatest of men
have wished to accomplish in prose.

If any great national or natural convulsion could or should
overwhelm your country in such sort as to sweep Great Britain
from the kingdoms of the earth, and leave only that, after all,
the most living of human things, a *dead language* to be studied
and read, and imitated by the wise of future and far generations, upon foreign shores ; if your literature should become
the learning of mankind, divested of party cabals, temporary
fashions, and national pride and prejudice ;—an Englishman,

anxious that the posterity of strangers should know that there had been such a thing as a British Epic and Tragedy, might wish for the preservation of Shakespeare and Milton; but the surviving World would snatch Pope from the wreck, and let the rest sink with the people. He is the moral poet of all civilization; and as such, let us hope that he will one day be the national poet of mankind. He is the only poet that never shocks; the only poet whose *faultlessness* has been made his reproach.

The reader is not called upon to believe in Byron's real sincerity in such assertions. They are different in manner from the earlier portion of the article. They show a more conscious and studied effort. His most intimate friends did not believe they represented fully his convictions.[1] Evidently he was writing for effect. Such things were but a part of his scheme of amusement [2] and purpose to outdo his antagonists.[3]

The second letter [4] was written in consequence of the

[1] " I think at times that Byron ' protests too much,' and is seeking to convince himself against his will of the merits of the older school . . . I think that it is possible that he felt at last that the future and, in a way, the truth of poetry was with the innovators."—Ellis, *Samuel Rogers and his Circle*, 192 & 194. Moore records in his diary at the time :—" Looked again over his letter on Bowles. It is amusing to see through his design in thus depreciating all the present school of poetry. Being quite sure of his own hold upon fame, he contrives to loosen that of all his contemporaries, in order that they may fall away entirely from his side and leave him unencumbered, even by their floundering."— *Memoirs* III, 227 f.

[2] " My intention was to make fun of all these fellows; but how I succeeded, I don't know."—*L. & J.* V, 274.

[3] Cf., " Pope was the tolerant yet steady adherent of the most bigoted of sects; and Cowper the most bigoted and despondent sectary that ever anticipated damnation to himself or others. Is this harsh ? I know it is, and I do not assert it as my opinion of Cowper *personally*, but to *show what might* be said, with just as great an appearance of truth and candour as all the odium which has been accumulated upon Pope in similar speculations."—Earlier passage in the Letter.

[4] " I enclose you another letter on ' *Bowles*.' But I premise that it is not like the former, and that I am not at all sure how *much*, if *any*, of it should be published. Upon this point you can consult with Mr. Gifford, and think *twice* before you publish it all at."—*L. & J.* V, 265. A few days later he says, the letter " will *not* do for publication (I suspect) being as the Apprentices say, ' Damned *low*.' "—*L. & J.* V. 269.

receipt and perusal of other tracts of the controversy. It
is saner, more orderly, nearly as long, and its subject is
better suited for discussion. It is a defence of Pope's
moral character, against the Cockney subdivision of the
" Naturals,"[1] and hence is very little critical. It contains
some good advice to Bowles, how to conduct himself under
criticism, and reflects some interesting practices of Byron.
It is evidence against Byron's judgment of himself that he
is always flippant in prose. In the copious addenda to it
some passages occur that are worthy of note.

In further criticism of the poetry of his age he says:

> In the present day, then, there have sprung up two sorts
> of Naturals ;—the Lakers, who whine about Nature because they
> live in Cumberland ; and their *under-sect* (which some one has
> maliciously called the " Cockney School "), who are enthusiastical
> for the country because they live in London. It is to be ob-
> served, that the rustical founders are rather anxious to disclaim
> any connection with their metropolitan followers, whom they
> ungraciously review, and call cockneys, atheists, foolish fellows,
> bad writers, and other hard names not less ungrateful than
> unjust. I can understand the pretentions of the aquatic gentle-
> men of Windermere to what Mr. Braham terms " *entusymusy*,"
> for lakes, and mountains, and daffodils, and buttercups ; but
> I should be glad to be apprized of the foundation of the London
> propensities of their imitative brethren to the same " high
> argument." Southey, Wordsworth, and Coleridge have rambled
> over half Europe, and seen Nature in most of her varieties
> (although I think that they have occasionally not used her
> very well) ; but what on earth—of earth, and sea, and Nature—
> have the others seen ? Not a half, nor a tenth part so much
> as Pope. While they sneer at his Windsor Forest, have they
> ever seen anything of Windsor except its *brick* ?

The distinction in taste that he makes between these men
and the higher order of poets of the day, as well as Pope,

---

[1] Cf. *L. & J.* V, 337, 338.

is basic, and his manner of setting it forth admirable. His exception of Hunt, the leader of the group, is only by courtesy.[1]

The grand distinction of the under forms of the new school of poets is their *vulgarity*. By this I do not mean that they are *coarse*, but " shabby-genteel," as it is termed. A man may be *coarse* and yet not *vulgar*, and the reverse. Burns is often coarse, but never *vulgar*. Chatterton is never vulgar, nor Wordsworth, or the higher of the Lake school, though they treat of low life in all its branches. It is in their *finery* that the new under school are *most* vulgar, and they may be known by this at once. . . . Far be it from me to presume that there ever was, or can be, such a thing as an *aristocracy* of *poets*; but there *is* a nobility of thought and of style, open to all stations, and derived partly from talent, and partly from education,— which is to be found in Shakespeare, and Pope, and Burns, no less than in Dante and Alfieri, but which is nowhere to be perceived in the mock birds and bards of Mr. Hunt's little chorus. If I were asked to define what this gentlemanliness is, I should say that it is only to be defined by *examples*—of those who have it, and those who have it not. In *life*, I should say that most *military* men have it, and few *naval*;—that several men of rank have it, and few lawyers;—that it is more frequent among authors than divines (when they are not pedants); that *fencing*-masters have more of it than dancing masters, and singers than players; and that (if it be not an Irishism to say so) it is far more generally diffused among women than among men. In poetry, as well as writing in general, it will never *make* entirely a poet or a poem; but neither poet nor poem will ever be good for anything without it. It is the *salt* of society, and the seasoning of composition. *Vulgarity* is far worse than downright *blackguardism*; for the latter comprehends

---

[1] Cf. *L. & J.* IV, 237 f., & V, 337. Only a few months later Hunt was to engage in the enterprise of the *Liberal* with Byron and Shelley. Cf., Keats's criticism, " Hunt does one harm by making fine things petty and beautiful things hateful." Haydon and others have spoken of Hunt in the same way.

wit, humour, and strong sense at times; while the former is a
sad abortive attempt at all things, " signifying nothing." It
does not depend upon low themes or even low language, for
Fielding revels in both;—but is he ever *vulgar* ? No. You
see the man of education, the gentleman, and the scholar,
sporting with his subject,—its master, not its slave. Your
vulgar writer is always most vulgar the higher his subject. . . .
It is a thing to be felt more than explained. Let any man
take up a volume of Mr. Hunt's subordinate writers, read (if
possible) a couple of pages, and pronounce for himself, if they
contain not the kind of writing which may be likened to
" shabby-genteel " in actual life. When he has done this, let
him take up Pope; and when he has laid him down, take up
the cockneys again—if he can.

The same studied laudation of Pope occurs in the conclusion of the letter.[1] The foundation of this admiration in
Byron, to wit, a true appreciation of classical decorum,
which many of the romantic writers lacked—including, in
practice, Byron himself—is eminently praiseworthy. But
the extent to which he expresses his approbation, in disregard of all restraint classical and otherwise, in his effort to
outdo Bowles and the Cockney defamers, resolves his whole
attitude in to a paltry hero-worship and nothing more.

Neither time, nor distance, nor grief, nor age, can ever diminish
my veneration for him, who is the great moral poet of all time,
of all climes, of all feelings, and of all stages of existence. The
delight of my boyhood, the study of my manhood, perhaps (if
allowed to me to attain it), he may be the consolation of my
age. His poetry is the Book of Life. Without canting, and
yet without neglecting religion, he has assembled all that a good
and great man can gather together of moral wisdom cloathed
(*sic*) in consummate beauty. Sir William Temple observes,
' that of all the numbers of mankind that live within the compass

---

[1] Captain Medwin reports Byron as saying :—" I have often thought
of erecting a monument to him at my own expense in Westminster
Abbey, and hope to do so yet."—*Conversations*, 243.

of a thousand years, for one man that is born capable of making a *great poet*, there may be a *thousand* born capable of making as great generals and ministers of state as any in story.' Here is a statesman's opinion of poetry: it is honourable to him, and to the art. Such a "poet of a thousand years" was *Pope*. A thousand years will roll away before such another can be hoped for in our literature. But it can *want* them—he himself is a literature.

The controversy, indeed, was not worthy of the great talent and vehemence employed in it. The discussion was not always dignified. From the nature of the special topic, it became a contention merely. Byron was not "piping hot"[1] as he is usually described as being. He affected a rancor greater than he felt. He had more confidence in his controversial ability than in any other of his powerful assets,[2] he had a quarrel with most things English, and he loved a fight.[3] In the engagement he deliberately over-stated sometimes, but none knew that he did so better than himself. Finally, he had not mastered his theme—a little recasting and revision would have worked wonders—but he was mainly in the right, whatever his manner of setting forth his position.[4]

As has been stated, these letters receive about all the consideration that Byron gets as a critic, yet they represent no more than ten days' time in his full literary career!

---

[1] Cf., " Ye who are belted and alert to go
Where bays, won only in hard battles, grow,
Asthmatic Wordsworth, Byron piping-hot,
Leave in the rear, and march with manly Scott," etc.
—W. S. Landor, " To Recruits." Etc.

[2] Cf. *L. & J.* IV, 326-7, and *ibid.* V, 376, 398-9.

[3] See *L. & J.* VI, 4, etc.

[4] " I am too warm a controversialist."—*L. & J.* VI, 211. To what extent he was influenced by his grand model, the reader may judge:— " I have been reading ' Johnson's Lives,' a book I am very fond of. I look upon him as the profoundest of critics, and had occasion to study him when I was writing to Bowles."—Captain Medwin, *Conversations,* 242.

m

Opinion of them has never been high, but it has grown slightly more favorable since their production.

Gifford says of the first letter:

It will be unsafe to publish it as it stands. The letter is not very refined, but it is vigorous and to the point. Bowles requires checking. I hope, however, that Lord B. will not continue to squander himself thus. When will he resume his majestic march, and shake the earth again ? [1]

W. H. Prescott, writing on the controversy at the time, says somewhat sneeringly:

We know not where his lordship learned his logic, but it is certainly a much more concise system than any with which we have yet been acquainted.[2]

Sir Egerton Brydges, writing at the time of Byron's death, avers:

This was, probably, written hastily, and not originally intended for publication ; at any rate, it is written inelegantly and clumsily, and is not worthy of Lord Byron's genius and taste. The *opinions* are such as I have always contended, and always shall contend, to be mainly right ; but they are badly argued and illustrated ; deduced from principles imperfectly understood, arranged in a confused manner, and often expressed with an awkwardness and even vulgarity which quite surprises me.[3]

Byron's biographer, Leslie Stephen, in the *Dictionary of National Biography,* grants in passing

The vigorous, though perverse, letters to Bowles on the Pope controversy.

Professor Courthope gives some commendation:

Nor was it so much reckless bravado, as a sincere critical perception of the value of classical form, that made him speak

---

[1] *Memoir of John Murray* I, 420.
[2] *North American Review*, October, 1821.
[3] *Letters*, 377.

disparagingly of the works of himself and his contemporaries in comparison with the poetry of Pope.[1]

And Professor Saintsbury indeed deals severely but in doing so makes pretty large concessions:

> Let us confine ourselves to that unquestionably remarkable *Letter to John Murray* on Bowles and Pope, which is admittedly his critical diploma-piece. There are of course very good things in it. Byron was a genius; and your genius will say genial things now and then, whatsoever subject he happens to be treating. But he cannot in the very least maintain himself at the critical point.... Never was such critical floundering.... Suffice it to say, that to take him seriously as critic is impossible.[2]

Saintsbury is right, to a certain extent, if Byron as critic is to be judged only by his controversial—hardly his *critical*—" diploma-piece." But this is an unfair light in which to view him as critic, because by it his work is considered only in part, and in that part which represents him only as controversialist.

The Liberal Byron's achievements in formal criticism are over at this point. What remains was little more than a project, though it promised a regular literary occupation for his later years. This was the ill-omened enterprise of *The Liberal.*

The plan of the journal included other aims than criticism and so far as the plan was executed they were paramount. But undeniably the primary object of the venture was critical.[3]

---

[1] *A History of English Poetry* VI, 260.

[2] *A History of Criticism* III, 281 f.

[3] The idea, traceable to Leigh Hunt, prevails in some quarters that Byron acted from mercenary motives in founding *The Liberal.* " He expected very large returns from ' The Liberal ' . . . this plan of a periodical publication was no sudden business; he had proposed it more than once, and to different persons; and his reasons for it were, that he thought he should get both money and fame."—Leigh Hunt,

Definite proposal of such an undertaking is contained in a Christmas correspondence with Moore in 1820.

I have been thinking of a project for you and me, in case we both get to London again, which (if a Neapolitan war don't suscitate) may be calculated as possible for one of us about the spring of 1821. I presume that you, too, will be back by that time, or never; but on that you will give me some index. The project, then, is for you and me to set up jointly a *newspaper*—nothing more nor less—weekly, or so, with some improvement or modifications upon the plan of the present scoundrels, who degrade that department,—but a *newspaper*, which we will edite in due form, and, nevertheless, with some attention. There must always be in it a piece of poesy from one or other of us *two*, leaving room, however, for such dilettanti rhymers as may be deemed worthy of appearing in the same column: but *this* must be a *sine qua non*; and also as much prose as we can compass. We will take an *office*—our names *not* announced, but suspected—and, by the blessing of Providence, give the age some new lights upon policy, poesy, biography, criticism, morality, theology, and all other *ism, ality*, and *ology* whatsoever.[1]

Lord Byron, 85 f. " Power, money, and notoriety were Byron's chief objects."—Barnette Miller, *Leigh Hunt's Relations*, 96. Byron unquestionably was anxious to secure funds at the time, but he knew too well the fortunes of periodical writing in general, and the hazard of a venture of the kind for himself in his great unpopularity then, to expect great financial profit from the undertaking. Leigh Hunt later confessed to injustice in his work on Byron.

[1] *L. & J.* V, 143. The critical aim at this point of development seems to have been only a part of a much larger whole, but from the fuller explanation which follows in the connection manifestly criticism is uppermost in Byron's mind, and the other objects, excepting the *sine qua non* poetry, are but incidental. Trelawny declares the object, upon maturity of the plan, to have been critical:—" That he might occasionally use it for criticising and attacking those who offended him . . . Byron had a hankering to try his powers in those hand-to-hand conflicts then in vogue, even in the great Reviews."—*Records*, 181. *Blackwood's*, in anticipation of the first appearance of the magazine, recognized its critical cast:—" You must be careful how you wreak your disdain on the principles of Lord Byron's later poetry, as he will soon have it in his power to make fierce reprisals on you and the other

Moore's misgivings were too strong to allow him to form such an alliance with his noble friend.   Shelley knew of the latter's wishes, and upon Moore's declination proposed the name of Leigh Hunt, and agreed to support the journal with his own pen.   Hunt readily consented to become one of the triumvirate.   Such was the illustrious body of promoters, editors, and proprietors of the new journal,[1] two geniuses and a compound of conceit and cockney humors. Any friend of the publication well might quake for its success upon review of such a personnel.

This was the condition of affairs in the first part of the year 1822.   Byron and Shelley had been in Italy for some time.   Hunt closed his London connection, contrary to the expectation of his southern partners, and appeared on the scene in June.   Plans were well under way for the first issue,[2] when a genuine calamity befell the enterprise in the accidental death of Shelley by drowning in the bay of Spezia.[3]

Byron again applied to Moore.

Leigh Hunt is sweating articles for his new Journal; and both he and I think it somewhat shabby in *you* not to contribute.

dissenters. You have, perhaps, heard of the Journal which is to be written by him at Pisa, and sent over here for publication, in order that the balance of critical power may be restored, which has preponderated lately too much on the Tory side."   A latter day writer asserts the critical claim of the magazine, after the burial of the matter for nearly a century:—" Not unnaturally, therefore, the idea occurred to him that the founding of a critical review, in alliance with an able and friendly newspaper, would effect his purpose, and at the same time give him an opportunity for exercising those powers of literary criticism and satire, of the possession of which he had already given such convincing proof."—Alexander Brecknock, *The Pilgrim Poet*, 100.

[1] Shelley was to be the silent partner. " You shall be the sleeping partner if you will; only it shall be with a Cleopatra, and your dreams shall be worth the giving of kingdoms."—Leigh Hunt.   These men were in residence in Pisa.   John Hunt was to print and publish the journal in London.

[2] It had been decided to call the new magazine *The Liberal*.   Cf. *L. & J.* V, 214.

[3] " May-day Night; A Poetical Translation from Goethe's Faust," in the first number, was by Shelley.

Will you become one of the *properrioters*? "Do, and we go snacks." I recommend you to think twice before you respond in the negative.[1]

With Moore's continued detachment the fate of the journal was sealed. Byron and Hunt were men of extreme humors. They had been attracted to each other by political sympathies as early as 1816 but within two years Byron had become disaffected. Hunt had made the egotistical discovery that "the texture of Byron's mind resembled his own to a thread," but the men were totally uncongenial, and the fact spelled disaster for the publication.

The initial number appeared on October 15, 1822, with the title: *The Liberal: Verse and Prose from the South.* It was the climax of its career. By the following month Byron was beginning to conceive of himself, by some species of hallucination, as a martyr to the enterprise.[2]

I am afraid the Journal *is* a *bad* business, and won't do; but in it I am sacrificing *myself* for others—*I* can have no advantage in it. I believe the *brothers H.* to be honest men; I am sure that they are poor ones. They have not a rap; they pressed me to engage in this work, and in an evil hour I consented: still I shall not repent if I can do them the least service.[3]

Despite his generous assertions he began straightway to try to rid himself of what had become a burdensome alliance.[4]

Three other numbers appeared in January, April, and July of the following year, with support from Byron in such productions as the *Morgante Maggiore*, *The Blues*,

---

[1] *L. & J.* VI, 109.

[2] The editor of Byron's *Correspondence* (II, 210) says, "He was dissuaded by Hobhouse from taking a partnership in *The Liberal.*"

[3] *L. & J.* VI, 122 f. Cf. *Correspondence* II, 240.

[4] Cf., "He embarks in an obnoxious publication to provoke censure, and leaves it to shift for itself for fear of scandal."—Wm. Hazlitt, *The Spirit of the Age,* 104. In his well-known hostility to Byron, Hazlitt is hardly just.

and some cantos of *Don Juan*. He assisted Hunt financially as well. But at the fourth number the journal expired under the united opprobrium of the press and the estrangement of its editors.

The only number of the four that could claim our interest is the first. It contains two regular articles from Byron's hand. The first is the *Vision of Judgment*, which stands as the consummation of his long war with Southey. It deals with literary matters, and may be reckoned as the very acme of controversial skill in verse, but in its critical character it is no more than extravaganza. The second article looks significant—" A Letter to the Editor of *My Grandmother's Review* "[1]—but the critical quality is only apparent. It is but a " farrago of unconnected nonsense," signed " Wortley Clutterbuck," and was intended only to confound the editor of the *British Review*, William Roberts, in his resentment at an implied reference to him as bribe-taker in *Don Juan*.[2] Nothing critical from Byron's pen appeared in the subsequent numbers.

Byron's aim of making the journal a literary censor, interpreter, or expositor, never matured. The whole plan is entitled to consideration as criticism only in its projection. And, as his great poem, in which he appears as spectator and judge of the world's abuses, was then finished, so far as it was to be finished, the enterprise of *The Liberal* was his last critical venture of any kind.

---

[1] " The letter is written in great haste, and amidst a thousand vexations."—*L. & J.* IV, 347.
[2] Canto I, 209 f. Cf. *L. & J.* V, 92.

CHAPTER VII

MISCELLANEOUS CRITICISM

There is so much heart in the praise which you bestow, and so little ill-nature in your censure—though fraught with the *severity* of truth, that even those blamed could hardly be offended, although they might feel it.—James Hogg, Letter to Byron, Oct. 11, 1814.

Byron's best criticism is to be found in his *obiter dicta*.[1] These are concerned chiefly with individual authors and single productions, and are almost wholly contemporaneous.

A Survey   Byron had some critical grasp and appreciation of the classical literatures. An occasional striking judgment, as we shall see, arises from his notice of the Greek and Latin authors. He has dropped enough hints on Italian literature to form a scanty judgment. Italian was the most poetical of languages,[2] and the people were the most poetical in temperament among modern nations,[3] but modern Italian prose was not at all equal to the older prose of the language,[4] and in the whole course of their history the Italians had had no real tragic drama.[5] He knew Italian literature of the middle period better, and admired it more, than he did English literature

---

[1] " Byron, with next to no real critical power, could bring dazzling resources of wit and rhetoric to the support of any random opinion, traditional or revolutionary, he might happen by whim or habit to entertain."—Sidney Colvin, *John Keats*, 480.
[2] See Chapter II, 46 f., and V, 95 f.
[3] See *L. & J.* III, 29.
[4] See *L. & J.* IV, 209.
[5] See *L. & J.* V, 64. Cf. *Correspondence* II, 204.

of the same period. No better criticism is to be found in his writings, as we shall see, than that which he makes upon the great medieval and Renaissance Italians. He had a slight personal acquaintance, by correspondence only, with Goethe, and admired him long. He dedicated (or attempted to dedicate) to him three plays—*Marino Faliero, Sardanapalus,* and *Werner*—; but he has left no definitive opinion of the great German.[1] Schiller, Grillparzer, and the Schlegels, on whom be has left some partial judgments, were known to him by translations only, and in this indirect way were esteemed.[2] Otherwise, he has hardly touched German literature in any specific manner.[3] French literature interested him only for the same period as did English literature, and then only in individual authors such as Voltaire, Rousseau, and Madame De Staël. And the literature of the Spanish peninsula attracted his critical attention only in the instance of the great figure Cervantes.

Byron had no real acquaintance with the literary men and monuments of the old and middle periods of his own language. He is said to have read Chaucer in his Dulwich days, but his works are devoid of critical reference to "the father of the English language."[4] *Huon of Bordeaux* is cited once;[5] and Geoffrey of Monmouth is called "a noted liar in his way"[6] and is honored with mention in *Don Juan.*[7] The "old Mysteries" are sometimes alluded to,

---

[1] See *L. & J.* V, 36, 100 f., etc.

[2] See *L. & J.* III, 356, IV, 92-3, V, 171-2, 191-4, etc.

[3] Cf. *The Waltz,* 72 f.

[4] For the only references to Chaucer in Byron's writings, see *Hints from Horace,* 81 & 428, Preface to *The Vision of Judgment, L. & J.* IV, 276, and *Correspondence* II, 92. Cf. Moore, *Life* I, 148, for a boyish objection to Chaucer.

[5] *The Deformed Transformed* I, i, 527. Byron's knowledge was perhaps from Sotheby's play, *Oberon: or, Huon de Bordeaux,* rather than from the romance itself.

[6] *L. & J.* I, 201.

[7] Canto XVI, 5.

though only casually.   Otherwise, the whole middle English
period is a void to him.[1]   At least it cannot be said of his
romanticism that he was a medieval revivalist.

The first half of the modern period is likewise little
known to him.   Spenser, whose verse form he adopted and
mastered, and indeed preferred to all others,[2] is nowhere
criticised.[3]   Shakespeare is the subject of frequent quotation
and reference but of the rarest critical mention.[4]   The great

[1] See *L. & J.* II, 349, for a quotation from " Clym o' the Clow, or
Robin Hood."
[2] See Chapter V, 101 f.
[3] " Spenser he could not read; at least he said so.   All the gusto
of that most poetical of the poets went with him for nothing.   I lent
him a volume of the ' Fairy Queen,' and he said he would try to like
it.   Next day he brought it to my study-window, and said, ' Here,
Hunt, here is your Spenser.   I cannot see anything in him.' "—Leigh
Hunt, *Lord Byron*, 77.
[4] Opinion of Byron's attitude toward Shakespeare varies.   Certainly
he depreciated the great " blackguard," perhaps on account of his
birth, and undoubtedly because of the liberties he took with regular
drama.   " He affected to doubt whether Shakespeare was so great
a genius as he has been taken for, and whether fashion had not a great
deal to do with it; an extravagance, of which none but a patrician
author could have been guilty."—Leigh Hunt, *Lord Byron*, 45.   " This
puts me in mind of Lord Byron saying to me the other day, ' What
do you think of Shakespeare, Moore?   I think him a dammed humbug.'
Not the first time I have heard him speak slightingly of Shakespeare."
—Thomas Moore, *Diary*, Oct. 15, 1819.   " Passed the evening with
Byron, who declaimed against Shakespeare, and Dante and Milton,
and said Voltaire was worth a thousand such."—John C. Hobhouse,
Recollections of a Long Life III, 6.   It is doubtful that he felt any
real envy of " his British godship."   " He even seemed to regard it
as a piece of presumption in Shakespeare *to be preferred before him*
as a dramatic author."—Wm. Hazlitt, *New Monthly Magazine*, April,
1826.   Hazlitt was, of course, hostile to Byron.   There is no question
that Byron knew Shakespeare well, and there is every evidence that
he appreciated fully his great poetry.   " It was this same desire of
astonishing people that led him to depreciate Shakespeare, which I
have frequently heard him do, though from various reflections of his in
conversation, and the general turn of his mind, I am convinced that he
had not only deeply read, but deeply felt the beauties of our immortal
poet."—Lady Blessington, *Conversations*, 162.   Ernst Zabel makes a total
of four hundred and seven quotations from or references to Shakespeare in Byron's complete works, *Byrons Kenntnis von Shakespeare
und sein Urteil über ihn.*   Cf., Hermann Engel, *Byrons Stellung zu
Shakespeare.*

Elizabethan dramatists are never more definitely characterized than as "our irregular dramatists," "the older
writers," and the like.[1] Milton is mentioned often, and is
criticised for his verse form,[2] for special elements,[3] and once
an appreciation of *Paradise Lost* is attempted,[4] but there is
no proof that Byron ever read Milton after his Cambridge
career.[5] Dryden is extolled frequently because of his
association with Pope, but there is nowhere in Byron a
finished estimate of him or any of his works. As far as
Byron's critical interest goes, there were only two or three
literary figures in England before Dryden.[6] Even of the
Augustan Age proper, of which he has given such testimony
of admiration, he has left little definite criticism. And
of Pope himself, who was well-nigh a divinity to him both
moral and literary, he has made no adequate characterization,[7] but he has written more *about* Pope than about
any other man of letters.

---

[1] Cf., *L. & J.* II, 183, etc. He even confessed to never having read
Marlowe's *Dr. Faustus.* See *L. & J.* IV, 174.

[2] Reply to *Blackwood's, L. & J.* IV, 490 f., etc.

[3] Letter to Murray on Bowles, *L. & J.* V, 555, etc.

[4] *Hints from Horace,* 199-212.

[5] "Since I was twenty I have never read Milton."—Preface to *Cain.*

[6] Byron's acquaintance with older English literature belongs to his
boyhood. See Moore's *Life* I, 144-148. And cf. *ibid.,* 144, for a really
judicious characterization of Burton's *Anatomy of Melancholy.* But his
interest did not survive his minority. The reader is at once reminded
of Johnson who believed that English poetry began with Waller (Cf.,
Thomas Seccombe, *The Age of Johnson,* 15). Byron considered Johnson
the greatest critic in English literature (See Second Letter to Bowles,
note 1, etc.). But the resemblance was more from an agreement of
tastes doubtless, than from a definite influence of Johnson on Byron
in this respect.

[7] In Byron's copy of Ruffhead's *Life of Pope,* which was preserved
by his friend Francis Hodgson, occur some notes in Byron's hand-
writing, evidently of the Cambridge period, which purport to be criticism
but which cannot in any way be said to be estimates. The nearest
approach to a judgment is the commentary on the *Rape of the Lock,*
which professes only to cite sources of material in the poem. See Rev.
James T. Hodgson, *Memoir* I, 97 f. For Byron's canonization of Pope
see chapter VI, 161 f., and 166 f.

Byron's criticism then of men and works in his native language applies to his contemporaries, or at most to those who immediately preceded him.[1] His commentary there is abundant, in his poetry, in his prefaces and notes, in his conversations, and in a well-nigh constant stream in his letters and journals.[2] There is hardly a figure of the time, great or small, who has escaped his attention. Here and there he makes a stroke with consummate art, and yet full portraits are as rare as the few names he has entirely omitted from the roster.

His judgments are marked by a strong individuality. Some of them, as in the early satire, are dependent upon public opinion, that is, authoritative opinion. Others are as positively contradictory of the popular view. It is doubtful in his last years, during his residence in Italy, if he knew public opinion in England, but his criticisms at the time are not therefore necessarily the worse.

Byron's utterances of the kind belong to the conversational type of criticism.[3] They represent little forethought or premeditation. Usually they are a few phrases dropped here and there " as sailors lend money."[4] If a single one of them had cost him a second effort of the mind, he probably would not have made it.[5] When one is found

---

[1] " Not an inconsiderable portion of his writings, both in prose and verse, represents him as the critic of his contemporaries, and the censor and satirist of his age."—E. P. Whipple, *North American Review*, January, 1845.

[2] " These *Letters* are chiefly noteworthy for the extent and variety of the literary allusions which they contain."—Lewis Bettany, *Confessions of Lord Byron*, viii.

[3] " One of the things that most annoyed me in London was the being continually asked to give my opinion on the works of contemporaries. I got out of the difficulty as well as I could, by some equivocal answer that might be taken in two ways."—Lady Blessington, *Conversations*, 274 f.

[4] Byron is " a magnificent-minded fellow, who does not wait for the scales to weigh what he says, but gives praise, as sailors lend money, by handfuls."—Thomas Moore, Letter to Rogers, Jan. 13, 1814.

[5] Cf., " His criticism is that of Boileau, and when deliberate is generally absurd."—John Nichol, *Byron*, 204.

to be commonplace, as is often the case, the reader passes it by unnoticed; when one is felicitous, he records it as " the expression of an irresistible mental impetus . . . . . . where reflection could not modify or improve the judgment."[1] Few are vague or indefinite, but now and then some are at odds with each other.[2] The whole is impressionistic criticism in a somewhat exaggerated vein.[3]

A careful study of Byron's utterances on men and books will disclose two or three interesting facts. After the leveling processes of time, he is recognized in the main as right. The present day notion of his " marvellously erratic judgments about men and books "[4] is derived clearly from exceptional cases. And his estimates in substance, whatever their manner, compare favorably with those of any critic of his own age. It need hardly be added that an injustice frequently done a critic of the literature of his own age, is to consider the subject matter properly in its time but to remove the critic to the student's own day. Byron has suffered greatly from this method of treatment.

The Age In his works at various periods of his career Byron has left evidence of an evolution, almost a revolution, in his feeling toward the literature, specifically the poetry, of his age.

His first estimate, after the ill-tempered view of the *English Bards and Scotch Reviewers*, is a representation in

[1] P. E. More, *Atlantic Monthly*, December, 1898.

[2] Cf., " Opinions are made to be changed, or how is truth to be got at."—*L. & J.* IV, 118.

[3] Cf., " His taste was capricious in the extreme. His opinion of any person, or any institution, or any aspiration, varied with the physical variations of his body, and was often very different after a debauch from what it was after a ride. No one could infer his judgment of to-morrow from his judgment of to-day. The friend that appeared in the eulogy of one week was likely to point the squib of the next. His consistency in criticism was according to his constancy in hatred."— E. P. Whipple, *North American Review*, January, 1845.

[4] W. P. Trent, *The Authority of Criticism*, 218.

diagram in his journal for November 22, 1813. The figure is doubly interesting because it represents as well popular opinion. The order of the names is at once striking because of its marked difference from that in which the modern critic would place them.

He [Scott] is undoubtedly the Monarch of Parnassus, and the most *English* of bards. I should place Rogers next in the living list (I value him more as the last of the *best* school)—Moore and Campbell both *third*—Southey and Wordsworth and Coleridge—the rest, οἱ πολλοι—thus:—

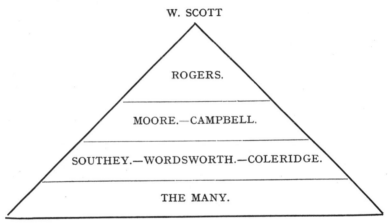

There is a triangular *Gradus ad Parnassum*!—the names are too numerous for the base of the triangle. Poor Thurlow has gone wild about the poetry of Queen Bess's reign—*c'est dommage.* I have ranked the names upon my triangle more upon what I believe popular opinion, than any decided opinion of my own. For, to me, some of Moore's last *Erin* sparks—" As a beam o'er the face of the waters "—"When he who adores thee "— " Oh blame not "—and " Oh breathe not his name "—are worth all the Epics that ever were composed.[1]

---

[1] *L. & J.* II, 343 f.

A dual valuation of Byron as critic attaches to this estimate,—he is still reliant upon public opinion, and he is
romantic in his deliberate judgment.[1]

Four years further of maturing thought on the subject
brings the critic to the conviction, as positive as it is apparently sudden,[2] that the spirit of the day is radically wrong,
even for himself and his peers.

With regard to poetry in general, I am convinced, the more
I think of it, that he and *all* of us—Scott, Southey, Wordsworth,
Moore, Campbell, I,—are all in the wrong, one as much as
another; that we are upon a wrong revolutionary poetical system,
or systems, not worth a damn in itself, and from which none
but Rogers and Crabbe are free; and that the present and next
generations will finally be of this opinion.   I am the more
confirmed in this by having lately gone over some of our classics,
particularly *Pope*, whom I tried in this way,—I took Moore's
poems and my own and some others, and went over them side
by side with Pope's, and I was really astonished (I ought not
to have been so) and mortified at the ineffable distance in point
of sense, harmony, effect, and even *Imagination*, passion and
Invention, between the little Queen Anne's man, and us of the
Lower Empire.   Depend upon it, it is all Horace then, and
Claudian now, among us; and if I had to begin again, I would
model myself accordingly.[3]

It is manifestly a pronouncement for Pope and classical
poetry.   Posterity must condemn and correct.

Half a year later he is less severe in his judgment, and
in his moderation and characteristic self-absolvement, he
is indeed nearer his real conviction.   He writes to Moore:

---

[1] He never approaches the habit of deliberation more than in his
diaries and journals.

[2] Cp. *L. & J.* III, 25.

[3] *L. & J.* IV, 169.   Gifford has the following high praise to say
of the passage:—" There is more good sense, and feeling and judgment in this passage, than in any other I ever read, or Lord Byron
wrote."

I called Crabbe and Sam the fathers of present Poesy; and said, that I thought—except them—*all* of " *us youth* " were on a wrong tack.   But I never said that we did not sail well. Our fame will be hurt by *admiration* and *imitation*.   When I say *our*, I mean *all* (Lakers included), except the postscript of the Augustans.   The next generation (from the quantity and facility of imitation) will tumble and break their necks off our Pegasus, who runs away with us; but we keep the *saddle*, because we broke the rascal and can ride.   But though easy to mount, he is the devil to guide; and the next fellows must go back to the riding-school and the manège, and learn to ride the " great horse." [1]

Scott at the time was engaged with his novels and was no longer a productive poet, hence his position on the pyramid is lost.   Crabbe [2] and Rogers occupy the summit.   It is notable that romantic poetry still has Byron's approval but his critical conscience is alive to the thought that for permanent effects a course of greater restraint had been wiser. There is observable, as well, a feeling of security and self-dependence developed within the four or five important years.

But within a year's time, stung to rebellion by the continual depreciation of his early model, Pope, he becomes the critical dogmatist of the older creed.

Your whole generation are not worth a canto of the *Rape of the Lock*, or the *Essay on Man*, or the *Dunciad*, or " anything that is his." [3]

Read him—most of you *don't*—but *do*—and I will forgive you; though the inevitable consequence would be that you would burn all I have ever written, and all your other wretched

---

[1] *L. & J.* IV, 196 f.

[2] Strangely enough, Crabbe was omitted from the pyramid.   His place in Byron's estimate should have been with Rogers.   He is the one poet who won Byron's admiration early and retained it unchanged, without friendship or favor, to the end.

[3] *L. & J.* IV, 225.

Claudians of the day (except Scott and Crabbe) into the bargain. I wrong Claudian, who *was* a *poet*, by naming him with such fellows; but he was the *ultimus Romanorum*, the tail of the Comet, and these persons are the tail of an old Gown cut into a waistcoat for Jackey; but being both *tails*, I have compared one with the other, though very unlike, like all Similies.[1]

His next is after the broadside to *Blackwood's*, while the contest about Pope is on.

There never was such a *Set* as your *ragamuffins* (I mean *not* yours only, but everybody's). What with the Cockneys, and the Lakers, and the *followers* of Scott, and Moore, and Byron, you are in the very uttermost decline and degradation of literature. I can't think of it without all the remorse of a murderer. I wish that Johnson were alive again to crush them![2]

Two weeks later:

You are taken in by that false stilted trashy style, which is a mixture of all the styles of the day, which are *all bombastic* (I don't except my *own*—no one has done more through negligence to corrupt the language); but it is neither English nor poetry. Time will show.[3]

After dispatching his last missive in the controversy he is contemptuous of all literature of the day because of its failure to reflect the right experience in the lives of its makers.[4] Scott is excepted for his novels, and Moore and Byron for the sources if not the system of their poetry.

I have no patience with the sort of trash you send me out by way of books; except Scott's novels, and three or four other things, I never saw such work or works. Campbell is lecturing, Moore idling, Southey twaddling, Wordsworth driveling, Coleridge

[1] *L. & J.* IV, 278.
[2] *L. & J.* V, 76.
[3] *L. & J.* V, 82.
[4] See Chapter V, 92 f. for Byron's insistence upon experience as the groundwork of poetry.

n

muddling, Joanna Baillie piddling, Bowles quibbling, squabbling, and sniveling. Milman will *do*, if he don't cant too much, nor imitate Southey : the fellow has poesy in him ; but he is envious, and unhappy, as all the envious are. Still he is among the best of the day. Barry Cornwall will do better by and bye, I dare say, if he don't get spoilt by green tea, and the praises of Pentonville and Paradise Row. The pity of these men is, that they never lived either in *high life*, nor in *solitude* : there is no medium for the knowledge of the *busy* or the *still* world. If admitted into high life for a season, it is merely as *spectators*—they form no part of the Mechanism thereof. Now Moore and I, the one by circumstances, and the other by birth, happened to be free of the corporation, and to have entered into its pulses and passions, *quarum partes fuimus*. Both of us have learnt by this much which nothing else could have taught us.[1]

His impatience, however, has subsided, as he calmly makes an entry in his journal later in the year.

One of my notions, different from those of my contemporaries, is, that the present is not a high age of English Poetry : there are *more* poets (soi-disant) than ever there were, and proportionally *less* poetry. This *thesis* I have maintained for some years, but, strange to say, it meeteth not with favour from my brethren of the Shell. Even Moore shakes his head, and firmly believes that it is the grand Era of British Poesy.[2]

This is one of the most remarkable judgments in all Byron, made as it was in his mature years, opposing as it did almost an established fact, and combatting the opinion of those on whom he relied most for his own.

But the fire of the reformer is gone, and the conditions but furnish material for the facetiousness of *Don Juan*, with only a recurring hint of the combatant, and finally a renunciation altogether of the censor's rod.

[1] *L. & J.* V, 362 f.
[2] " Detached Thoughts," *L. & J.* V, 441.

Sir Walter reigned before me; Moore and Campbell
Before and after; but now grown more holy,
The Muses upon Sion's hill must ramble
With poets almost clergymen, or wholly;
And Pegasus has a psalmodic amble
Beneath the very Reverend Rowley Powley,
Who shoes the glorious animal with stilts,
A modern Ancient Pistol—' by these hilts! '

Still he excels that artificial hard
Labourer in the same vineyard, though the vine
Yields him but vinegar for his reward,—
That neutralised dull Dorus of the Nine;
That swarthy Sporus, neither man nor bard;
That ox of verse, who *ploughs* for every line:—
Cambyses' roaring Romans beat at least
The howling Hebrews of Cybele's priest.—

Then there's my gentle Euphues; who, they say,
Sets up for being a sort of *moral me*;
He'll find it rather difficult some day
To turn out both, or either, it may be.
Some persons think that Coleridge hath the sway;
And Wordsworth has supporters, two or three;
And that deep-mouthed Bœotian ' Savage Landor '
Has taken for a swan rogue Southey's gander.

John Keats, who was killed off by one critique,
Just as he really promised something great,
If not intelligible, without Greek
Contrived to talk about the gods of late,
Much as they might have been supposed to speak.
Poor fellow! His was an untoward fate;
'Tis strange the mind, that very fiery particle,
Should let itself be snuffed out by an article.

The list grows long of live and dead pretenders
To that which none will gain—or none will know
The conqueror at least; who, ere Time renders

n 2

His last award, will have the long grass grow
Above his burnt-out brain, and sapless cinders.
If I might augur, I should rate but low
Their chances ;—they're too numerous, like the thirty
Mock tyrants, when Rome's annals waxed but dirty.

This is the literary *lower* empire,
Where the praetorian bands take up the matter ;—
A " dreadful trade," like his who " gathers samphire,"
The insolent soldiery to soothe and flatter,
With the same feelings as you'd coax a vampire.
Now, were I once at home, and in good satire,
I'd try conclusions with those Janizaries,
And show them *what* an intellectual war is.

I think I know a trick or two, would turn
Their flanks ;—but it is hardly worth my while,
With such small gear to give myself concern :
Indeed I've not the necessary bile ;
My natural temper's really aught but stern,
And even my Muse's worst reproof's a smile ;
And then she drops a brief and modern curtsy,
And glides away, assured she never hurts ye.[1]

His last judgment is from a conversation with Kennedy
late in the year 1823. It echoes his former faith, but
prejudice has become only a wholesome preference, and there
is evidence of poise and reason and breadth and a spirit of
toleration that before were everywhere absent.

I have not the least prejudice against the style of our older
writers, I am quite accustomed to it, and prefer the force and
energy of their language, to the soft harmonious periods of the
present day, which have more sound than sense.[2]

---

[1] Canto XI, 57 f. The " Reverend Rowley Powley " is the Reverend
George Croly. " That ox of verse " is H. H. Milman, and " my gentle
Euphues " is the poet's school fellow, Bryan Waller Procter.
[2] *Conversations*, 206.

Well-balanced criticism was ahead, if the passage can be taken as an index at all.[1]

The Lake Poets Byron has more to say of the Lake group of poets than of any other school or movement in poetry. He knew individual writers and productions better than he did the larger currents and tendencies of literature. The Lake poets more than any others represented the poetry of the age to him, hence his opinion of them varies as does his opinion of the age.[2] The value of his criticism is not equal to the attention he gave these writers, casual as it was, in the course of his life.

His ultimate hostility toward the Lakers arose from two main causes. He did not know them intimately as men and individuals, as he knew most of the other literary celebrities of the time, and in his opinion, they constituted the leadership in the opposition to the poetry of Pope.[3] The question of literary envy may be dismissed with little consideration, not because Byron disclaimed it,[4] but because in his intense subjectivity he was well-nigh incapable of suffering from it. The setting of the tide away from himself toward the Lake trio aroused in him the spirit of combativeness only, not of envy.

His adverse judgments of the Lakers in the early satire[5]

[1] For his expressions on the age, in the controversy on Pope, see Chapter VI, 144 f., 164.
[2] His anathemas against them in his controversial writings are almost negligible as criticism. See Chapter VI, 142 f.
[3] Byron's latter day critical faith was grounded in this opposition. Cf.,   " Thou shalt believe in Milton, Dryden, Pope;
Thou shalt not set up Wordsworth, Coleridge, Southey," etc.
—*Don Juan* I, 205.

[4] " I really have *no* literary envy."—*L. & J.* III, 59. Cp., " His jealousy of Wordsworth and others, who were not town-poets, was more creditable to him, though he did not indulge it in the most becoming manner. He pretended to think worse of them than he did."—Leigh Hunt, *Lord Byron*, 132.
[5] See Chapter IV.

and his vituperations against them in his more sustained
critical writings[1] represent his greatest strictures. Unfortunately the two constitute his best known opinions of
the men. At other times he could accord them merit not
unbefitting their talents and rank, although he was never
able to do them full justice. His greatest error on the
whole subject was in allowing his impressions of Southey,
the least worthy of the three, to extend to and include the
others.

His first comment after *English Bards and Scotch Reviewers* is on Southey in 1811. It is in the same manner
and tone as the satire, and really differs from it only in
being in prose.

I should think X *plus* Y at least as amusing as the *Curse of
Kehama*, and much more intelligible. Master Southey's poems
are, in fact, what parallel lines might be—viz. prolonged *ad
infinitum* without meeting anything half so absurd as themselves.[2]

Early in the autumn of 1813 he met Southey, and, as
in the case of most of those whom he had attacked early and
become acquainted with later, his attitude changed immediately. He records the event in a favorable account of
Southey's " epic appearance."

Yesterday, at Holland House, I was introduced to Southey—
the best-looking bard I have seen for some time. To have that
poet's head and shoulders, I would almost have written his

---

[1] See Chapter VI, 142 f. Compare the following :—" Upon the principle of *adisse quem laeseris* he took every opportunity, and broke through
every decency in literature, and even common manners, to malign,
degrade, and, as far as in him lay, to destroy the public and private
characters of those great men. He did this in works published by himself
in his own lifetime, and what is more, he did it in violation of his
knowledge and convictions to the contrary."—H. N. Coleridge, Preface
to Specimens of the *Table Talk of Samuel Taylor Coleridge* VI, 251.
[2] *L. & J.* II, 74 f.

Sapphics. He is certainly a prepossessing person to look on, and a man of talent, and all that, and—*there* is his eulogy.[1]

Before the season was over he made a judgment of the new laureate, from which modern opinion would hardly dissent:

Southey, I have not seen much of. His appearance is *Epic*; and he is the only existing entire man of letters. All the others have some pursuit annexed to their authorship. His manners are mild, but not those of a man of the world, and his talents of the first order. His prose is perfect. Of his poetry there are various opinions: there is, perhaps, too much of it for the present generation; posterity will probably select. He has *passages* equal to any thing. At present, he has a *party*, but no *public*—except for his prose writings. The life of Nelson is beautiful.[2]

In the light of Southey's ascendancy at the time, the passage is not a mean instance of critical detachment and judgment by permanent worth.

In 1815 Southey is excepted among all the writers of Oriental tales as the only one who has done anything worth while.

Nobody but S****y has done anything worth a slice of bookseller's pudding, and *he* has not luck enough to be found out in doing a good thing.[3]

His first criticism of Wordsworth after the pilgrimage is almost adequate for the great romantic leader.

There must be many " fine things " in Wordsworth; but I should think it difficult to make *six* quartos (the amount of the whole) all fine, particularly the Pedlar's portion of the poem; but there can be no doubt of his powers to do almost any thing.[4]

[1] *L. & J.* II, 266.
[2] Journal, *L. & J.* II, 331.
[3] *L. & J.* III, 169.
[4] *L. & J.* III, 131.

A year later he still speaks favorably, although Wordsworth's production has not justified the expectations which his early works inspired. By this time Wordsworth's greatest work was over.

At that time I gave him credit for a promise, which is unfulfilled. I still think his capacity warrants all you say of *it* only, but that his performances since *Lyrical Ballads* are miserably inadequate to the ability which lurks within him: there is undoubtedly much natural talent spilt over the *Excursion*; but it is rain upon rocks—where it stands and stagnates, or rain upon sands—where it falls without fertilizing. Who can understand him? Let those who do, make him intelligible. Jacob Behmen, Swedenborg, and Joanna Southcote, are mere types of this arch-apostle of mystery and mysticism.[1]

In 1816 Byron did Wordsworth the honor, in a poem entitled " Churchill's Grave," to imitate his style. On the manuscript sheet of the poem Byron recorded the following complimentary criticism.

The following poem (as most that I have endeavoured to write) is founded on a fact; and this detail is an attempt at a serious imitation of the style of a great poet—its beauties and its defects : I say the *style* ; for the thoughts I claim as my own. In this, if there be any thing ridiculous, let it be attributed to me, at least as much as to Mr. Wordsworth ; of whom there can exist few greater admirers than myself. I have blended what I would deem to be the beauties as well as defects of his style ; and it ought to be remembered that, in such things, whether there be praise or dispraise, there is always what is called a compliment, however unintentional.[2]

---

[1] *L. & J.* III, 239. See the remainder of the letter for some minor criticism of Wordsworth.

[2] In reviewing the *Prisoner of Chillon* (*Quarterly Review*, October, 1816) Scott found some resemblances in the poem to some passages in Wordsworth. Interestingly enough, he found " Churchill's Grave " to be modeled after Southey's eclogues.

Byron's first prose utterances upon Coleridge are a little
disparaging because of the " Manichean's " lectures on the
new poetry against the practice of such as Rogers and
Campbell.   But he writes to Coleridge in 1815 in very high
commendation of his play, *Remorse*, and encourages him to
turn his hand to tragic drama.   Byron at the time was on
the management of Drury Lane Theatre.

If I may be permitted, I would suggest that there never was
such an opening for tragedy.   In Kean, there is an actor worthy
of expressing the thoughts of the characters which you have
every power of embodying ; and I cannot but regret that the
part of Ordonio was disposed of before his appearance at Drury
Lane.   We have had nothing to be mentioned in the same
breath with *Remorse* for very many years.[1]

In October of the same year he characterizes Coleridge
in a letter to Moore as

A man of wonderful talent . . . who has been worse used by
the critics than ever we were.[2]

And a year later he declares to Murray:

I won't have any one sneer at " Christabel ": it is a fine
wild poem.[3]

Byron's favorable opinion of the Lake trio did not last
beyond his residence in England.   Thereafter he not unnaturally felt a distaste for most things English, and in their
systematic opposition to the older poetical regime, and to
Pope specifically, he found cause for disliking them.   But
for his exile and the intemperate affair of the controversy,
into both of which he was driven, or considered himself
driven, he probably would have continued his esteem of the

[1] *L. & J.* III, 191.
[2] *L. & J.* III, 232.
[3] *L. & J.* III, 369.   Cf. footnote to line 522 of *The Siege of Corinth*,
and *L. & J.* IV, 31.   It was on Byron's recommendation that *Christabel*
was finally published by Murray in 1816.

Lake group, consented to if not actually championed the tendencies of the age, and at most become nothing more than a wholesome conservator of the best principles of the older style of writing. But as circumstances developed, beginning with his second pilgrimage he became the champion of Pope and the avowed antagonist of " Southey and Co."

Early in 1817 he is silent upon Southey's poetry but profuse in denouncing his politics.

Southey's *Wat Tyler* is rather awkward; but the Goddess Nemesis has done well. He is—I will not say what, but I wish he was something else. I hate all intolerance, but most the intolerance of Apostacy, and the wretched vehemence with which a miserable creature, who has contradicted himself, lies to his own heart, and endeavours to establish his sincerity by proving himself a rascal—*not* for changing his opinions, but for persecuting those who are of less malleable matter. It is no disgrace to Mr. Southey to have written *Wat Tyler*, and afterwards to have written his birthday or Victory odes (I speak only of their *politics*), but it is something, for which I have no words, for this man to have endeavoured to bring to the stake (for such would he do) men who think as he thought, and for no reason but because they think so still, when he has found it convenient to think otherwise. * * * * * I am all for moderation, which profession of faith I beg leave to conclude by wishing Mr. Southey damned—not as a poet but as a politician.[1]

In the following year he is unduly hard on Wordsworth for somewhat the same reason, and extends his ill-usage to Wordsworth's poetry.

Did you read his skimble-skamble about Wordsworth being at the head of his own *profession*, in the *eyes* of *those* who followed it ? I thought that poetry was an *art*, or an *attribute*, and not a *profession ;*—but be it one, is that * * * * * * at the head of *your* profession in your *eyes* ? I'll be curst if he is of *mine*, or ever shall be. He is the only one of us (but of us he is not)

[1] *L. & J.* IV, 117.

whose coronation I would oppose.   Let them take Scott,
Campbell, Crabbe, or you, or me, or any of the living, and
throne him ;—but not this new Jacob Behmen, this * * * * * *
whose pride might have kept him true, even had his principles
turned as perverted as his *soi-disant* poetry.[1]

His next judgment is from *Don Juan* in the same year.
It comprises a large part of the dedication and is addressed
to Southey " in good, simple, savage verse," but it treats
the whole group in loose critical fashion.   The tone, nowhere
vehement, is in keeping with the general spirit of the great
poem, which " censures but not vituperates," and fittingly
precedes the years of intolerance just ahead.

> Bob Southey ! You're a poet—Poet-laureate,
> And representative of all the race ;
> Although 'tis true that you turned out a Tory at
> Last,—yours has lately been a common case,;
> And now, my Epic Renegade ! what are ye at ?
> With all the Lakers, in and out of place ?
> A nest of tuneful persons, to my eye
> Like " four and twenty Blackbirds in a pye ;
>
> Which pye being opened they began to sing "
> (This old song and new simile holds good),
> "A dainty dish to set before the King,"
> Or Regent, who admires such kind of food ;—
> And Coleridge, too, has lately taken wing,
> But like a hawk encumbered with his hood,—
> Explaining Metaphysics to the nation—
> I wish he would explain his Explanation.
>
> You, Bob ! are rather insolent, you know,
> At being disappointed in your wish
> To supersede all warblers here below,
> And be the only Blackbird in the dish ;
> And then you overstrain yourself, or so,

---

[1] *L. & J.* IV, 238.

And tumble downward like the flying fish
Gasping on deck, because you soar too high, Bob,
And fall, for lack of moisture, quite a-dry, Bob!

And Wordsworth, in a rather long " Excursion "
(I think the quarto holds five hundred pages),
Has given a sample from the vasty version
Of his new system to perplex the sages;
'Tis poetry—at least by his assertion,
And may appear so when the dog-star rages—
And he who understands it would be able
To add a story to the Tower of Babel.

You—Gentlemen! by dint of long seclusion
From better company, have kept your own
At Keswick, and, through still continued fusion
Of one another's minds, at last have grown
To deem as a most logical conclusion,
That Poesy has wreaths for you alone:
There is a narrowness in such a notion,
Which makes me wish you'd change your lakes for Ocean.

I would not imitate the petty thought,
Nor coin my self-love to so base a vice,
For all the glory your conversion brought,
Since gold alone should not have been its price.
You have your salary; was't for that you wrought?
And Wordsworth has his place in the Excise.
You're shabby fellows—true—but poets still,
And duly seated on the Immortal Hill.

Your bays may hide the baldness of your brows—
Perhaps some virtuous blushes;—let them go—
To you I envy neither fruit nor boughs—
And for the fame you would engross below,
The field is universal, and allows
Scope to all such as feel the inherent glow:
Scott, Rogers, Campbell, Moore, and Crabbe, will try
'Gainst you the question with posterity.

For me, who, wandering with pedestrian Muses,
Contend not with you on the wingéd steed,
I wish your fate may yield ye, when she chooses,
The fame you envy, and the skill you need;
And, recollect, a poet nothing loses
In giving to his brethren their full meed
Of merit—and complaint of present days
Is not the certain path to future praise.

He that reserves his laurels for posterity
(Who does not often claim the bright reversion)
Has generally no great crop to spare it, he
Being only injured by his own assertion;
And although here and there some glorious rarity
Arise like Titan from the sea's immersion,
The major part of such appellants go
To—God knows where—for no one else can know.

If, fallen in evil days on evil tongues,
Milton appealed to the Avenger, Time,
If Time, the Avenger, execrates his wrongs,
And makes the word " Miltonic" mean " *Sublime*",
He deigned not to belie his soul in songs,
Nor turn his very talent to a crime ;
He did not loathe the Sire to laud the Son,
But closed the tyrant-hater he begun.

Think'st thou, could he—the blind Old Man—arise
Like Samuel from the grave, to freeze once more
The blood of monarchs with his prophecies,
Or be alive again—again all hoar
With time and trials, and those helpless eyes,
And heartless daughters—worn—and pale—and poor;
Would *he* adore a sultan ? *he* obey
The intellectual eunuch Castlereagh ?

In Canto III a year later he returns to the subject and treats it in like manner. From this point on Southey is the special object of his execration, but he criticises Words-

worth most,[1] while Coleridge is not much more than the
subject of incidental mention.

> All are not moralists, like Southey, when
> He prated to the world of " Pantisocrasy " ;
> Or Wordsworth unexcised, unhired, who then
> Seasoned his pedlar poems with Democracy ;
> Or Coleridge long before his flighty pen
> Let to the Morning Post its aristocracy ;
> When he and Southey, following the same path,
> Espoused two partners (milliners of Bath).

> Such names at present cut a convict figure,
> The very Botany Bay in moral geography ;
> Their loyal treason, renegado rigour,
> Are good manure for their more bare biography ;
> Wordsworth's last quarto, by the way, is bigger
> Than any since the birthday of typography ;
> A drowsy, frowzy poem, called the " Excursion,"
> Writ in a manner which is my aversion.

> He there builds up a formidable dyke
> Between his own and other's intellect ;
> But Wordsworth's poem, and his followers, like
> Joanna Southcote's Shiloh and her sect,
> Are things which in this century don't strike
> The public mind,—so few are the elect ;
> And the new births of both their stale virginities
> Have proved but Dropsies, taken for Divinities.

> But let me to my story : I must own,
> If I have any fault, it is digression—
> Leaving my people to proceed alone,
> While I soliloquise beyond expression ;
> But these are my addresses from the throne,
> Which put off business to the ensuing session :—

[1] For a full study of the relationship of Byron and Wordsworth,
see F. H. Pughe, *Studien über Byron und Wordsworth.* Cf. *L. & J.* V,
101 f., 230, etc., and, *infra*, 247.

Forgetting each omission is a loss to
The world, not quite so great as Ariosto.

I know that what our neighbours call "*longueurs*,"
(We've not so good a *word*, but have the *thing*,
In that complete perfection which insures
An epic from Bob Southey every spring—)
Form not the true temptation which allures
The reader; but 'twould not be hard to bring
Some fine examples of the *Epopée*,
To prove its grand ingredient is *Ennui*.

We learn from Horace, " Homer sometimes sleeps " ;
We feel without him,—Wordsworth sometimes wakes,—
To show with what complacency he creeps,
With his dear " *Waggoners*," around his lakes.
He wishes for " a boat " to sail the deeps—
Of ocean ?—No, of air ; and then he makes
Another outcry for " a little boat,"
And drivels seas to set it well afloat.

If he must fain sweep o'er the ethereal plain,
And Pegasus runs restive in his "Waggon,"
Could he not beg the loan of Charles's Wain ?
Or pray Medea for a single dragon ?
Or if, too classic for his vulgar brain,
He feared his neck to venture such a nag on,
And he must needs mount nearer to the moon,
Could not the blockhead ask for a balloon ?

" Pedlars," and " Boats," and "Waggons " ! Oh ! ye shades
Of Pope and Dryden, are we come to this ?
That trash of such sort not alone evades
Contempt, but from the bathos' vast abyss
Floats scumlike uppermost, and these Jack Cades
Of sense and song above your graves may hiss—
The " little boatman " and his *Peter Bell*—
Can sneer at him who drew "Achitophel " ! [1]

---

[1] Stanzas 93-100.

There is indeed more of the buffoon, as Byron pleased often to call himself, in such passages than of the sane umpire of letters, and yet there is a critical element involved that cannot be wholly ignored.

The next citation represents him in the period of the conflict proper where his feelings are too strong for good criticism. His language is vivid but not critical.

I love Scott and Moore, and all the better brethren; but I hate and abhor that puddle of water worms whom you have taken into your troop.[1]

A few weeks after his part in the controversy is finished he makes one of the characters in *The Blues* utter a prophecy in regard to the Lakers.

Sir, your taste is too common; but time and posterity
Will right these great men, and this age's severity
Become its reproach.[2]

The assertion, which Byron made ironically, contained indeed a truth, contrary to his satirical purpose and beyond his possible conjecture.

Toward the end of his life Byron showed a tendency to distinguish Southey from the other Lakers as the object of his dislike. To have confused them at all was a great error in his critical judgment, though intelligible in Byron from his habit of superficial inquiry and hasty conclusion.

I have reduced my hates to two—that venomous reptile Brougham, and Southey the apostate.[3]

His last critical judgment of the trio is upon Coleridge. As he rated him above the others, it is fitting that his final

---

[1] *L. & J.* V, 18.
[2] Eclogue Second, 99 f.
[3] Trelawny, *Records*, 205. See the *Vision of Judgment* for his final word on Southey. For Byron's challenge to Southey to a duel, see *L. & J.* VI, 10, 17, 29, and *Correspondence* II, 212, 215.

estimate shoud be the best thing he says of any member of the group, or the whole of it, anywhere in his career.

Coleridge is the Sosia in "Amphytrion";—he does not know whether he is himself or not. If he had never gone to Germany, nor spoilt his fine genius by the transcendental philosophy and German metaphysics, nor taken to write lay sermons, he would have made the greatest poet of the day. What poets had we in 1795 ? Hayley had got a monopoly, such as it was. Coleridge might have been anything : as it is, he is a thing " that dreams are made of." [1]

Individual Authors In *English Bards and Scotch Reviewers* Byron criticised Scott for receiving money in somewhat liberal amounts for his works. But all animus toward the man passed away early. In 1813, as we have seen, Byron placed him on the very pinnacle of the English Parnassus. At this time Scott was abandoning poetry for fiction, and Byron was succeeding him in the popular favor.[2] Ever afterwards, by a warm and close friendship and a well-placed literary admiration, though adverse in political sympathies, the younger poet held the older in the very highest esteem.

A piece of critical commentary of Byron's on two of Scott's poems belongs with the satire.

Never was any plan so incongruous and absurd as the groundwork of this production. The entrance of Thunder and Lightning, prologuising to Bayes' tragedy, unfortunately takes away the merit of originality from the dialogue between Messieurs the Spirits of Flood and Fell in the first canto. Then we have the amiable William of Deloraine, " a stark mosstrooper," videlicet, a happy compound of poacher, sheep-stealer, and

---

[1] Captain Medwin, *Conversations*, 215 f.
[2] Cf., *L. & J.* II, 400, and:—" I encouraged him in this project, and asked him why he had ever relinquished poetry. ' Because Byron *bet me*,' said he, pronouncing the word, *beat*, short."—Lockhart, *Life of Sir Walter Scott* X, 119. Cf. *ibid*. V, 22 f.

highwayman. The propriety of his magical lady's injunction not to read can only be equalled by his candid acknowledgment of his independence of the trammels of spelling, although, to use his own elegant phrase, " 'twas his neck-verse at Harribee," i. e., the gallows. The biography of Gilpin Horner, and the marvellous pedestrian page, who travelled twice as fast as his master's horse, without the aid of seven-leagued boots, are *chefs d'œuvre* in the improvement of taste. For incident we have the invisible, but by no means sparing box on the ear bestowed on the page, and the entrance of a Knight and Charger into the castle, under the very natural disguise of a wain of hay. Marmion, the hero of the latter romance, is exactly what William of Deloraine would have been, had he been able to read and write. The poem was manufactured for Messrs. Constable, Murray, and Miller, worshipful Booksellers, in consideration of the receipt of a sum of money; and truly, considering the inspiration, it is a very creditable production. If Mr. Scott will write for hire, let him do his best for his pay-masters, but not disgrace his genius, which is undoubtedly great, by a repetition of Black-Letter Ballad imitations.[1]

It is the last hostile judgment made against Scott individually.

Even before his acquaintance with Scott, Byron could write enthusiastically to Hodgson from Greece:

I see the *Lady of the Lake* advertised. Of course it is in his old ballad style, and pretty. After all, Scott is the best of them. The end of all scribblement is to amuse and he certainly succeeds there. I long to read his new romance.[2]

The *Waverley* novels appealed to Byron from the first and held his interest and admiration for life. Indeed he had no very high opinion of contemporary fiction except

---

[1] A marginal note by Byron, to the passages attacking *Marmion* and the *Lay*, in one of the early editions of *English Bards and Scotch Reviewers*, printed in later editions.
[2] *L. & J.* I, 299.

Scott's.[1] It is easy to understand, from his interest in history, from the familiar subjects treated in the novels,[2] and from their powerful style, why he was so enthusiastic over the great series.[3]

Waverley is the best and most interesting novel I have redde since—I don't know when. I like it as much as I hate *Patronage*, and *Wanderer*, and *O'Donnell*, and all the feminine trash of the last four months. Besides, it is all easy to me, because I have been in Scotland so much (though then young enough too), and feel at home with the people, Lowland and Gael.[4]

Two years later he writes:

The Antiquary is not the best of the three, but much above all the last twenty years, saving its elder brothers.[5]

After Byron's expatriation Scott favorably reviewed *Childe Harold's Pilgrimage* III and *The Prisoner of Chillon* in courageous disregard of the popular outcry against Byron at the time. Byron's appreciation of the championship was indeed great, but it did not in the least affect the judicial saneness of his criticism.

[1] Byron himself attempted a novel early. " I have written 214 pages of a novel."—October 26, 1807, *L. & J.* I, 147. His trial at a ghost story from his pact with the Shelleys is well known. For his fragment, see *L. & J.* III, 446 f.

[2] Cf. *L. & J.* V, 98 f., VI, 4 f., etc.

[3] He was under no delusion in regard to the use Scott made of history. Charged as he was himself at almost every turn of his life with plagiarism, he was a little sensitive on the subject. " I have a great respect for Sir Walter, but I have read enough to know how much of his works are his own property, and how much he takes from others. No author is more successful in appropriation."—Wm. Parry, *The Last Days of Lord Byron*, 222. But the fact was no blemish to the novels or stigma upon the character of the "Ariosto of the North," as Byron denominated Scott.

[4] *L. & J.* III, 110 f.

[5] *L. & J.* III, 371. A keen critical acumen must be accorded him for the detection as early as 1815, when such critics as Hazlitt (see *Works* VII, 130), and such poets as Moore and Wordsworth (See *Diary* of Moore, III, 160), were in doubt as late as 1819, of the authorship of the Waverley novels. Cf. *L. & J.* VI, 4, III, 167 f., and Medwin, *Conversations*, 245 f., and cp. *Correspondence* II, 38.

Some weeks ago I wrote to you my acknowledgments of
W(alter) S(cott)'s article. Now I know it to be his, it cannot
add to my good opinion of him, but it adds to that of myself.
He, and Gifford, and Moore, are the only *regulars* I ever knew
who had nothing of the *Garrison* about their manner: no
nonsense, nor affectations, look you! As for the rest whom I
have known, there was always more or less of the author about
them—the pen peeping from behind the ear, and the thumbs a
little inky, or so.[1]

For the remainder of his life Byron had only praise for
Scott[2] and Scott's works.

Pray send me W. Scott's new novels. What are their names
and characters? I read some of his former ones, at least once
a day, for an hour or so. The last are too hurried: he forgets
Ravenswood's name, and calls him *Edgar* and then *Norman*;
and Girder, the Cooper, is styled now *Gilbert* and now *John*;
and he don't make enough of Montrose; but Dalgetty is excellent, and so is Lucy Ashton, and the bitch her mother. What
is *Ivanhoe*? and what do you call his other? are there *two*?
Pray make him write at least two a year: I like no reading
so well.[3]

Read the conclusion, for the fiftieth time (I have read all
W. Scott's novels at least fifty times), of the third series of
Tales of My Landlord—grand work—Scotch Fielding, as well
as great English poet—wonderful man! I long to get drunk
with him.[4]

Scott is certainly the most wonderful writer of the day. His
novels are a new literature in themselves, and his poetry as

---

[1] *L. & J.* IV, 85.
[2] Cf., *L. & J.* V, 17.
[3] *L. & J.* IV, 415. Cf. *ibid.*, 411-12.
[4] *L. & J.* V, 151. The " fifty times " is, of course, exaggeration.
He modifies the number to " forty times " in a letter to Murray two
months later. Lady Blessington says, " He generally reads his novels
three times."—*Conversations*, 231. Cf., "When I removed from Ravenna
to Pisa the other day, and sent on my library before, they were the
only books that I kept by me, although I already have them by heart."—
L. & J. VI, 5.

good as any—if not better (only on an erroneous system)—
and only ceased to be so popular, because the vulgar learned
were tired of hearing "Aristides called the Just," and Scott
the Best, and ostracised him.[1]

In his last estimates he is a little extravagant, though
not more so than the opinion of the time gave him excuse
for being.

You disclaim "jealousies"; but I would ask, as Boswell
did of Johnson, " of *whom could* you be *jealous* ? " of none of
the living certainly, and (taking all and all into consideration)
of which of the dead ? [2]

> Having wound up with this sublime comparison,
> Methinks we may proceed upon our narrative,
> And, as my friend Scott says, " I sound my warison " ;
> Scott, the superlative of my comparative—
> Scott, who can paint your Christian knight or Saracen,
> Serf—lord—man, with such skill as none would share it, if
> There had not been one Shakespeare and Voltaire,
> Of one or both of whom he seems the heir.[3]

He said that he quite equalled, nay, in his opinion surpassed,
Cervantes.[4]

He could, of course, bestow no higher praise on any man
than to compare him with Pope. This he did of Scott
and of no other person in literature.

Pope's *Homer* is the very best translation that ever was,
or ever will be ; there is nothing like it in the world, be assured.
It is quite delightful to find Pope's character coming round
again ; I forgive Gifford everything for that. Puritan as he is,
he has too much good sense not to know that, even if all the
lies about Pope were truths, his character is one of the best

[1] Diary, *L. & J.* V, 167 f.
[2] *L. & J.* VI, 4.
[3] *Don Juan* XV, 59.
[4] Lady Blessington, *Conversations*, 60.

among literary men.   There is nobody now like him, except Watty, and he is as nearly faultness as ever human being was.[1]

The " Irish Anacreon," Thomas Moore, stood a little closer in personal ties to Byron than did Sir Walter Scott, and he is second only to Scott in Byron's critical esteem. Excepting Hobhouse, with whom the relationship was personal more than literary, Moore was the longest and closest associate of Byron's life.   The strength of the attachment led Byron during the first years of their friendship to over-rate Moore's talent, though not more so than the elite literary public itself was doing.   But the gist of his critical opinion of Moore is a nearer approach to a right judgment by permanent standards than would be expected, nearer indeed than is true in the case of Scott.

Moore figured prominently in the early satire under his pen name of Thomas Little.   But there he was ridiculed for an incident in his literary career rather than for any literary shortcomings.[2]   The first attempt at a characteri-

---

[1] Charles Mackay, *Medora Leigh*, 251, on the authority of a member of the party in Greece.   Byron's championship of the personal character of Scott, of his own volition against an ardent admirer, is a delight to all who appreciate the real sermon that Scott lived:—" There is one part of your observations in the pamphlet which I shall venture to remark upon ;—it regards Walter Scott.   You say that ' his character is little worthy of enthusiasm,' at the same time that you mention his productions in the manner they deserve.   I have known Walter Scott long and well, and in occasional situations which call forth the *real* character—and I can assure you that his character *is* worthy of admiration—that of all men he is the most *open*, the most *honorable*, the most *amiable*.   With his politics I have nothing to do : they differ from mine, which renders it difficult for me to speak of them.   But he is *perfectly sincere* in them : and Sincerity may be humble, but she cannot be servile.   I pray you, therefore, to correct or soften that passage.   You may, perhaps, attribute this officiousness of mine to a false affectation of *candour*, as I happen to be a writer also.   Attribute it to what motive you please, but *believe* the *truth*.   I say that Walter Scott is as nearly a thorough good man as man can be, because I *know* it by experience to be the case."—*L. & J.* VI, 220 f.   The detractor was Henri Beyle (Stendhal) who knew Byron at Milan in 1816.

[2] " In that thing of mine, the *English Bards*, at the time when I was angry with all the world, I never ' disparaged your parts.' "—*L. & J.* II, 254.

zation after the satire is a bit of facetious verse written just
after the pilgrimage.

ON MOORE'S LAST OPERATIC FARCE,
OR FARCICAL OPERA

Good plays are scarce,
So Moore writes *farce* :
The poet's fame grows brittle—
We knew before
That *Little's* Moore,
But now 'tis Moore that's little.[1]

Two months later he became acquainted with Moore.
Soon after the event he writes to Harness that Moore is

The epitome of all that is exquisite in poetical or personal
accomplishments.[2]

This enthusiasm of the newly acquired friendship did not
diminish as long as Byron remained in England,[3] nor was
it ever abated, save for Moore's larger works, for which
Byron's admiration later was tempered.

Byron was responsible in greater measure than has been
recognized for the production of Moore's masterpiece, *Lalla
Rookh.*   It was a part of his own laudable purpose to exploit
the East in English poetry.

[I] have always regretted that you don't give us an *entire*
work, and not sprinkle yourself in detached pieces—beautiful,
I allow, and quite *alone* in our language, but still giving us a
right to expect a *Shah Nameh* (is that the name ?) as well as
gazelles.   Stick to the East ;—the oracle, Stael, told me it was
the only poetical policy.   The North, South, and West, have
all been exhausted; but from the East, we have nothing but

---

[1] September 14, 1811, not published till 1830.
[2] *L. & J.* II, 77 f.   Cf. Dedication of the *Corsair.*
[3] Cf. *L. & J.* III, 153.

Southey's unsaleables,—and these he has contrived to spoil, by adopting only their most outrageous fictions. His personages don't interest us, and yours will. You will have no competitor; and, if you had, you ought to be glad of it. The little I have done in that way is merely a " voice in the wilderness " for you; and if it has had any success, that also will prove that the public are orientalising, and pave the path for you.[1]

Moore has a peculiarity of talent, or rather talents,—poetry, music, voice, all his own; and an expression in each, which never was, nor will be, possessed by another. But he is capable of still higher flights in poetry. By the by, what humour, what—every thing, in the " *Post-Bag* ! " There is nothing Moore may not do, if he will but seriously set about it.[2]

I certainly am of opinion that you have not yet done all *you* can do, though more than enough for any one else. I want, and the world expects, a longer work from you.[3]

He is fastidious over the title, when the work is about to appear.

I like a tough title myself—witness the *Giaour* and *Childe Harold*, which choked half the blues at starting * *. I wish you had not called it a " *Persian Tale.*" Say a " Poem," or " Romance," but not " Tale." [4]

On the same day he expresses himself freely to Murray, with a god-fatherly anxiety for the success of the poem.

Lalla Rookh—you must recollect that, in the way of title, *The Giaour* has never been pronounced to this day; and both it and *Childe Harold* sounded very formidable and facetious to the blue-bottles of wit and honour about town, till they were taught and startled into a proper deportment; and therefore *Lalla Rookh*, which is very orthodox and oriental, is as good a title as need be, if not better. I could wish rather that he had

[1] *L. & J.* II, 254 f.
[2] Journal, *L. & J.* II, 333.
[3] *L. & J.* II, 302.
[4] *L. & J.* IV, 76 f. Cf. *ibid.*, 62.

not called it " a *Persian tale* "; firstly, because we have had Turkish tales, and Hindoo tales, and Assyrian tales, already ; and tale is a word of which it repents me to have nicknamed poesy. Fable would be better ; and, secondly, 'Persian tale' reminds one of the lines of Pope on Ambrose Phillips ; though no one can say, to be sure, that this tale has been " turned for half-a-crown " ; still it is as well to avoid such clashings. " Persian *story* "—why not ?—or romance ? I feel as anxious for Moore as I could do for myself, for the soul of me, and I would not have him succeed otherwise than splendidly.[1]

His first taste of the work was from an outline and extracts which Murray had sent him. His satisfaction overflows to both Murray and Moore.

I have got the sketch and extracts from *Lallah Rookh*, which I humbly suspect will knock up *Ilderim*, and shew young gentlemen some thing more than having been across a Camel's hump is necessary to write a good Oriental tale. The plan, as well as the extract I have seen, please me very much indeed, and I feel impatient for the whole.[2]

You have caught the colours as if you had been in the rainbow and the tone of the East is perfectly preserved. I am glad you have changed the title from " Persian Tale " * * * * I suspect you have written a devilish fine composition, and I rejoice in it from my heart ; because " the Douglas and the Percy both together are confident against a world in arms." I hope you won't be affronted at my looking on us as " birds of a feather " ; though, on whatever subject you had written, I should have been very happy in your success.[3]

Of the extracts I can but judge as extracts, and I prefer the " Peri " to the " Silver Veil." He seems not so much at home in his versification of the " Silver Veil," and a little embarrassed with his horrors ; but the Conception of the Character of the Imposter is fine, and the plan of great scope for his genius

[1] *L. & J.* IV, 85 f.
[2] *L. & J.* IV, 146.
[3] *L. & J.* IV, 148.

—and I doubt not that as a whole, it will be very Arabesque and beautiful.[1]

Disappointment began with his first acquaintance with the full work.

I am very glad to hear of its popularity, for Moore is a very noble fellow in all respects, and will enjoy it without any of the bad feeling which success—good or evil—sometimes engenders in the men of rhyme. Of the poem itself, I will tell you my opinion when I have mastered it : I say of the *poem*, for I don't like the *prose* at all—at all ; and in the mean time, the " Fire worshippers " is the best, and the " Veiled Prophet " the worst, of the volume.[2]

His later comment to Moore is more favorable, but there is no attempt to express an appreciation which he does not feel.

Your passion is fully effective; and all poetry of the *Asiatic* kind—I mean Asiatic, as the Romans called " Asiatic oratory," and not because the scenery is Oriental—must be tried by that test only.   I am not quite sure that I shall allow the Miss Byrons (legitimate or illegitimate) to read *Lalla Rookh*—in the first place, on account of this said *passion* ; and, in the second, that they mayn't discover that there was a better poet than papa.[3]

Evidently the poem had not fulfilled his expectations.[4]

After *Lalla Rookh* Moore never again occupied quite so high a position in Byron's favor, although their friendship continued in all its former strength.   This lower estimate is creditable to Byron's critical sense.   His later comments

---

[1] *L. & J.* IV, 151.
[2] *L. & J.* IV, 169.
[3] *L. & J.* V, 310.
[4] Cf., " He talked of our mutual friend Moore, and of his *Lalla Rookh*, which he said though very beautiful had disappointed him ; adding that Moore would go down to posterity by his Melodies, which were all perfect."—Lady Blessington, *Conversations*, 41.

are mainly upon Moore's lyrical compositions, which as
early as 1813 he had called " My matins and vespers."

> When Julia sate within as pretty a bower
> As e'er held houri in that heathenish heaven
> Described by Mahomet, and Anacreon Moore,
> To whom the lyre and laurels have been given,
> With all the trophies of triumphant song—
> He won them well, and may be wear them long ![1]

Galignani has just sent me the Paris edition of your works
(which I wrote to order), and I am glad to see my old friends
with a French face. I have been skimming and dipping, in
and over them, like a swallow, and as pleased as one. It is the
first time that I had seen the Melodies without music ; and, I
don't know how, but I can't read in a music-book—the crotchets
confound the words in my head, though I recollect them perfectly when *sung*. Music assists my memory through the ear,
not through the eye ; I mean, that her quavers perplex me upon
paper, but they are a help when heard. And thus I was glad
to see the words without their borrowed robes ;—to my mind
they look none the worse for their nudity.[2]

But, with regard to *you*, I thought that you had always been
allowed to be a *poet*, even by the stupid as well as the envious
—a bad one, to be sure—immoral, florid, Asiatic, and diabolic-
ally popular,—but still always a poet, *nem. con.* This discovery
therefore, has to me all the grace of novelty, as well as of consolation (according to Rochefoucault), to find myself *no*-poetised
in such good company. I am content to " err with Plato " ;
and can assure you very sincerely, that I would rather be received
a *non*-poet with you, than be crowned with all the bays of the
(*yet*-uncrowned) Lakers in their society.[3]

Despite the long, close, and uninterrupted friendship,
and the influence that personal relations were known to

[1] *Don Juan* I, 104.
[2] *L. & J.* V, 41.
[3] *L. & J.* VI, 29.

wield over Byron's saner judgment, his critical estimate of
Moore, in his later years, is one which present opinion would
be slow to change.[1]

The only poet of really first rank who ever came intimately
into Byron's life was Shelley. But Byron has least of all
to say of Shelley as an author, and almost nothing of him
as a man and a friend. At the same time, he is known to
have held him in high esteem, both as a poet and as a man.[2]

The cause of this extraordinary silence is complex.
Shelley was under as severe social, literary, and religious
proscription as Byron. Public championship of him would
have done Shelley little good and Byron himself none.[3]
Shelley was Byron's junior by four years, and Byron was
not given to acknowledging younger genius than his own.[4]
And, finally, in his cursory way of dealing with men and
works, Byron was perhaps never aware of the full extent
of Shelley's powers.[5] There is no evidence at any time in
Byron's life that he made any real study of Shelley's works.

---

[1] For a full account of Byron's relation with Moore, see Edgar
Dawson, *Byron und Moore*.

[2] Shelley's temporary intimidation in the presence of Byron is well
known. But he at least came to believe that Byron had a high opinion
of his muse. In proposing the sale to a publisher of his " Laon and
Cynthia," he urges the project as " an arrangement which, if there
be any truth in the opinions of my friends Lord Byron and Mr. Leigh
Hunt of my powers, cannot be disadvantageous to you."—R. Ingpen,
Letters II, 559.

[3] Cf., " Shelley he did not dare to acknowledge, even as a visitor."—
Leigh Hunt, *Lord Byron*, 227.

[4] Cf. *L. & J.* V, 68. Trelawny has dropped a hint of at least a
drawing-room envy of Shelley by Byron, which has received some
recognition. Cf., " On his side Byron, though too sincere and honest
to depreciate Shelley's poetic genius, was not exactly the man to seek
to glorify a serious rival in a field which he could generously afford to
divide with Tom Moore."—Helen R. Angeli, *Shelley and His Friends
in Italy*, 221. Cf. also, J. A. Symonds, *Shelley* (E. M. L.), 162.

[5] Cf., " We may perceive in the poetry of the two men deep and
radical differences, indicating a spiritual difference between them much
more deep, which may explain the little notice which Byron took of
Shelley's poetry."—Charles Kingsley, *Fraser's Magazine*, November,
1853. Cf. *L. & J.* IV, 273, and V, 435, 496.

He valued him as a companion and a friend but did not fathom him fully as a poet. But whatever commentary he has left is at least critically favorable.

His first declaration is only a partial defense of Shelley against detraction, as late as 1820. This was after Shelley's climacteric year as a productive poet.

Surely he has talent and honour, but is crazy against religion and morality. His tragedy is sad work ; but the subject renders it so. His *Islam* had much poetry. You seem lately to have got some notion against him.[1]

He depreciates the *Cenci* as a play the following year, because it does not conform with his ideas of drama, but he recognizes its great poetical value in the body of Shelley's work.

You also know my high opinion of your own poetry,—because it is of *no* school. I read *Cenci*—but, besides that I think the *subject* essentially *un*dramatic, I am not an admirer of our old dramatists *as models*. I deny that the English have hitherto had a drama at all. Your *Cenci*, however, was a work of power, and poetry.[2]

Two judgments before Shelley's death, recorded by Medwin, are sound criticism.

The " Cenci " is equally horrible, though perhaps the best tragedy modern times have produced. It is a play,—not a poem, like " Remorse " and " Fazio "; and the best proof of its merit is, that people are continually quoting it. What may not be expected from such a beginning ?[3]

There's Shelley has more poetry in him than any man living ; and if he were not so mystical, and would not write Utopias and set himself up as a Reformer, his right to rank as a poet, and very highly too, could not fail of being acknowledged. . . . .

[1] *L. & J.* V, 74.
[2] *L. & J.* V, 268.
[3] *Conversations*, 111 f.

The works he wrote at seventeen are much more extraordinary than Chatterton's at the same age.[1]

The remainder of what he has to say is in defense of Shelley's character against the popular outcry. His utterances in this way are the more notable because they are directed chiefly against Moore.

As to poor Shelley, who is another bugbear to you and the world, he is, to my knowledge, the *least* selfish and the mildest of men—a man who has made more sacrifices of his fortune and feelings for others than any man I ever heard of. With his speculative opinions I have nothing in common, nor desire to have.[2]

In your last letter you say, speaking of Shelley, that you would almost prefer the " damning bigot " to the " annihilating infidel." Shelley believes in immortality, however—but this by the way.[3]

His expressions after Shelley's death are in the same vein.

You were all brutally mistaken about Shelley, who was, without exception, the *best* and least selfish man I ever knew. I never knew one who was not a beast in comparison.[4]

You will have heard by this time that Shelley and another gentleman (Captain Williams) were drowned about a month ago (a *month* yesterday), in a squall off the Gulf of Spezia. There is thus another man gone, about whom the world was ill-naturedly, and ignorantly, and brutally mistaken. It will, perhaps, do him justice *now*, when he can be no better for it.[5]

You are all mistaken about Shelley. You do not know how mild, how tolerant, how good he was in Society ; and as perfect a Gentleman as ever crossed a drawing-room, when he liked, and where he liked.[6]

---

[1] *Ibid.*, 290 f.   Cf., " ' Pooh ! ' replied Byron, ' your poetry, my dear Shelley, is lovely; but your ideas are, if you will pardon me, Utopian.' "—Jane Clermont, reported by Wm. Graham, *Last Links*, 21.
[2] *L. & J.* VI, 32.
[3] *L. & J.* VI, 35.
[4] *L. & J.* VI, 99.
[5] *L. & J.* VI, 99.
[6] *L. & J.* VI, 157.   Cf. *ibid.*, 175.

It may be that a sense of the great wrong he had done Shelley, in his own regrettable conduct toward the mother of Allegra,[1] sealed Byron's lips to further commentary on the junior poet. But as remarked above, Byron was doubt-less simply unaware of the full power of the genius which for a while made a part of his life and elevated the tone and spirit of his poetry.[2]

It was unfortunate for Keats as the protégé of Hunt and the Cockneys that his verse came to Byron's attention in connection with the furor over the poetry of Pope. And before Byron was really disengaged from the controversy, the news came of Keats's death, and thus all chance for either helpful or harmful criticism was over.

Byron's private utterances at the time are more exe-cratory than his abuses in the controversy.

No more Keats, I entreat :—Flay him alive; if some of you don't, I must skin him myself : there is no bearing the drivelling idiotism of the Mankin.[3]

This was in October, 1820. A month later he writes :

The *Edinburgh* praises Jack Keats or Ketch, or whatever his names are : why, his is the * of Poetry—something like the pleasure an Italian fiddler extracted out of being suspended daily by a Street Walker in Drury Lane. This went on for some weeks : at last the Girl went to get a pint of Gin—met another, chatted too long, and Cornelli was *hanged outright before she returned.* Such like is the trash they praise, and such will be the end of the * * poesy of this miserable Self-polluter of the human Mind.[4]

---

[1] Cf. *L. & J.* V, 74-5, footnote *ibid.*, 73 f., and Professor Dowden's *Life of Shelley* II, 423 f., and Cp. *Correspondence* II, 179 f.

[2] See M. Eimer, *Die persönlichen Beziehungen zwischen Byron und den Shelleys,* for a fuller study of the subject.

[3] *L. & J.* V, 96. Cf., " Johnny Keats's *p-ss a bed* poetry," earlier in the same letter.

[4] *L. & J.* V, 109.

Again in less than a week:

Mr. Keats, whose poetry you enquire after, appears to me what I have already said : such writing is a sort of mental * * * * — * * * * * his *Imagination*. I don't mean he is *indecent*, but viciously soliciting his own ideas into a state, which is neither poetry nor anything else but a Bedlam vision produced by raw pork and opium.[1]

And in postscript to the next letter following he adds:

Of the praises of that little dirty blackguard Keates in the *Edinburgh*, I shall observe as Johnson did when Sheridan the actor got a *pension* : " What ! has *he* got a pension ?   Then it is time that I should give up *mine* ! "   Nobody could be prouder of the praises of the *Edinburgh* than I was, or more alive to their censure, as I showed in *E (nglish) B (ards) and S (cotch) R(eviewers)*. At present *all the men* they have ever praised are degraded by that insane article.   Why don't they review and praise " Solomon's Guide to Health " ? it is better sense and as much poetry as Johnny Keates.[2]

These passages, amid all the criticism to be found in Byron's works, seem most the result of malevolence and ill-nature. In fact, he was softened into moderation only by the news that Keats was no longer alive to suffer under any infliction.

A show of reparation for his savagery is made to the memory of Keats in a letter to Murray when Byron's share in the controversy is over.

Is it true, what Shelley writes me, that poor John Keates died at Rome of the *Quarterly Review* ?   I am very sorry for it, though I think he took the wrong line as a poet, and was spoilt by Cockneyfying, and Suburbing, and versifying Tooke's Pantheon and Lempriere's Dictionary.[3]

[1] *L. & J.* V, 117.
[2] *L. & J.* V, 120 f.   Keats's plebeian origin, indicated in the word " blackguard," was perhaps partial ground for Byron's rancor.   He uses the word of both Shakespeare and Otway.   See *L. & J.* V, 89.
[3] *L. & J.* V, 269.

Partial apology for his treatment of Keats is made to Shelley on the same date.

> I was provoked by his *attack* upon *Pope*, and my disapprobation of *his own* style of writing.[1]

But a fair critical estimate of Keats never came from Byron's hand.

The banker poet, Samuel Rogers, touched Byron's life and literary career at many points with more than a mere formal intimacy. During the years of lionizing in England, Rogers was nearly as familiar a companion of Byron as was Moore. He was one of the select few living poets honored with eulogy in the early satire,[2] and as " the last of the *best* school " he occupied a position only a little lower than Scott and above both Moore and Campbell on the pyramidal Parnassus of 1813. This exalted place in Byron's estimation he retained until the Italian residence, when a close personal contact being no longer possible Byron's impulses were to relegate him to a position more befitting his talents as they are esteemed to-day. He never fell in Byron's judgment, however, to a place lower than his merit.

Byron early recognized the qualities of Rogers's poetry that are conceded to-day as constituting his chief claim to memory—his elegance and refinement.

> I have been reading *Memory* again, the other day, and *Hope* together, and retain all my preference for the former. His elegance is really wonderful—there is no such thing as a vulgar line in his book.[3]

Two months later he is represented as an author of superb taste and urbanity.

---

[1] *L. & J.* V, 268.   Cf. Chapter VI, 148, *L. & J.* V, 331, and *Don Juan* XI, 60.

[2] See Chapter IV, 72.

[3] September 5, 1813, *L. & J.* II, 260.   Cf. *L. & J.* II, 124, and "Lines Written on a Blank Leaf of *The Pleasures of Memory*," 1812.

Rogers is silent,—and, it is said, severe. When he does talk, he talks well ; and, on all subjects of taste, his delicacy of expression is pure as his poetry. If you enter his house—his drawing-room—his library—you of yourself say, this is not the dwelling of a common mind. There is not a gem, a coin, a book thrown aside on his chimney-piece, his sofa, his table, that does not bespeak an almost fastidious elegance in the possessor. But this very delicacy must be the misery of his existence. Oh the jarrings his disposition must have encountered through life ![1]

"The fairy *Jacqueline,*" as an expression of the character of the poet, is in Byron's opinion the best of all Rogers's poems.

You could not have made me a more acceptable present than *Jacqueline.* She is all grace and softness and poetry ; there is so much of the last, that we do not feel the want of *story*, which is simple, yet enough. I wonder that you do not oftener unbend to more of the same kind. I have some sympathy with the *softer* affections, though very little in *my* way, and no one can depict them so truly and successfully as yourself.[2]

In 1817 Byron becomes fairly convinced that English poetry is on a wrong tack. Early in the year Rogers and Crabbe are called " the fathers of present poesy," and later the former is designated as the " Grandfather of living Poetry." Both are exempt from the lawless tendencies of the age. At the same time, Byron is content to find in himself and Moore a poetical kinship and sympathy with Rogers.

Rogers whom . . . . I regard as our poetical papa. You are his lawful son, and I the illegitimate.[3]

In April of the same year he says of Rogers:

He is the Tithonus of poetry—immortal already. You and I must wait for it.[4]

---

[1] Journal, *L. & J.* II, 331.
[2] *L. & J.* III, 101. The poem was published with *Lara,* " Larry and Jackey," facetiously called by Byron.
[3] *L. & J.* IV, 89.
[4] *L. & J.* IV, 102 f.

It is the last unqualified praise he gives to Rogers. After-wards his speech is clearly subdued.

Rogers's characteristics become a part of the facetiousness of *Don Juan*. The sultana's door opens noiselessly,

> The hinges being as smooth as Rogers' rhymes.[1]

In the first letter to Bowles Rogers is

> The last Argonaut of classic English poetry, and the Nestor of our inferior race of living poets.[2]

To Trelawny he is characterized as but

> A banker and poetiser. He feeds the needy critics and they dub him poet.[3]

And in the " Detached Thoughts " he is described as

> " The *worst* good man with the *best* natured Muse." His Muse being all Sentiment and Sago and Sugar.[4]

Byron's last judgment of Rogers deserves attention.

> If Rogers has not fixed himself in the higher fields of Parnassus, he has, at least, cultivated a very pretty flower-garden at its base.[5]

The figure recalls the poetical pyramid, but Rogers is shifted to a position that is his by modern consent.

Byron has not left sufficient material on the few other celebrated poets of his time for an estimate. He held Campbell in the highest esteem all his life, but he admired him without characterizing him.[6] In his journal of December 5, 1813, is found not a literary judgment but an

---

[1] Canto V, 89. Cf., for harsher spirit, " Question and Answer," 1818.
[2] *L. & J.* V, 537.
[3] *Records*, 33.
[4] *L. & J.* V, 420. An estrangement had sprung up between them, from Byron's imputing some slanderous talk to Rogers. Cf. *L. & J.* IV, 202-3, V, 372, 420, etc.
[5] Lady Blessington, *Conversations*, 353.
[6] See *L. & J.* V, 25-6, for some corrections of Campbell as critic and literary historian.

interesting little critical formula incidental to some personal talk on Campbell.

C * * [Campbell] looks well,—seems pleased, and dressed to *sprucery*. A blue coat becomes him,—so does his new wig. He really looked as if Apollo had sent him a birthday suit, or a wedding-garment, and was witty and lively. He abused Corinne's book, which I regret ; because, firstly, he understands German, and is consequently a fair judge ; and, secondly, he is *first-rate*, and, consequently, the best of judges. I reverence and admire him ; but I won't give up my opinion—why should I ? I read *her* again and again, and there can be no affectation in this. I cannot be mistaken (except in taste) in a book I read and lay down, and take up again ; and no book can be totally bad which finds *one*, even *one* reader, who can say as much sincerely.[1]

Crabbe won Byron's heartiest favor at the outset, and held it undiminished to the end, but he is never drawn even in outline. Perhaps the famous line from the satire,

Though Nature's sternest painter, yet the best,

is compensation for the whole after silence.

Burns is but the subject of brief appreciation here and there, as will be seen. Blake the mystic is never mentioned—naturally enough. Cowper is in part venerated and in part condemned,[2] but never estimated. Gray and Goldsmith are extolled whenever they are named, but are not delineated entire nor judged in any of their qualities.

These great names, on which Byron is so provokingly silent, are well known to constitute the majority of the group that he admired most and longest. He talks most of those in whom he found excuse for censure. From this

---

[1] *L. & J.* II, 364. Cf. *ibid.* III, 128, and V, 167.
[2] Cf., *English Bards and Scotch Reviewers*, 808 f., *L. & J.* V, 25, 558, etc.

fact comes the suggestion that his criticism is mainly destructive.

Of the group of journalists, critics, and editor-poets of the day, Leigh Hunt is the only one whom Byron attempts to set forth in his literary character. The great northern "anthropophagus," Jeffrey, was the chief object of attack in the satire, but thereafter he was the recipient only of praise from Byron's pen. Byron's relation was much closer to Gifford, the great English editor, from whom he received many helpful suggestions while his works were going through the press. But his expressions upon the man are only so many encomiums of the living monarch of literature, as those upon Pope are obeisances to the dead, which reflect little credit upon the " critic and censor of the age."

> From Mr. G(ifford) every comma is an obligation for which thank him in my name and behalf.[1]

And within a few weeks of his death a decade later:

> It is not true that I ever *did, will, would, could,* or *should* write a satire against Gifford, or a hair of his head. I always considered him as my literary father, and myself as his " prodigal son "; and if I have allowed his " fatted calf " to grow to an ox before he kills it on my return, it is only because I prefer beef to veal.[2]

Byron's scattered commentary upon Hunt deals mainly with him as a poet.[3] Early in 1814 a critical opinion is given of one of Hunt's effusions.

[1] *L. & J.* III, 3.
[2] *L. & J.* VI, 329. Cf., " You, Mr. Gifford, have had the honour, such as it is, of being praised uniformly by the noble Lord ; and, in that distinction, it seems, you stand proudly preëminent, for there is hardly any other living writer to whom he has not dealt out nearly as much abuse as adulation."— John Watkins, *Byron*, viii. Cf. *L. & J.* I, 202, II, 27, 41, 221, III, 17-18, and V, 371-2.
[3] His treatment of Hunt as leader of the Cockneys and editor of *The Liberal* has been seen, Chapter VI, 164 f. For a full account of the relationship of the two men, see W. F. Schirmer, *Die Beziehungen zwischen Byron und Leigh Hunt*.

I send you Hunt, with his Ode ; the thoughts are good, but the expressions *buckram* except here and there.[1]

As in the case of Moore's *Lalla Rookh,* Byron guided the *Rimini* through the routine of its production,[2] and was rewarded with its dedication. In the sympathy of their friendship at the time he was gratified with the poem.

Pray let me have the rest of *Rimini.* You have two excellent points in that poem—originality and Italianism. I will back you as a bard against half the fellows on whom you have thrown away much good criticism and eulogy ; but don't let your bookseller publish in *quarto* ; it is the worst size possible for circulation. I say this on bibliopolical authority.[3]

There is a substratum of poetry, which is a foundation for solid and durable fame. The objections (*if* there be objections, for this is a *pre*sumption, and not an *as*sumption) will be merely as to the mechanical part, and such, as I stated before, the usual consequences of either novelty or revival.[4]

Leigh Hunt's poem is a devilish good one—quaint, here and there, but with the substratum of originality, and with poetry about it, that will stand the test.[5]

Disillusionment came with the estrangement in their personal relations. *Rimini* was included in his general condemnation of Hunt as poet, critic, and literary theorist.

Hunt's letter is probably the exact piece of vulgar coxcombry you might expect from his situation. He is a good man, with some poetical elements in his chaos ; but spoilt by the Christ-Church Hospital and a Sunday newspaper,—to say nothing of the Surrey gaol, which conceited him into a martyr. But he is a good man. When I saw *Rimini* in MS., I told him that I

---

[1] *L. & J.* III, 69. Cf. *ibid.,* 200.
[2] " He subsequently called on me in the prison several times, and used to bring books for my Story of Rimini, which I was then writing." —Leigh Hunt, *Lord Byron,* 4. Cf. *L. & J.* III, 200, 244, 246, 251, etc.
[3] *L. & J.* III, 242.
[4] *L. & J.* III, 265 f.
[5] *L. & J.* III, 267.

deemed it good poetry at bottom, disfigured only by a strange style. His answer was, that his style was a system, or *upon system*, or some such cant ; and, when a man talks of system, his case is hopeless : so I said no more to him, and very little to any one else. He believes his trash of vulgar phrases tortured into compound barbarisms to be *old* English ; and we may say of it as Aimwell says of Captain Gibbet's regiment, when the Captain calls it an " old corps,"—" the *oldest* in Europe, if I may judge by your uniform." He sent out his *Foliage* by Percy Shelley * * *, and, of all the ineffable Centaurs that were ever begotten by Self-love upon a Night-mare, I think " this monstrous Sagittary " the most prodigious. *He* (Leigh Hunt) is an honest charlatan, who has persuaded himself into a belief of his own impostures, and talks Punch in pure simplicity of heart, taking himself (as poor Fitzgerald said of *him*self in *Morning Post*) for *Vates* in both senses, or nonsenses, of the word.[1]

His last remarks upon Hunt are almost valueless as criticism. What might have been a judicious estimate was precluded by their unfortunate association in *The Liberal*, in which both men were at fault but neither was willing to accept his part of the blame. In a total estimate of his literary character, it is to be noted, Hunt, according to Byron, was the exact counterpart of Rogers, who was a perfect example of the *gentilhomme* of letters.

" Rimini " has a great deal of merit. There never were so many fine things spoiled as in " Rimini."[2]

As to any community of feeling, thought, or opinion, between L. H. and me, there is little or none : we meet rarely, hardly ever ; but I think him a good principled and able man, and must do as I would be done by. I do not know what world he has lived in, but I have lived in three or four ; and none of them like his Keats and Kangaroo *terra incognita*.[3]

[1] *L. & J.* IV, 237 f. Cf. *L. & J.* V, 588.
[2] Captain Medwin, *Conversations*, 323.
[3] *L. & J.* VI, 157. Cf. *ibid.*, 167 f.

Occasional Judgments Scattered throughout Byron's poetry and in almost continuous succession in his letters and journals are striking passages on literary subjects, which often constitute notable criticism.

The first of all such isolated bits is a criticism of an humble poem which had for its subject Byron himself. The passage is one of the very earliest fragments of critical writing that came from Byron's pen. It is substantially a private review of the poem to Byron's friend Hobbouse.

A Birthday Ode has been addressed to me by a country school-master, in which I am likened to the Sun, or Sol, as he classically saith ; the people of Newstead are compared to Laplanders. I am said to be a Baron, and a Byron, the truth of which is indisputable. Feronia is again to reign (she must have some woods to govern first), but it is altogether a very pleasant performance, and the author is as superior to Pye, as George Gordon to George Guelph. To be sure some of the lines are too short, but then, to make amends, the Alexandrines have from fifteen to seventeen syllables, so we may call them Alexandrines the great.[1]

From his interest in satire, in connection with the *Hints from Horace,* he says of Juvenal, whom he has been reading in his friend Hodgson's translation:

I have been reading *Juvenal* and *Lady Jane,* etc., for the first time since my return. The Tenth Sat* has always been my favourite, as I suppose indeed of everybody's. It is the finest recipe for making one miserable with his life, and content to walk out of it, in any language. I should think it might be redde with great effect to a man dying without much pain, in preference to all the stuff that ever was said or sung in churches.[2]

Sometimes he is capable of a little quaint, harmless humor that has more critical point in its make-up than the spirit

[1] *L. & J.* I, 167.
[2] *L. & J.* II, 32.

of the composition would indicate. His fellow traveler and subsequent biographer, John Galt, is the subject in one instance of such pleasantry.

There is a book entitled *Galt, his Travels in ye Archipelago*, daintily printed by Cadell and Davies, ye which I could desiderate might be criticised by you, inasmuch as ye author is a well-respected esquire of mine acquaintance, but I fear will meet with little mercy as a writer, unless a friend passeth judgment. Truth to say, ye boke is ye book of a cock-brained man, and is full of devises crude and conceitede, but peradventure for my sake this grace may be vouchsafed unto him. Review him myself I can not, will not, and if you are likewise hard of heart, woe unto ye boke ! ye which is a comely quarto.[1]

If Byron was equipped for criticism of any literary phase or element more than another it was Orientalism in English literature. He says of William Beckford's romance of *Caliph Vathek* :

For correctness of costume, beauty of description, and power of imagination, it far surpasses all European imitations, and bears such marks of originality that those who have visited the East will find some difficulty in believing it to be more than a translation. As an Eastern tale, even Rasselas must bow before it ; his " Happy Valley " will not bear a comparison with the " Hall of Eblis." [2]

He met the Edgeworths, father and daughter, during his London residence after his return from the pilgrimage. He says of *Patronage*, with some of the smartness of the social dandy, just at the time when Miss Edgeworth was the best known English novelist :

I have redde *Patronage*. It is full of praises of Lord Ellen-

---

[1] *L. & J.* II, 101 f.
[2] Note to the *Giaour*. The opinion is noteworthy as being against Byron's later idol, Johnson, in favor of a pronounced romantic. Cf. *Childe Harold* I, 22 f.

borough ! ! !—from which I infer near and dear relations at the
bar, and has much of her heartlessness and little of her humours
(wit she has none), and she must live more than 3 weeks in London
to describe *good* or (if you will) high society ; the *ton* of her book
is as vulgar as her father—and no more attractive than her
eyes.[1]

The result of Lady Caroline Lamb's resentment against
Byron was his portraiture in her novel *Glenarvon.*   Byron's
dispassionate criticism of the work could hardly have been
gratifying to its pathetic authoress in her nervous anxiety
to know his opinion.

It seems to me, that if the authoress had written the *truth*,
and nothing but the truth—the whole truth—the romance
would not only have been more *romantic*, but more entertaining.
As for the likeness, the picture can't be good—I did not sit
long enough.[2]

He turns to " the honored file " of classical writers for
the levity of *Don Juan,* and derides them singly for the purpose of condemning as unwholesome the whole group.

> Ovid's a rake, as half his verses show him,
> Anacreon's morals are a still worse sample,
> Catullus scarcely has a decent poem,
> I don't think Sappho's Ode a good example,
> Although Longinus tells us there is no hymn
> Where the Sublime soars forth on wings more ample ;
> But Virgil's songs are pure, except that horrid one
> Beginning with " *Formosum Pastor Corydon.*"

---

[1] *L. & J.* III, 11.   Cf., " I admire them (the Edgeworth novels) ;
but they excite no feeling, and they leave no love—except for some
Irish steward or postillion.   However, the impression of intellect and
prudence is profound—and may be useful."—Diary, *L. & J.* V, 179 f.
R. L. Edgeworth, the father, was the author of a little volume, *Poetry
Explained for the Use of Young People,* published when Byron was
fourteen years of age, but there is scant evidence that Byron was
acquainted with the work.
[2] *L. & J.* IV, 12.   Cf. *ibid.* III, 338 f., and IV, 94.

Lucretius' irreligion is too strong
For early stomachs, to prove wholesome food;
I can't help thinking Juvenal was wrong,
Although no doubt his real intent was good,
For speaking out so plainly in his song,
So much indeed as to be downright rude;
And then what proper person can be partial
To all those nauseous epigrams of Martial.[1]

Sometimes in the choice of great subject matter he cajoles the reader into expecting a great judgment, but as often he perversely turns aside to maintain the spirit of his unique poem.

Milton's the prince of Poets—so we say;
A little heavy, but no less divine:
An independent being in his day—
Learned, pious, temperate in love and wine;
But, his life falling into Johnson's way,
We're told this great High Priest of all the Nine
Was whipt at college—a harsh sire—odd spouse,
For the first Mrs. Milton left his house.[2]

There is a very noticeable tendency in his diaries and journals to thoughtfulness and reflection, not usually acknowledged to be a habit of the man. It represents sometimes the difference between Byron the poser and Byron the real man. What he has to say of Johnson's *Vanity of Human Wishes* is in this manner of meditative criticism. From the instance, notwithstanding the high regard in which he held his subject, it will be observed that he is not always successful in the vein.

Dined. Read Johnson's *Vanity of Human Wishes*,— all the examples and mode of giving them sublime, as well as the latter part, with the exception of an occasional couplet. I do not so

[1] Canto I, 42-3.
[2] *Don Juan* III, 91.

much admire the opening. I remember an observation˙ of Sharpe's (the *Conversationist*, as he was called in London, and a very clever man,) that the first line of this poem was super-fluous, and that Pope (the best of poets, *I* think), would have begun at once, only changing the punctuation—

" Survey mankind from China to Peru."

The former line, " Let observation," etc. is certainly heavy and useless. But 'tis a grand poem—and *so true*!—true as the 10th of Juvenal himself. The lapse of ages *changes* all things —time—language—the earth—the bounds of the sea—the stars of the sky, and every thing " about, around, and underneath " man, *except man himself*, who has always been, and always will be, an unlucky rascal. The infinite variety of lives conduct but to death, and the infinity of wishes lead but to disappoint-ment.[1]

He is more effective in this manner a few weeks later on the subject of Dante's gentleness, in refutation of Schlegel's charge that Dante is wanting in gentleness.

Why, there is gentleness in Dante beyond all gentleness, when he is tender. It is true that, treating of the Christian Hades or Hell, there is not much scope or site for gentleness—but who *but* Dante could have introduced any " gentleness " at all into *Hell* ? Is there any in Milton's ? No—and Dante's Heaven is all love, and glory, and majesty.[2]

In further criticism of the same critic, incidentally giving a judgment of a well-recognized masterpiece, he says :

I have found out, however, where the German is right—it is about the *Vicar of Wakefield*. " Of all romances in miniature (and, perhaps, this is the best shape in which Romance can appear) the *Vicar of Wakefield* is, I think, the most exquisite." He *thinks* !—he might be sure. But it is very well for a Schlegel.[3]

---

[1] Diary, *L. & J.* V, 161 f.
[2] Diary, *L. & J.* V, 194.
[3] Diary, *L. & J.* V, 194. In his letters and journals Byron employs the *Vicar of Wakefield*, by way of reference and quotation, in evident critical appreciation, more than any other single literary work.

His reference to Gray in one of the missives in the controversy, while it is somewhat novel, is not so much an exaltation of the *Elegy* as a disparagement of romantic odes, springing from Byron's mistaken notion of defending his own classical tenet.

Had Gray written nothing but his Elegy, high as he stands, I am not sure that he would not stand higher; it is the cornerstone of his glory : without it his odes would be unsufficient for his fame.[1]

His encomium of Horace Walpole, inspired as it was by the sympathy of position, has the elements of sound criticism, although it is a little too extravagant in parts.

It is the fashion to underrate Horace Walpole ; firstly, because he was a nobleman, and secondly, because he was a gentleman ; but, to say nothing of the composition of his incomparable letters, and of the *Castle of Otranto*, he is the " Ultimus Romanorum," the author of the *Mysterious Mother*, a tragedy of the highest order, and not a puling love-play. He is the father of the first romance and of the last tragedy in our language, and surely worthy of a higher place than any living writer, be he who he may.[2]

When he touches upon Pope, all restraint is abandoned. Then only his imagery and picturesqueness count.

As to Pope, I have always regarded him as the greatest name in our poetry. Depend upon it, the rest are barbarians. He is a Greek Temple, with a Gothic Cathedral on one hand, and a Turkish Mosque and all sorts of fantastic pagodas and conventicles about him. You may call Shakespeare and Milton pyramids, if you please, but I prefer the Temple of Theseus or the Parthenon to a mountain of burnt brickwork.[3]

His explanation of the quality of Sheridan's wit is as

[1] *L. & J.* V, 554.
[2] Advertisement to *Marino Faliero*.
[3] *L. & J.* V, 274.

valuable as it is illuminating, because a thing of the kind cannot be ascertained from the printed page, and Byron made his judgment from intimate contact and observation.

Sheridan's humour, or rather wit, was always saturnine, and sometimes savage : he never laughed (at least that I saw, and I watched him).[1]

Byron's acquaintance with fiction was greater than with any other prose form. He regarded the novel of the eighteenth century in somewhat the same way as he regarded the poetry of the same time. Excepting Scott's, the best days of English fiction were over. Fielding, "the *prose* Homer of Human nature,"[2] was his favorite among the giants of the older period. His meditations upon Fielding in his "Detached Thoughts" are worthy of note.

I have lately been reading Fielding over again. They talk of Radicalism, Jacobinism, etc., in England (I am told), but they should turn over the pages of "Jonathan Wild the Great." The inequality of conditions, and the littleness of the great, were never set forth in stronger terms ; and his contempt for Conquerors and the like is such, that, had he lived *now*, he would have been denounced in "the Courier" as the grand Mouthpiece and Factionary of the revolutionists. And yet I never recollect to have heard this turn of Fielding's mind noticed, though it is obvious in every page.[3]

The remarkable juvenile work of his friend Lewis he praises in a way that has been justified by the permanence of the book.

"The Monk" is perhaps one of the best in any language, not excepting the German. It only wanted one thing, as I told Lewis, to have rendered it perfect. He should have made the

---

[1] "Detached Thoughts," *L. & J.* V, 460-1.
[2] Diary, *L. & J.* V, 149.
[3] *L. & J.* V, 465.

dæmon really in love with Ambrosio : this would have given it a human interest.[1]

Byron's knowledge of the Bible is everywhere recognized. The Scriptures appealed to him, particularly the Old Testament parts, as much for their literary value as for their historical or sacred contents. Kennedy transmits the following appreciation of the witch of Endor scene :

> I have always thought this the finest and most finished witch-scene that ever was written or conceived ; and you will be of my opinion, if you consider all the circumstances and the actors in the case, together with the gravity, simplicity, and dignity of the language.[2]

The passage is one of the last criticisms that Byron made.

Eulogia   The very highest reaches of criticism that Byron ever attained are to be found in several incidental tributes to literary talent and achievement, occurring chiefly in his poetry. These passages are interpretative in nature and appreciative in spirit, and from the genius expended in them are a part of our creative literature itself.

Following the fine apotheosis of the youthful White in *English Bards and Scotch Reviewers*, which has already been cited,[3] is a tribute to one whom Byron admired early and honored long, Samuel Rogers.

LINES WRITTEN ON A BLANK LEAF OF THE
" PLEASURES OF MEMORY "

> Absent or present, still to thee,
> My friend, what magic spells belong !
> As all can tell, who share, like me,
> In turn thy converse, and thy song.

[1] Captain Medwin, *Conversations*, 229. Cp. *L. & J.* II, 368.
[2] *Conversations*, 154.
[3] See Chapter IV, 74.

But when the dreaded hour shall come
By Friendship ever deemed too nigh,
And ' Memory ' o'er her Druid's tomb
Shall weep that aught of thee can die,

How fondly will she then repay
Thy homage offered at her shrine,
And blend, while ages roll away,
Her name immortally with *thine* ! [1]

In one of the " Hebrew Melodies " Byron celebrates the
minstrelsy of the shepherd poet of Scripture in a fine
strain.

THE HARP THE MONARCH MINSTREL SWEPT

The Harp the Monarch Minstrel swept,
The King of men, the loved of Heaven,
Which Music hallowed while she wept
O'er tones her heart of hearts had given,
Redoubled be her tears, its chords are riven !
It softened men of iron mould,
It gave them virtues not their own ;
No ear so dull, no soul so cold,
That felt not, fired not to the tone,
Till David's Lyre grew migthier than his Throne !

It told the triumphs of our King,
It wafted glory to our God ;
It made our gladdened valleys ring,
The cedars bow, the mountains nod ;
Its sound aspired to Heaven and there abode !
Since then, though heard on earth no more,
Devotion and her daughter Love,
Still bid the bursting spirit soar
To sounds that seem as from above,
In dreams that day's broad light can not remove.

[1] Dated April 19, 1812, first published, 1816.

The orator, dramatist, and courtly wit, Richard Brinsley Sheridan, was a member of the inner circle to which Byron belonged in his London convivial days. Byron has commemorated Sheridan's great and varied powers in several very fine appreciations. The first associates him with the more picturesque figure of Burns.

Read Burns today. What would he have been, if a patrician ? We should have had more polish—less force—just as much verse, but no immortality—a divorce and a duel or two, the which had he survived, as his potations must have been less spirituous, he might have lived as long as Sheridan, and outlived as much as poor Brinsley. What a wreck is that man ! and all from bad pilotage ; for no one had ever better gales, though now and then a little too squally. Poor dear Sherry ! I shall never forget the day he and Rogers and Moore and I passed together ; when *he* talked, and *we* listened, without one yawn, from six till one in the morning.[1]

In his journal a month later, in addition to a general encomium, he gives an interesting insight into the softer side of Sheridan's nature.

Lord Holland told me a curious piece of sentimentality in Sheridan. The other night we were all delivering our respective and various opinions on him and other *hommes marquans,* and mine was this :—" Whatever Sheridan has done or chosen to do has been, *par excellence,* always the *best* of its kind. He has written the *best* comedy (*School for Scandal*), the *best* drama (in my mind, far before that St. Giles's lampoon, the *Beggar's Opera*), the best farce (the *Critic*—it is only too good for a farce), and the best Address (Monologue on Garrick), and, to crown all, delivered the very best Oration (the famous Begum Speech) ever conceived or heard in this country." Somebody told S. this the next day, and on hearing it he burst into tears ![2]

---

[1] *L. & J.* II, 320. Dr. Otto Matthiae, *Characteristics of Lord Byron,* construes the whole criticism as referring to Burns.
[2] *L. & J.* II, 377.

Upon Sheridan's death in 1816 Byron pronounced a eulogy, in his well-known *Monody*, with superb critical power and without exaggeration, that has few equals.

> Of human feelings the unbounded lord
>
> . . . .
>
> The matchless dialogue, the deathless wit,
> Which knew not what is was to intermit ;
> The glowing portraits, fresh from life, that bring
> Home to our hearts the truth from which they spring
>
> . . . .
>
> The worthy rival of the wondrous *Three* !
> Whose words were sparks of Immortality ! etc.

Madame de Staël was also for a while among the famous literati with whom Byron associated in London. His reverie upon her works at the time is in his very best meditative manner.

After all, what is a work—any—or every work—but a desert with fountains, and, perhaps, a grove or two, every day's journey ? To be sure, in Madame, what we often mistake, and "pant for," as the "cooling stream," turns out to be the "*mirage*" (critice *verbiage*) ; but we do, at last, get to something like the temple of Jove Ammon, and then the waste we have passed is only remembered to gladden the contrast.[1]

In musing, several years after her death, upon his acquaintance with her, he says :

In knew Madame de Staël well—better than she knew Italy ; but I little thought that, one day, I should *think with her thoughts* in the country where she has laid the scenes of her most attractive production. She is sometimes right, and often wrong, about Italy and England ; but almost always true in delineating the heart, which is of but one nation, and of no country,—or, rather of all.[2]

---

[1] Journal, *L. & J.* II, 326. Cf. *L. & J.* III, 11.
[2] A manuscript note in Countess Guiccioli's *Corinne*.

Byron's appreciation of great private letters as literature—to which he has become so distinguished a contrib-
utor himself—before the general recognition of the type,
is a credit to his critical judgment. His opinion of the
correspondence of Walpole has already been indicated. His
judgment of the letters of Burns is as sound.

They are full of oaths and obscene songs. What an anti-
thetical mind!—tenderness, roughness,—delicacy, coarseness—
sentiment, sensuality—soaring and grovelling, dirt and deity—
all mixed up in that one compound of inspired clay![1]

The Third and Fourth cantos of *Childe Harold* are as well
stored with these eulogistic treasures as the early cantos
are rich in the associations of history and tradition. The
climax of all Byron's criticism is attained in the Third.

> Here the self-torturing sophist, wild Rousseau,
> The apostle of Affliction, he who threw
> Enchantment over Passion, and from Woe
> Wrung overwhelming eloquence, first drew
> The breath which made him wretched; yet he knew
> How to make Madness beautiful, and cast
> O'er erring deeds and thoughts a heavenly hue
> Of words, like sunbeams, dazzling as they past
> The eyes, which o'er them shed tears feelingly and fast.

> His love was Passion's essence—as a tree
> On fire by lightning; with ethereal flame
> Kindled he was, and blasted; for to be
> Thus, and enamoured, were in him the same.
> But his was not the love of living dame,
> Nor of the dead who rise upon our dreams,
> But of ideal Beauty, which became
> In him existence, and o'erflowing teems
> Along his burning page, distempered though it seems.

---

[1] Journal, *L. & J.* II, 376 f.

This breathed itself to life in Julie, *this*
Invested her with all that's wild and sweet ;
This hallowed, too, the memorable kiss
Which every morn his fevered lip would greet,
From hers, who but with friendship his would meet ;
But to that gentle touch, through brain and breast
Flashed the thrilled Spirit's love-devouring heat ;
In that absorbing sigh perchance more blest
Than vulgar minds may be with all they seek possest.

His life was one long war with self-sought foes,
Or friends by him self-banished ; for his mind
Had grown Suspicion's sanctuary, and chose
For its own cruel sacrifice the kind,
' Gainst whom he raged with fury strange and blind.
But he was phrensied,—wherefore, who may know ?
Since cause might be which Skill could never find ;
But he was phrensied by disease or woe
To that worst pitch of all, which wears a reasoning show.

For then he was inspired, and from him came,
As from the Pythian's mystic cave of yore,
Those oracles which set the world in flame,
Nor ceased to burn till kingdoms were no more :
Did he not this for France ? which lay, before,
Bowed to the inborn tyranny of years ?
Broken and trembling to the yoke she bore,
Till by the voice of him and his compeers,
Roused up to too much wrath, which follows o'er-grown
fears ?[1]

Rousseau was a better subject for critical delineation
by Byron than any other that came under the latter's spell,
and Byron was better suited for the task than any other
critic of his time. Representing the extremes of romanti-

---

[1] Stanzas 77-81. Cf., *ibid.*, note 21, and *L. & J.* III, 335. " This
whole passage is a masterpiece of psychological criticism."—P. E. More,
Cambridge *Byron*.

cism of their respective countries, the two men had numerous parallels in their lives and characters. The close resemblance between them was pointed out to Byron many
times. He disclaimed it,[1] but really it was gratifying to
him. In the innate sympathies of the men there is explanation enough for Byron's masterly analysis. But from other
instances in Byron's criticism, in similar vein, that press it
close for honors, it cannot be called mere introspection, or
self-delineation, and nothing else.[2]

The great passages on Voltaire and Gibbon from the same
canto are almost as good.

> Lausanne! and Ferney! ye have been the abodes
> Of Names which unto you bequeathed a name;
> Mortals, who sought and found, by dangerous roads,
> A path to perpetuity of Fame:
> They were gigantic minds, and their steep aim
> Was, Titan-like, on daring doubts to pile
> Thoughts which should call down thunder, and the flame
> Of Heaven again assailed—if Heaven, the while,
> On man and man's research could deign do more than smile.

> The one was fire and fickleness, a child
> Most mutable in wishes, but in mind
> A wit as various,—gay, grave, sage, or wild,—
> Historian, bard, philosopher, combined;
> He multiplied himself among mankind,
> The Proteus of their talents; But his own
> Breathed most in ridicule,—which, as the wind,
> Blew where it listed, laying all things prone,—
> Now to o'erthrow a fool, and now to shake a throne.

[1] Cf., " Detached Thoughts," *L. & J.* V, 408 f., and *L. & J.* I, 192 f.

[2] Cf., " Ce que Lord Byron dit là de Rousseau est bien autrement vrai de lui-même."—Countess D'Haussonville, *Les dernières Années de Lord Byron*, 67.

The other, deep and slow, exhausting thought,
And hiving wisdom with each studious year,
In meditation dwelt—with learning wrought,
And shaped his weapon with an edge severe,
Sapping a solemn creed with solemn sneer;
The lord of irony,—that master-spell,
Which stung his foes to wrath, which grew from fear,
And doomed him to the zealot's ready Hell,
Which answers to all doubts so eloquently well.[1]

The Prophecy of Dante supplies the " matchless portraitures " of the great Italians.

But out of the long file of sonneteers
There shall be some who will not sing in vain,
And he, their Prince, shall rank among my peers,
And Love shall be his torment; but his grief
Shall make an immortality of tears,
And Italy shall hail him as the Chief
Of Poet-lovers, and his higher song
Of Freedom wreathe him with as green a leaf.
But in a farther age shall rise along
The banks of Po two greater still than he;
The world which smiled on him shall do them wrong
Till they are ashes, and repose with me.
The first will make an epoch with his lyre,
And fill the earth with feats of Chivalry:
His Fancy like a rainbow, and his Fire,
Like that of Heaven, immortal, and his Thought
Borne onward with a wing that cannot tire:
Pleasure shall, like a butterfly new caught,
Flutter her lovely pinions o'er his theme,
And Art itself seem into Nature wrought
By the transparency of his bright dream.—
The second, of a tenderer, sadder mood,

---

[1] Stanzas 105-7.

Shall pour his soul out o'er Jerusalem;
He, too, shall sing of Arms, and Christian blood
Shed where Christ bled for man; and his high harp
Shall, by the willow over Jordan's flood,
Revive a song of Sion, and the sharp
Conflict, and final triumph of the brave
And pious, and the strife of Hell to warp
Their hearts from their great purpose, until wave
The red-cross banners where the first red Cross
Was crimsoned from His veins who died to save,
Shall be his sacred argument; the loss
Of years, of favour, freedom, even of fame
Contested for a time, while the smooth gloss
Of Courts would slide o'er his forgotten name,
And call Captivity a kindness—meant
To shield him from insanity or shame—
Such shall be his meek guerdon! who was sent
To be Christ's Laureate—they reward him well!
Florence dooms me but death or banishment,
Ferrara him a pittance and a cell,
Harder to bear and less deserved, for I
Had stung the factions which I strove to quell;
But this meek man who with a lover's eye
Will look on Earth and Heaven, and who will deign
To embalm with his celestial flattery
As poor a thing as e'er was spawned to reign,
What will *he* do to merit such a doom?
Perhaps he'll *love*,—and is not Love in vain
Torture enough without a living tomb?
Yet it will be so—he and his compeer,
The Bard of Chivalry, will both consume
In penury and pain too many a year,
And, dying in despondency, bequeath
To the kind World, which scarce will yield a tear,
A heritage enriching all who breathe
With the wealth of a genuine Poet's soul.
And to the country a redoubled wreath,

Unmatched by time ; not Hellas can unroll
Through her olympiads two such names, though one
Of hers be mighty ;—and is this the whole
Of such men's destiny beneath the Sun ?[1]

Finally, one of the last cantos of *Don Juan* provides an
inimitable study of Cervantes and the effect of his great
work on his country's literature and institutions.

Of all tales ' tis the saddest—and more sad,
Because it makes us smile : his hero's right,
And still pursues the right ;—to curb the bad
His only object, and ' gainst odds to fight
His guerdon : ' tis his virtue makes him mad !
But his adventures form a sorry sight ;—
A sorrier still is the great moral taught
By that real Epic unto all who have thought.

Redressing injury, revenging wrong,
To aid the damsel and destroy the caitiff ;
Opposing singly the united strong,
From foreign yoke to free the helpless native :—
Alas ! must noblest views, like an old song,
Be for mere Fancy's sport a theme creative.
A jest, a riddle, Fame through thin and thick sought !
And Socrates himself but Wisdom's Quixote ?

Cervantes smiled Spain's chivalry away ;
A single laugh demolished the right arm
Of his own country ;—seldom since that day
Has Spain had heroes.   While Romance could charm,
The World gave ground before her bright array ;

---

[1] Canto III, 98-160. Cf. *Childe Harold* IV, 30-41. Even a hostile
critic like Hazlitt can say of passages of the kind :—" The names of
Tasso, of Ariosto, of Dante . . . lose nothing of their pomp or their
lustre in his hands, and when he begins and continues a strain of
panegyric on such subjects, we indeed sit down with him to a banquet
of rich praise, brooding over imperishable glories, ' Till Contemplation
has her fill.' "—*The Spirit of the Age.*

And therefore have his volumes done such harm,
That all their glory, as a composition,
Was dearly purchased by his land's perdition.[1]

Criticism of Manuscripts No study of Byron as critic is complete without a consideration of his criticism of manuscripts and advance pages of
works. The extent and influence of this kind of criticism
is in large part indeterminable because of its privacy. The
rôle was unsought by Byron, but there is good evidence
that he acquitted himself in it with becoming spirit and
talent, whether or not results were always gratifying to
those concerned. From Byron's rank in the popular esteem
of the time, the demands made upon him for this kind of
work must have been considerable.

Applications for such criticism came from two sources,
from his admirers among men of letters[2] and other aspir-
ing authors, and from his publishers. The latter, after
his identification with the house of John Murray, may be
regarded as a pretty constant thing.

As early as 1811 Byron is asked by his publisher, Caw-
thorne, for an opinion on a work by a celebrated author.

He wants me to read the MS (if he obtains it), which I shall
do with great pleasure ; but I should be very cautious in ventur-
ing an opinion on her whose *Cecilia* Dr. Johnson superintended.
If he lends it to me, I shall put it in the hands of Rogers and
Moore, who are truly men of taste.[3]

After a reading of *Roncesvaux*, a poem on the old Roland
material by J. H. Merivale in 1814, he responds to the author
magnanimously.

---

[1] Canto XIII, 9-11.
[2] The influence of Byron's hand in this employment has already
been seen in two notable cases, the *Lalla Rookh* of Moore and the
Story of Rimini of Leigh Hunt.
[3] *L. & J.* II, 87 f. Cf. *ibid.*, 88.

I have redde *Roncesvaux* with very great pleasure, and (if I were so disposed) see very little room for criticism. There is a choice of two lines in one of the last cantos,—I think " Live and protect " better, because " Oh who ? " implies a doubt of Roland's power or inclination. I would allow the—but that point you yourself must determine on—I mean the doubt as to where to place a part of the Poem, whether between the actions or no . . . . You have written a very noble Poem, and nothing but the detestable taste of the day can do you harm—but I think you will beat it. Your measure is uncommonly well-chosen and wielded.[1]

Two or three months later, with a little casual judgment of his own, he refers the work of an unknown author to Murray for criticism and answer.

I send you a poem as sent to me in MS for criticism, with the Author's letter, and will feel obliged if you will send it back to the man tomorrow (see his address in the letter) with any or no answer. The title and Subject would be thought original; but in Rochester's poems mention is made of a *play* with the like delicate appellation. Who the man is I know not ; by his letter he seems silly, and by his poem, insane.[2]

He says of Hoppner's elegy sent to him at Venice in 1817:

I think your Elegy a remarkably good one, not only as a composition, but both the politics and poetry contain a far greater proportion of truth and generosity than belongs to the times, or to the professors of these opposite pursuits, which usually agree only in one point, as extremes meet. I do not know whether you wished me to retain the copy, but I shall retain it till you tell me otherwise ; and am very much obliged by the perusal.[3]

Late in his Italian residence he solicits Moore in highly humorous fashion in behalf of his friend Taaffe's work on Dante.

[1] *L. & J.* III, 5. Cf. *ibid.* II, 123, 143, etc.
[2] *L. & J.* III, 74.
[3] *L. & J.* IV, 189.

There is here Mr. Taaffe, an Irish genius, with whom we are acquainted. He hath written a really *excellent* Commentary on Dante, full of new and true information and much ingenuity. But his verse is such as it hath pleased God to endue him withal. Nevertheless, he is so firmly persuaded of its equal excellence, that he won't divorce the Commentary from the traduction, as I ventured delicately to hint,—not having the fear of Ireland before my eyes, and upon the presumption of having shotten very well in his presence (with common pistols too, not with my Manton's) the day before.

But he is eager to publish all, and must be gratified, though the Reviewers will make him suffer more tortures than there are in his original. Indeed, the *Notes* are well worth publication; but he insists upon the translation for company, so that they will come out together, like Lady C**t chaperoning Miss**. I read a letter of yours to him yesterday, and he begs me to write to you about his Poeshie. He is really a good fellow, apparently, and I dare say that his verse is very good Irish.

Now, what shall we do for him ? He says that he will risk part of the expense with the publisher. He will never rest till he is published and abused—for he has a high opinion of himself —and I see nothing left but to gratify him, so as to have him abused as little as possible ; for I think it would kill him. You must write, then, to Jeffrey to beg him *not* to review him, and I will do the same to Gifford, through Murray. Perhaps they might notice the Comment without touching the text. But I doubt the dogs—the text is too tempting.[1]

Murray had formed the habit of applying to him, as the greatest of his authors, as early as December, 1813, for opinions on projected works.

I have redde through your Persian Tales, and have taken the liberty of making some remarks on the *blank* pages. There are many beautiful passages, and an interesting story ; and I cannot give you a stronger proof that such is my opinion, than by the *date* of the *hour—two o'clock*,—till which it has kept me

[1] *L. & J.* V, 475 f.

awake *without a yawn.* The conclusion is not quite correct in *costume* : there is no *Mussulman suicide* on record—at least for *love.* But this matters not. The tale must have been written by some one who has been on the spot, and I wish him, and he deserves, success. Will you apologise to the author for the liberties I have taken with his MS ? Had I been less awake to, and interested in, his theme, I had been less obtrusive : but you know *I* always take this in good part, and I hope he will. It is difficult to say what *will* succeed, and still more to pronounce what *will not. I* am at this moment in *that uncertainty* (on your *own* score) ; and it is no small proof of the author's powers to be able to *charm* and *fix* a *mind's* attention on similar subjects and climates in such a predicament.[1]

From Italy in 1817 he writes on a mission of the kind:

Mr. Maturin's bankrupt tragedy . . . . is the absurd work of a clever man. I think it might have done upon the stage, if he had made Manuel (by some trickery, in a masque or vizor) fight his own battle, instead of employing Molineux as his champion ; and, after defeating Torrismond, have made him spare the son of his enemy, by some revulsion of feeling, not incompatible with a character of extravagant and distempered emotions. But as it is, what with the Justiza, and the ridiculous conduct of the whole *dram. pers.* (for they are all as mad as Manuel, who surely must have had greater interest with a corrupt bench than a distant relation and heir presumptive, somewhat suspect of homicide), I do not wonder at its failure. As a play, it is impracticable ; as a poem, no great things.[2]

By 1820 there is an intimation that he is growing a little restive under so much enquiry and request from Murray.

---

[1] *L. & J.* II, 299. The Tales were by Gally Knight, a Cambridge friend, whom Byron elsewhere has characterized as " translating his way up Parnassus," and, " Between whom and Sotheby there is the difference of the foam of a washing-tub from the froth of a syllabub."
[2] *L. & J.* IV, 134 f. A month later he says of *Manuel,* " With the exception of a few capers, it is as heavy a nightmare as was ever bestrode by indigestion."

Why do you ask me for opinions of your ragamuffins ? You see what you get by it ; but recollect, I never give opinions till required.[1]

The nature and value of this mode of criticism are in great part unknown because it was often written on the manuscripts, and when the benefit was derived the criticism was lost. But it seemed valuable to a shrewd publisher like Murray, and his estimate is not to be contemned.

Critical Extravaganza The audacity that characterizes Byron's criticism as a whole amounts now and then to the abandonment of all restraint.[2] He is dominated at such times by some splenetic mood—caused, it may have been, by physical discomfort or mental unquiet or by some discord to his super-refined sensibilities—and a wish to startle by some unexpected turn of phrase and thought. The special character of such criticism is its abnegation of all taste and decorum. From the somewhat savage *jeux d'esprit* impulse behind, criticism of the kind need of course never be taken very seriously.

Before his return from the first pilgrimage Byron indulges in a little critical license with the protégé, singularly enough, of the future Lady Byron.

EPITAPH FOR JOSEPH BLACKETT
Late poet and shoemaker

Stranger ! behold, interred together,
The *souls* of learning and of leather.
Poor Joe is gone, but left his *all* ;
You'll find his relics in a *stall*.
His works were neat, and often found
Well stitched, and with *morocco* bound.

---

[1] *L. & J.* V, 84. Cf. *ibid.* III, 60, 246, VI, 7, etc.
[2] "Auch in Bezug auf Bücher und ihre Verfasser hatte er seine Launen."—Karl Elze, *Byron*, 376.

Tread lightly—where the bard is laid
He cannot mend the shoe he made ;
Yet is he happy in his hole,
With verse immortal as his *sole*.
But still to business he held fast,
And stuck to Phoebus to the *last*.
Then who shall say so good a fellow
Was only " leather and prunella " ?
For character—he did not lack it ;
And if he did, ' twere shame to " Black-it."[1]

Critical discrimination is shown in the individual items, and emphatic point in the conclusion of some " Versicles " of March, 1817.

I read the " Christabel ";
     Very well :
I read the " Missionary ";
     Pretty-very :
I tried at " Ilderim ";
     Ahem !
I read a sheet of " Marg'ret of *Anjou* ";
     Can you ?
I turned a page of Webster's " Waterloo ";
     Pooh ! Pooh !
I looked at Wordsworth's milk-white " Rylstone Doe ";
     Hillo !
I read " Glenarvon," too, by Caro. Lamb—
     God damn !

In a provokingly clever way that has few parallels, he writes at Murray's request the well-known " civil and delicate declension for the medical tragedy " of Byron's physician, Dr. Polidori. He found zest for the task in his own distaste for the man.

---

[1] Malta, May 16, 1811.

Dear Doctor, I have read your play,
Which is a good one in its way,—
Purges the eyes and moves the bowels,
And drenches handkerchiefs like towels
With tears, that, in a flux of grief,
Afford hysterical relief
To shattered nerves and quickened pulses,
Which your catastrophe convulses.

I like your moral and machinery;
Your plot, too, has such scope for Scenery;
Your dialogue is apt and smart;
The play's concoction full of art;
Your hero raves, your heroine cries,
All stab, and every body dies.
In short, your tragedy would be
The very thing to hear and see;
And for a piece of publication,
If I decline on this occasion,
It is not that I am not sensible
To merits in themselves ostensible,
But—and I grieve to speak it—plays
Are drugs—mere drugs, Sir—now-a-days.
I had a heavy loss by *Manuel,*—
Too lucky if it prove not annual.—
And Sotheby, with his *Orestes,*
(Which, by the by, the old Bore's best is),
Has lain so very long on hand,
That I despair of all demand.
I've advertised, but see my books,
Or only watch my Shopman's looks;—
Still *Ivan, Ina,* and such lumber,
My back-shop glut, my shelves encumber.

There's Byron too, who once did better,
Has sent me, folded in a letter
A sort of—it's no more a drama
Than *Darnley, Ivan,* or *Kehama;*

So alter'd since last year his pen is,
I think he's lost his wits at Venice.

. . . .

. . . .

In short, sir, what with one and t'other,
I dare not venture on another.
I write in haste; excuse each blunder;
The Coaches through the street so thunder!
My room's so full—we've Gifford here
Reading MS., with Hookham Frere,
Pronouncing on the nouns and particles
Of some of our forthcoming Articles.

The *Quarterly*—Ah, Sir, if you
Had but the genius to review! —
A smart Critique upon St. Helena,
Or if you only would but tell in a
Short compass what—but, to resume;
As I was saying, Sir, the room—
The Room's so full of wits and bards,
Crabbes, Campbells, Crokers, Freres, and Wards
And others, neither bards nor wits:
My humble tenement admits
All persons in the dress of Gent.,
From Mr. Hammond to Dog Dent.

A party dines with me today,
All clever men, who make their way;
Crabbe, Malcolm, Hamilton and Chantrey,
Are all partakers of my pantry.
They're at this moment in discussion
On poor De Staël's late dissolution.
Her book, they say, was in advance—
Pray Heaven, she tell the truth of France!

. . . .

Thus run our time and tongues away.—
But, to return, sir, to your play:
Sorry, Sir, but I can not deal,

Unless 'twere acted by O'Neill.
My hands are full—my head so busy,
I'm almost dead—and always dizzy;
And so, with endless truth and hurry,
Dear Doctor, I am yours,

JOHN MURRAY [1]

There is good savagery in some stanzas parodying Wordsworth, " the grand metaquizzical poet."

There's something in a stupid ass,
And something in a heavy dunce;
But never since I went to school
I heard or saw so damned a fool
As William Wordsworth is for once.

And now I've seen so great a fool
As William Wordsworth is for once;
I really wish that Peter Bell
And he who wrote it were in hell,
For writing nonsense for the nonce.[2]

His prose contains occasional bits of the same kind of
writing. The " venerable Mokanna," Sotheby, is dubbed

That wretched leper of literature—that Itch of Scribbling
personified.[3]

Belvidera, the heroine of Otway's *Venice Preserved*, is

That maudlin bitch of chaste lewdness and blubbering curiosity[4]

And the German critic, Frederick Schlegel, is

Like Hazlitt, in English, who *talks pimples*—a red and white
corruption rising up (in little imitation of mountains upon maps),

---

[1] " Epistle from Mr. Murray to Dr. Polidori, August, 1817."
[2] " Epilogue," in Byron's hand, on the margin of *Peter Bell*, 1819,
published 1888.
[3] *L. & J.* IV, 228.
[4] *L. & J.* IV, 91.

but containing nothing, and discharging nothing, except their own humours.[1]

The rough vigor of all such criticism is partial atonement for its perversity.

Summary In *The Two Foscari* Byron makes the son, who never speaks jocularly though often bitterly, describe books as,

> Those lying likenesses of lying men.

Despite Byron's remonstrances against interpreting him in his characters, the line may be taken as indicating a certain inherent feeling in him toward all writing in its relation to its authors, and consequently explaining his generally adverse criticism of men and books. It was a part of his moral isolation from which he could not escape. On the other hand, when author or work occasionally pleased him, he gave praise with all the unabated fervor of his being. His judgments, then, show all the impressionism of his volatile nature, and they have all the force of his great genius.

After all, the critic is simply a man who knows a good book when he sees it, whether the book was written yesterday or a thousand years ago, and who, if the book is good, can also tell what is its class and degree of goodness.[2]

---

[1] Diary, *L. & J.* V, 191.
[2] Irving Babbitt, *Nation*, March 28, 1912.

CHAPTER VIII

OTHER ARTS

I speak merely as a *Formarum Spectator* . . . and can give my
opinion as Impartially as I would of a Statue.—*L. & J.* III, 45.

Byron's criticism in other departments than literature
adds nothing to the world's technical knowledge of art.[1]
He is never more than the dilettante in this kind of criticism. But occasionally his judgments on some kindred subjects, which were intimately associated with his experience
or inspired some of his great poetry, add something to the
world's appreciation of artistic things.

Oratory Byron's interest in orators and oratory was for
the greater part of his life close and personal.
His own gifts and early contemplation of a political career[2]
are sufficient explanation of his interest and opinions on
the subject. He regarded oratory as closely allied with

---

[1] For his idea of poetry as superior to other art forms and immaterial
records, see *The Island* II, 87 f.
[2] See Chapter II, 24, etc. His account of his own initial effort in
Parliament is worth recording for its critical content. " I have had many
marvellous eulogies repeated to me since, in person and by proxy,
from divers persons *ministerial*—yea, *ministerial*!—as well as oppo-
sitionists ; of them I shall only mention Sir F. Burdett. *He* says it
is the best speech by a *lord* since the ' *Lord* knowns when,' probably
from a fellow-feeling in the sentiments. Lord H. tells me I shall beat
them all if I persevere ; and Lord G. remarked that the construction
of some of my periods are (sic) very like *Burke's* ! ! And so much for
vanity. I spoke very violent sentences with a sort of modest impudence,
abused every thing and every body, and put the Lord Chancellor very
much out of humour : and if I may believe what I hear, have not lost
any character by the experiment. As to my delivery, loud and fluent
enough, perhaps a little theatrical. I could not recognize myself or
any one else in the newspapers."—*L. & J.* II, 105 f. Cf. *ibid.*, 318.
and " Detached Thoughts," *L. & J.* V, 414 f.

poetry, talent in the one art almost coinciding with talent in the other; and, as is to be expected, his view is exemplified in his own case.

Both *ancients* and *moderns* have declared that the two pursuits are so nearly similar as to require in a great measure the same Talents, and he who excels in the one, would on application succeed in the other. Lyttleton, Glover, and Young (who was a celebrated Preacher and a Bard) are instances of the kind. *Sheridan & Fox* also; *these* are *great Names.*[1]

There is sound judgment, well phrased and convincingly illustrated, in his explanation of the essentially democratic character of oratory, and its dependence upon circumstances and setting for effectiveness.

It is to be recollected, that the most beautiful and impressive doctrines of the divine Founder of Christianity were delivered, not in the *Temple*, but on the *Mount*. To waive the question of devotion, and turn to human eloquence,—the most effectual and splendid specimens were not pronounced within walls. Demosthenes addressed the public and popular assemblies. Cicero spoke in the forum. That this added to their effect on the mind of both orator and hearers, may be conceived from the difference between what we read of the emotions then and there produced, and those we ourselves experience in the perusal in the closet.[2]

The orator he esteemed no less highly than the poet, or any genius, and here and there in his writings is an echo of regret that he did not qualify for the rôle   It was his first choice, but he surrendered it because of unfavorable political conditions and because the career of the poet was, so to speak, thrust upon him.

I have never heard any one who fulfilled my Ideal of an Orator. Grattan would have been near it but for his Harlequin

[1] *L. & J.* I, 126. Cf. *ibid.* II, 242 f.
[2] *Childe Harold* III, note 19.

delivery. Pitt I never heard. Fox but once, and then he struck me as a debater, which to me seems as different from an Orator as an Improvisatore or a versifier from a poet. Grey is great, but it is not oratory. Canning is sometimes very like one. Windham I did not admire, though all the world did: it seemed such sophistry. Whitbread was the Demosthenes of bad taste and vulgar vehemence, but strong and English. Holland is impressive from sense and sincerity. Lord Lansdowne good, but still a debater only. Grenville I like vastly, if he would prune his speeches down to an hour's delivery. Burdett is sweet and silvery as Belial himself, and *I* think the greatest favourite in Pandemonium.[1]

Lord Chatham and Burke are the nearest approaches to Orators in England.[2]

Orators . . . . are things of Ages and not of Septennial or tiiennial reunions.[3]

National or racial character, he implies, has something to do with the gift of oratory.

I doubt greatly if the English *have* any eloquence, properly so called, and am inclined to think that the Irish *had* a great deal, and that the French *will* have, and have had in Mirabeau.[4]

And the great English legislative body was not, in his opinion, in any sense a school of oratory. Furthermore, eloquence was ineffective with it. In this view he is consistent with his notion of the rudimentary and democratic character of oratory.

The Impression of Parliament upon me was that it's [sic] members are not formidable as *Speakers*, but very much so as an *audience*; because in so numerous a body there may be little

---

[1] *L. & J.* V, 411 f.
[2] *L. & J.* V, 412.
[3] *L. & J.* V, 416. He probably would have included Patrick Henry as a real orator. Cf.,
  " Henry, the forest-born Demosthenes,
  Whose thunder shook the Philip of the seas."
                              —*Age of Bronze*, 384-5.
[4] *L. & J.* V, 412.

Eloquence (after all there were but *two* thorough Orators in all Antiquity, and I suspect still *fewer* in modern times), but must be a leaven of thought and good sense sufficient to make them *know* what is right, though they can't express it nobly.[1]

Cicero himself, and probably the Messiah, could never have alter'd the vote of a single Lord of the Bedchamber or Bishop.[2]

Acting Byron's associations with drama were lifelong,[3] and his connection with the stage, both officially and privately, was close for the whole of his life in England. He himself showed histrionic talent quite as early as he displayed oratorical powers.[4] His interest in the theater brought him membership in the Drury Lane management, which office he administered energetically until his untimely exile. His official position gave him opportunity to know some of the most celebrated actors of the day, and his commentary upon them and occasionally upon performances in which they figured often constitutes some interesting, if only ephemeral, criticism.

He says of acting itself :

I am acquainted with no *im*material sensuality so delightful as good acting.[5]

His first bit of dramatic criticism is concerned with the damning of a play at the Haymarket theater near the close

---

[1] *L. & J.* V, 415.

[2] *L. & J.* V, 416.

[3] See Chapters II, 32, and V, 106 f.

[4] "When I was a youth, I was reckoned a good actor. Besides ' Harrow Speeches ' (in which I shone) I enacted ' Penruddock ' in the 'Wheel of Fortune ' and ' Tristram Fickle ' in Allingham's farce of ' the Weathercock,' for three nights (the duration of our compact), in some private theatricals at Southwell in 1806, with great applause. The occasional prologue for our volunteer play was also of my composition. The other performers were young ladies and gentlemen of the neighbourhood; and the whole went off with great effect upon our good-natured audience."—" Detached Thoughts," *L. & J.* V, 445. Cf. *ibid.* I, 189, and V, 454.

[5] *L. & J.* III, 81. For the extreme effect of good acting on Byron see *L. & J.* IV, 339 f., 349.

of 1811. So affected was he that he wrote an entire letter about the experience to his friend Hobbouse.

I, this night, saw *Robert Coates* perform Lothario at the Haymarket, the house crammed, but bribery (a bank token) procured an excellent place near the stage.

Before the curtain drew up, a performer (all gemmen) came forward and thus addressed the house, Ladies, &c., " A melancholy accident has happened to the gentleman who undertook the part of Altamont—(here a dead stop—then—) this accident has *happened* to *his brother*, who fell this afternoon through a *loop-hole* into the *London Dock*, and was taken up dead, Altamont has just entered the house, distractedly, is— now dressing !!! and will appear in five minutes "!!! Such were verbatim the words of the apologist ; they were followed by a roar of laughter, and Altamont himself, who did not fall short of Coates in absurdity. Damn me, if I ever saw such a scene in my life ; the play was closed in 3rd act ; after Bob's demise, nobody would hear a syllable, he was interrupted several times before, and made speeches, every soul was in hysterics, and all the actors on his own model. You can't conceive how I longed for *you* ; your taste for the ridiculous would have been gratified to surfeit.

A farce followed in dumb-show, after Bob had been hooted from the stage, for a bawdy address he attempted to deliver between play and farce.

" Love à la mode " was damned, Coates was damned, everything was damned, and damnable.

His enacting I need not describe, you have seen him at Bath. But never did you see the *others*, never did you hear the *apology*, never did you behold the " distracted " survivor of a " brother neck-broken through a *loop-hole* in ye *London Docks*."

Like George Faulkner these fellows defied burlesque. Oh, Captain ! eye hath not seen, ear hath not heard, nor can the heart of man conceive to-night's performance.

Baron Geramb was in the stage box, and Coates in his address *nailed* the *Baron* to the infinite amusement of the audience, and the discomfiture of *Geramb*, who grew very wroth indeed.

I meant to write on other topics, but I must postpone. I can think, and talk, and dream only of these buffoons.
'Tis done, 'tis numbered with the things that were, "would, would it were to come " and you by my side to see it.[1]

A week later he writes enthusiastically of a fine performance by Kemble to his friend William Harness, the Shakespearean scholar:

Last night I saw Kemble in Coriolanus ;—he *was glorious*, and exerted himself wonderfully. By good luck I got an excellent place in the best part of the house, which was more than overflowing. Clare and Delawarr, who were there on the same speculation, were less fortunate. I saw them by accident,— we were not together. I wished for you, to gratify your love of Shakspeare and of fine acting to its fullest extent. Last week I saw an exhibition of a different kind in a Mr. Coates, at the Haymarket, who performed Lothario in a *damned* and damnable manner.[2]

In his journal of November 16, 1813, there is a notice on *Antony and Cleopatra*, which was being revived at Covent Garden. The perfect reflection of nature—though never commonplace nature—was his ideal of every art. Mrs. Fawcit's rendition of Cleopatra was gratifying to him.

Went last night with Lewis to see the first of *Antony and Cleopatra*. It was admirably got up, and well acted—a salad of Shakspeare and Dryden. Cleopatra strikes me as the epitome of her sex—fond, lively, sad, tender, teasing, humble, haughty, beautiful, the devil!—coquettish to the last, as well with the " asp " as with Antony. . . . . . Cleopatra, after securing him, says, " Yet go—it is your interest," etc.—how like the sex ! and the questions about Octavia—it is woman all over.[3]

Two weeks later he criticises upon the same basis a Turkish play that had been ascribed to him.

[1] *Correspondence* I, 64 f.
[2] *L. & J.* II, 90-1.
[3] *L. & J.* II, 319 f.

Saturday, I went with Harry Fox to *Nourjahad*; and, I believe, convinced him, by incessant yawning, that it was not mine. I wish the precious author would own it, and release me from his fame. The dresses are pretty, but not in costume;— Mrs. Horn's, all but the turban, and the want of a small dagger (if she is a sultana), *perfect*. I never saw a Turkish woman with a turban in my life—nor did any one else. The sultanas have a small poniard at the waist. The dialogue is drowsy— the action heavy—the scenery fine—the actors tolerable. I can't say much for their seraglio—Teresa, Phannio, or * * * were worth them all.[1]

At the close of the season, 1815, he gives to his friend Moore not so much a critique as a vivid semi-official account of the damning of a new play, Mrs. Wilmot's *Ina*.

Mrs. Wilmot's tragedy was last night damned. They may bring it on again, and probably will; but damned it was,— not a word of the last act audible. I went (*malgré* that I ought to have stayed at home in sackcloth for unc., but I could not resist the *first* night of anything) to a private and quiet nook of my private box, and witnessed the whole process. The first three acts, with transient gushes of applause, oozed patiently but heavily on. I must say it was badly acted, particularly by Kean, who was groaned upon in the third act,—something about "horror—such a horror" was the cause. Well! the fourth act became as muddy and turbid as need be; but the fifth—what Garrick used to call (like a fool) the *concoction* of a play—the fifth act stuck fast at the king's prayer. You know he says, "he never went to bed without saying them and did not like to omit them now." But he was no sooner upon his knees, than the audience got upon their legs—the damnable pit—and roared, and groaned, and hissed, and whistled. Well, that was choked a little; but the ruffian-scene—the penitent peasantry—and killing the bishop and princes—oh, it was all over! The curtain fell upon unheard actors, and the announce-

[1] *L. & J.* II, 354.

ment attempted by Kean for Monday was equally ineffectual. Mrs. Bartley was so frightened, that, though the people were tolerable quiet, the epilogue was quite inaudible to half the house. In short,—you know all. I clapped till my hands were skinless, and so did Sir James Mackintosh, who was with me in the box. All the world were in the house, from the Jerseys, Greys, etc., etc., downwards. But it would not do. It is, after all, not an *acting* play; good language, but no power.[1]

His generalizations upon players are most meager. He has more to say of individual actors than of the type.

Players are said to be an impracticable people. They are so.[2]

A year after his pilgrimage he writes a humorously exaggerated portrayal of William Betty, "the young Roscius," to his best of women friends, Lady Melbourne.

Betty is performing here, I fear very ill. His figure is that of a hippopotamus, his face like the bull and mouth on the panels of a heavy coach, his arms like fins fattened out of shape, his voice the gargling of an alderman with the quinsy, and his acting altogether ought to be natural, for it certainly is like nothing that *Art* has ever yet exhibited on the stage.[3]

His utterances upon Kean are almost a characterization. He writes to Webster upon Kean's appearance in the midseason of 1814:

There is a new actor named Kean come out; he is a wonder, and We are yet wise enough to admire him. He is Superior to Cooke certainly in many points, and will run Kemble hard; his Style is quite new, or rather *renewed*, being that of Nature.[4]

He had recorded in his journal the night before,

Just returned from seeing Kean in Richard. By Jove, he is a soul! Life—nature—truth without exaggeration or dim-

[1] *L. & J.* III, 195 f. Cf. *ibid.* III, 231 f., IV, 31, 134 f., etc.
[2] "Detached Thoughts," *L. & J.* V, 443.
[3] *Correspondence* I, 73. Cf. *L. & J.* I, 63 f.
[4] *L. & J.* III, 45.

inution.   Kemble's Hamlet is perfect;—but Hamlet is not Nature.   Richard is a man: and Kean is Richard.[1]

A little before the season is over, he says of Kean's Iago:

Was not Iago perfection ? particularly the last look.   I was *close* to him (in the orchestra), and never saw an English countenance half so expressive.[2]

His later criticism is of the great actor's conduct.   Byron had tried zealously to get Sotheby's *Ivan* produced.   The play was nearly ready for presentation, when, because of some differences with the management, Kean rejected his part, and Sotheby withdrew the play.

As for Kean he is an " *infidus Scurra*," and his conduct on this occasion is of a piece with all one ever heard of him.[3]

Other actors are criticised, for the most part, in a body, often including Kean.

I can conceive nothing better than Kemble, Cooke, and Kean, in their very different manners, or than Elliston in *Gentleman's* comedy, and in some parts of tragedy.   Miss O'Neill I never saw, having made and kept a determination to see nothing which should divide or disturb my recollection of Siddons.   Siddons and Kemble were the *ideal* of tragic action ; I never saw anything at all resembling them, even in *person* : for this reason we shall never see again Coriolanus or Macbeth.   When Kean is blamed for want of dignity, we should remember that it is a grace, not an art, and not to be attained by study.   In all, *not* SUPER-natural parts, he is perfect ; even his very defects belong, or seem to belong, to the parts themselves, and appear truer to nature.   But of Kemble we may say, with reference to his acting what the Cardinal de Retz said of the Marquis of Montrose, " that he was the only man he ever saw who reminded him of the heroes of Plutarch."[4]

[1] *L. & J.* II, 385 f.   Cf. *ibid.*, 387.
[2] *L. & J.* III, 81.   Cf. *ibid.*, 191, and *Correspondence* I, 281.
[3] *L. & J.* IV, 95.
[4] Preface to *Marino Faliero*, note 1.

Of Actors, Cooke was the most natural, Kemble the most supernatural, Kean a medium between the two, but Mrs. Siddons worth them all put together, of those whom I remember to have seen in England.[1]

Music Like many other poets, Byron lacked what is commonly called an ear for music.[2] But, notwithstanding the acknowledged absence of a high lyrical strain in his poetry,[3] music played no mean part in his life. His own musical accomplishments were less than mediocre— a little singing and nothing else[4]—but throughout his life music had all the fascination for him that one expects of extremely sensitive and emotional natures. His Italian residence improved his taste for music.[5] Mention in his letters of some musical entertainment or event is almost constant for the latter part of the period.[6] Opera then in his life took the place of the theatre in England, and he seems to have become sufficiently Italianate to warrant some very modest pretensions to a connoisseurship in the art.[7]

Some of his expressions of his appreciation of music at various periods of his life, and of its power over him, are worthy of recording.

[1] "Detached Thoughts," *L. & J.* V, 437. Cf., "An Occasional Prologue," 13-14, and "Drury Lane Address," 31-35. For slight mention of actresses like Mrs. Mardyn, Miss Kelly, and Miss Smith, see *L. & J.* III, 217, 223, V, 443, etc.

[2] Cf., "I can discover from a poet's versification whether or not he has an ear for music. . . . To instance poets of the present day;— from Bowles's and Moore's versification, I should know that they had fine ears for music; from Southey's, Wordsworth's, and Byron's, that they had no ears for it."—Samuel Rogers, *Table Talk*, 221 f. "Lord Byron, though he loved simple music, had no great organisation that way."—Thomas Moore, *Memoirs* V, 296.

[3] Needless to say, among his poems the *Hebrew Melodies* and several other individual poems were written to be set to music.

[4] He seems to have had some reputation for singing at Harrow and Southwell. See *L. & J.* I, 34, and cf. *ibid.* II, 301, and V, 409.

[5] Cf. *Hints from Horace*, 295-6, and *L. & J.* III, 79.

[6] Cf. *L. & J.* V, 154, 163, 176, 180, etc.

[7] Cf. *L. & J.* IV, 29, 357.

Our evenings we passed in music (he.was musical, and played on more than one instrument, flute and violoncello), in which I was audience.[1]

In the evening, four Swiss Peasant Girls of Oberhasli came and sang the airs of their country ; two of the voices beautiful—the tunes also : they sing too that *Tyrolese air* and song which you love, Augusta, because I love it—and I love, because you love it ; they are still singing. Dearest, you do not know how I should have liked this, were you with me. The airs are so wild and original, and at the same time of great sweetness.[2]

When I turn thirty, I will turn devout ; I feel a great vocation that way in Catholic churches, and when I hear the organ.[3]

Oh ! there is an organ playing in the street—a waltz, too! I must leave off to listen. They are playing a waltz which I have heard ten thousand times at the balls in London, between 1812 and 1815. Music is a strange thing.[4]

Now and then a musical notice occurs, full of flippancy and persiflage according to Byron's fashion, as in his account, to his publisher, of the opera at the Fenice Theatre on the occasion of the feast of St. Stephen in 1816.

The opera and its Syrens were much like all other operas and women, but the subject of the said opera was something edifying ; it turned—the plot and conduct thereof—upon a fact narrated by Livy of a hundred and fifty married ladies having *poisoned* a hundred and fifty husbands in the good old times. The bachelors of Rome believed this extraordinary mortality to be merely the common effect of matrimony or a pestilence ; but the surviving Benedicts, being all seized with the cholic, examined into the matter, and found that " their possets had been drugged " ; the consequence of which was much scandal and several suits at law. This is really and truly the subject of the Musical piece at

[1] *L. & J.* V, 169. The reference is to Long in the Cambridge period. Cf. *Correspondence* I, 297, 300.
[2] Journal, September 24, 1816, *L. & J.* III, 361.
[3] April 9, 1817, *L. & J.* IV, 99.
[4] Diary, February 2, 1821, *L. & J.* V, 199.

the Fenice ; and you can't conceive what pretty things are sung and recitativoed about the *horrenda strage*. The conclusion was a lady's head about to be chopped off by a Lictor, but (I am sorry to say) he left it on, and she got up and sung a trio with the two Consuls, the Senate in the back-ground being chorus. The ballet was distinguished by nothing remarkable, except that the principal she-dancer went into convulsions because she was not applauded on her first appearance.[1]

Rossini was his preference among the Italian composers of the day, although his operas were often ill rendered.

They have been crucifying *Othello* into an opera (*Otello*, by Rossini) : the music good, but lugubrious ; but as for the words, all the real scenes with Iago cut out, and the greatest nonsense inserted ; the handkerchief turned into a *billet-doux*, and the first singer would not *black* his face, for some exquisite reasons assigned in the preface. Scenery, dresses, and music very good.[2]

To the literature on dancing he contributed his judg-ment of *The Waltz*.[3] He himself was debarred from the accomplishment by his physical defect.[4] The fact doubt-less colored his view of the subject.[5] At the same time, there may have been a better cause for his disfavor, in the inferior practice of the art in England.

The whole town of Brientz were apparently gathered together in the rooms below ; pretty music and excellent Waltzing ; none but peasants ; the dancing much better than in England ; the English can't Waltz, never could, nor ever will.[6]

---

[1] *L. & J.* IV, 34 f.
[2] *L. & J.* IV, 214. Cf. *ibid.*, 204, *Correspondence* II, 111, and *Don Juan* XVI, 45, footnote.
[3] Cf. *L. & J.* II, 176, 178, 179, and *Don Juan* IV, 84-5.
[4] Cf. *L. & J.* III, 236, footnote 1.
[5] Cf. " Does Annabella (Miss Milbanke, The future Lady Byron) *waltz* ? It is an odd question, but a very essential point with me."— *Correspondence* I, 88.
[6] Journal, September 25, 1816, *L. & J.* III, 361. See *Don Juan* IV, 84-5, for an account of Italian dancers and dancing.

Painting Commensurate with the influence on his taste for classical music, the Italian residence developed in Byron an appreciation for painting and sculpture.[1] In Greece he was able to enjoy the products of art only amid their natural surroundings.[2] In Italy, on the other hand, he delighted in the many works of art independently of their setting. The Fourth Canto of *Childe Harold* is a memorial to the glory of Latin art,[3] with very many rich traditions indeed but without the beauty of natural setting found in Greece. Subsequently in the controversy with Bowles, it will be remembered, he supported, against his native sympathies really, the side of the question which argued in favor of artificial objects for poetical employment.[4]

It would be idle to say that he ever attained any kind of technical skill as a judge of art, or developed a critical taste for art.[5] He was never more than an amateur in any

---

[1] He " gazed upon the masterpieces of art with a more susceptible, and in spite of his disavowal, with a more learned eye, than can be traced in the effusions of any poet, who had previously expressed, in any formal manner, his admiration of their beauty."—John Wilson, 1845 edition of Byron's *Poems*. His appreciation of the paintings in Newstead Abbey found expression at least only in his residence in Italy. See *Don Juan* XIII, 68 f.

[2] " Relics of ancient art only appealed to Byron's imagination among their original and natural surroundings."—R. E. Prothero, *Byron's Letters and Journals* I, 290. Cf. *The Curse of Minerva*.

[3] " It necessarily treats more of works of art than of Nature."— *L. & J.* IV, 153.

[4] Cf. Chapter VI, 153 f.

[5] Cf., " I leave to learned fingers, and wise hands,
The Artist and his Ape, to teach and tell
How well his Connoisseurship understands
The graceful bend, and the voluptuous swell."
                              —*Childe Harold* IV, 53.
" For I have been accustomed to entwine
My thoughts with Nature, rather in the fields
Than Art in Galleries: though a work divine
Calls for my Spirit's homage, yet it yields
Less than it feels, because the weapon which it wields
Is of another temper."—*Childe Harold* IV, 61-2.

criticism of art. He was the better critic of himself in disclaiming at every turn any knowledge of the subject. What he really had, or came to have, was a deep, uncultivated, but susceptible feeling for certain works of art in whatever form they might be found. As in acting, his professed creed was nature in art, but it is more nearly correct to say that what he demanded was beauty in art. And in painting and sculpture, as in music, his appreciation was measured by the associations awakened in his own life and experience, by the resemblances which the objects bore to some actual beings he had known or to some images of his fancy.

Early in his Italian period he could still contemn painting, after a glimpse of the noble collection in the Manfrini Palace.

You must recollect, however, that I know nothing of painting; and that I detest it, unless it reminds me of something I have seen, or think it possible to see, for which [reason] I spit upon and abhor all the Saints and subjects of one half the impostures I see in the churches and palaces. . . . . Depend upon it, of all the arts, it is the most artificial and unnatural, and that by which the nonsense of mankind is the most imposed upon. I never yet saw the picture—or the statue—which came with a league of my conception or expectation; but I have seen many mountains, and Seas, and Rivers, and views, and two or three women, who went as far beyond it,—besides some horses; and a lion (at Veli Pasha's) in the Morea; and a tiger at supper in Exeter 'Change.[1]

But two years later in the *Prophecy of Dante* he makes the poet say:

> One noble stroke with a whole life may glow,
> Or deify the canvass till it shine
> With beauty so surpassing all below,
> That they who kneel to Idols so divine
> Break no commandment, for high Heaven is there

[1] April 14, 1817, *L. & J.* IV, 107.

Transfused, transfigurated : and the line
Of Poesy, which peoples but the air
With Thought and Beings of our thought reflected
Can do no more : then let the artist share
The palm, he shares the peril. . . . .
Art shall resume and equal even the sway
Which with Apelles and old Phidias
She held in Hellas' unforgotten day.[1]

Apparently the first real attention he ever gave to painting was in Flanders on his way to Italy from England after his exile.   He did not at all admire the Flemish school.   Rubens in particular he detested.

As for churches, and pictures, I have stared at them till my brains are like a guide-book :—the last (though it is heresy to say so) don't please me at all.   I think Rubens a very great dauber, and prefer Vandyke a hundred times over (but then I know nothing about the matter).   Rubens' women have all red gowns and red shoulders—to say nothing of necks, of which they are more liberal than charming ; it may all be very fine, and I suppose it may be Art, for 'tis not Nature.[2]

As for Rubens . . . his works, and his superb " tableaux," he seems to me (who by the way know nothing of the matter) the most glaring—flaring—staring—harlotry impostor that ever passed a trick upon the senses of mankind,—it is not nature— it is not art—with the exception of some linen (which hangs over the cross in one of his pictures) which, to do it justice, looked like a very handsome table-cloth—I never saw such an assemblage of florid night-mares as his canvas contains ; his portraits seemed clothed in pulpit cushions.[3]

When in Flanders, I never was so disgusted in my life as with Rubens, and his eternal wives and infernal glare of colours, as they appeared to me.[4]

---

[1] Canto IV, 28 f.
[2] *L. & J.* III, 332.
[3] *Correspondence* II, 5.
[4] *L. & J.* IV, 107.

Italian painting was at once more pleasing.

The Brera gallery of paintings has some fine pictures, but nothing of a collection. Of painting I know nothing; but I like a Guercino—a picture of Abraham putting away Hagar and Ishmael—which seems to me natural and goodly. The Flemish school such as I saw it in Flanders, I utterly detested, despised, and abhorred; it might be painting, but it was not nature; the Italian is pleasing and their *Ideal* very noble.¹ I also went over the Manfrini Palace, famous for its pictures. Amongst them, there is a portrait of *Ariosto* by *Titian*, surpassing all my anticipation of the power of painting or human expression : it is the poetry of portrait, and the portrait of poetry. There was also one of some learned lady, centuries old, whose name I forget, but whose features must always be remembered. I never saw greater beauty, or sweetness, or wisdom :—it is the kind of face to go mad for, because it cannot walk out of its frame. There is also a famous dead Christ and live apostles, for which Buonaparte offered in vain five thousand Louis ; and of which, though it is a *capo d'opera* of Titian, as I am no connoisseur, I say little, and thought less, except, of one figure in it. There are ten thousand others, and some very fine Giorgiones amongst them, etc., etc. There is an original Laura and Petrarch, very hideous both. Petrarch has not only the dress, but the features and air of an old woman, and Laura looks by no means like a young one, or a pretty one. What struck me most in the general collection was the extreme resemblance of the style of the female faces in the mass of pictures, so many centuries or generations old, to those you see and meet every day amongst the existing Italians. The queen of Cyprus and Giorgione's wife, particularly the latter, are Venetians as it were of yesterday ; the same eyes and expression, and, to my mind, there is none finer.²

Of the *Famiglia di Giorgione* in the same collection he says in his poetry at the time:

¹ *L. & J.* III, 377.
² *L. & J.* IV, 105 f.

And when you to Manfrini's palace go,
That picture (howsoever fine the rest)
Is loveliest to my mind of all the show ;
It may perhaps be also to *your* zest,
And that's the cause I rhyme upon it so ;
' Tis but a portrait of his Son, and Wife,
And self ; but *such* a Woman ! Love in Life !

Love in full and length, not love ideal,
No, nor ideal beauty, that fine name,
But something better still, so very real,
That the sweet Model must have been the same ;
A thing that you would purchase, beg, or steal,
Wer't not impossible, besides a shame :
The face recalls some face, as 'twere with pain,
You once have seen, but ne'er will see again ;

One of those forms which flit by us, when we
Are young, and fix our eyes on every face ;
And, oh ! the Loveliness at times we see
In momentary gliding, the soft grace,
The Youth, the Bloom, the Beauty which agree,
In many a nameless being we retrace,
Whose course and home we knew not, nor shall know,
Like the lost Pleiad seen no more below.[1]

The famous galleries at Florence, Bologna, and other
Italian cities, he visited and enjoyed, but he admired the
Venetian collection most and esteemed Titian and Giorgione
the greatest of Italian artists.

I went to the two galleries, from which one returns drunk
with beauty. The Venus is more for admiration than love ;
but there are sculpture and painting, which for the first time
at all gave me an idea of what people mean by their *cant*, and
what Mr. Braham calls " entusimusy " (i. e., enthusiasm) about
those two most artificial of the arts. What struck me most were,

---

[1] *Beppo*, stanzas 12-14.

the Mistress of Raphael, a portrait ; the mistress of Titian, a portrait ; a Venus of Titian in the Medici gallery—*the* Venus; etc.[1]

I have been picture-gazing this morning at the famous Domenichino and Guido, both of which are superlative.[2]

What a superb face there is in Guido's Innocents in the Gallery ! Not the *Shrieking* mother, but the *kneeling* one,—it is the image of Lady Ponsonby: who is as beautiful as Thought.[3]

I know nothing of pictures myself, and care almost as little ; but to me there are none like the Venetian—above all, Giorgione. I remember well his Judgment of Solomon in the Mariscalchi in Bologna. The real mother is beautiful, exquisitely beautiful.[4]

I re-visited the Florence Gallery, etc. My former impressions were confirmed ; but there were too many visitors there, to allow me to *feel* any thing properly. When we were (about thirty or forty) all stuffed into the Cabinet of Gems, and knick-knackeries, in a corner of one of the Galleries, I told R. that it "felt like being in the Watch-house." I left him to make his obeisances to some of his acquaintances, and strolled on alone— the only few minutes I could snatch of any feeling for the works around me.[5]

Sculpture Byron's sincerest appreciation in art was bestowed upon sculpture. Like painting, it elicited his interest most while he was in Italy, and it applied to the older period of Italian art.

> The kindled Marble's bust may wear
> More poesy upon its speaking brow
> Than aught less than the Homeric page may bear.[6]

His idea of the art, as of all arts, was that it must embody

---

[1] Florence, *L. & J.* IV, 113.
[2] Bologna, *L. & J.* IV, 313.
[3] *Correspondence* II, 49.
[4] *L. & J.* IV, 411.
[5] " Detached Thoughts," *L. & J.* V, 464. For his argument from the painter's art in the controversy, see *L. & J.* V, 549-50.
[6] *Prophecy of Dante* IV, 25 f.

and reflect nature,[1] but it might assemble and refine until the composite product surpassed models and attained an ideal form never realized in nature.

It is the great scope of the Sculptor to heighten nature into heroic beauty; *i. e.*, in plain English, to surpass his model.[2]

Of *sublimity*, I have never seen anything in human nature at all to approach the expression of sculpture, either in the Apollo, the Moses, or other of the sterner works of ancient or modern art.[2]

Canova among moderns he reckoned as one of the world's great masters, and his *Helen* as unsurpassed. This exaggerated estimate is as much the critical opinion of the age as it is Byron's own.

The *Helen* of Canova (a bust which is in the house of Madame the Countess d'Albrizzi, whom I know) is, without exception, to my mind, the most perfectly beautiful of human conceptions, and far beyond my ideas of human execution.

> In this beloved marble view
> Above the works and thoughts of Man,
> What Nature *could*, but *would not*, do,
> And Beauty and Canova *can*!
> Beyond Imagination's power,
> Beyond the Bard's defeated art,
> With Immortality her dower,
> Behold the *Helen* of the *heart*![3]

[1] Cf. His description of Haidee's lingering death in *Don Juan* IV, 61 f:—

> " The ruling passion, such as marble shows
> When exquisitely chiselled, still lay there,
> But fired as marble's unchanged aspect throws
> O'er the fair Venus, but forever fair;
> O'er the Laocoon's all eternal throes,
> And ever-dying Gladiator's air,
> Their energy like life forms all their fame,
> Yet looks not life, for they are still the same."

[2] Letter to Murray on Bowles, *L. & J.* V, 549 f. Cp., *Don Juan* II, 118.

[3] *L. & J.* IV, 14 f. Cf., " Europe—the World—has but one Canova." —Letter of dedication of *Childe Harold* to Hobhouse, and *L. & J.* V, 244.

His best appreciations are in his poetry, where he attains the high rank of interpreter in one art of the greatest products of another.   The superiority of sculpture in his esteem over the related arts is nowhere better shown than in this fact—it frequently inspired his great poetry.   There is no nobler form of criticism.

> There, too, the Goddess loves in stone, and fills
> The air around with Beauty—we inhale
> The ambrosial aspect, which, beheld, instils
> Part of its immortality—the veil
> Of heaven is half undrawn—within the pale
> We stand, and in that form and face behold
> What Mind can make, when Nature's self would fail;
> And to the fond Idolaters of old
> Envy the innate flash which such a Soul could mould.
>
> We gaze and turn away, and know not where,
> Dazzled and drunk with Beauty, till the heart
> Reels with its fulness: there—for ever there—
> Chained to the chariot of triumphal Art.
> We stand as captives, and would not depart.[1]
>
> I see before me the Gladiator lie:
> He leans upon his hand—his manly brow
> Consents to death, but conquers agony,
> And his drooped head sinks gradually low—
> And through his side the last drops, ebbing slow
> From the red gash, fall heavy, one by one,
> Like the first of a thunder-shower; and now
> The arena swims around him—he is gone,
> Ere ceased the inhuman shout which hailed the wretch
>   who won.
>
> He heard it, but he heeded not—his eyes
> Were with his heart—and that was far away;
> He recked not of the life he lost nor prize,

---

[1] *Childe Harold* IV, 49-50.

But where his rude hut by the Danube lay,
There were his young barbarians all at play,
There was their Dacian mother—he, their sire,
Butchered to make a Roman holiday—
All this rushed with his blood—Shall he expire
And unavenged?—Arise! ye Goths, and glut your ire![1]

Or, turning to the Vatican, go see
Laocoön's torture dignifying pain—
A Father's love and Mortal's agony
With an Immortal's patience blending:—Vain
The struggle—vain, against the coiling strain
And gripe, and deepening of the dragon's grasp
The Old Man's clench; the long envenomed chain
Rivets the living links,—the enormous Asp
Enforces pang on pang, and stifles gasp on gasp.[2]

Or view the Lord of the unerring bow,
The God of Life, and Poesy, and Light—
The Sun in human limbs arrayed, and brow
All radiant from his triumph in the fight;
The shaft hath just been shot—the arrow bright
With an Immortal's vengeance:—in his eye
And nostril beautiful Disdain, and Might
And Majesty, flash their full lightnings by,
Developing in that one glance the Deity.

But in his delicate form—a dream of Love,
Shaped by some solitary Nymph, whose breast
Longed for a deathless lover from above,
And maddened in that vision—are exprest
All that ideal Beauty ever blessed
The mind with in its most unearthly mood,

---

[1] *Childe Harold* IV, 140-1. The hostile critic Hazlitt, two years after Byron's death, pronounced this passage the finest in Byron:— "I think the finest stanza in Lord Byron is that where he describes the *Dying Gladiator*, who falls and does not hear the shout of barbarous triumph echoing from these very walls."—*Collected Works* IX, 234. Cf. *Don Juan* IV, 61.

[2] *Childe Harold* IV, 160.

When each conception was a heavenly Guest—
A ray of Immortality—and stood,
Starlike, around, until they gathered to a God !
And if it be Prometheus stole from Heaven
The fire which we endure—it was repaid
By him to whom the energy was given
Which this poetic marble hath arrayed
With an eternal Glory—which, if made
By human hands, is not of human thought—
And Time himself hath hallowed it, nor laid
One ringlet in the dust—nor hath it caught
A tinge of years, but breathes the flame with which 'twas
wrought.[1]

The reader will recognize familiar subjects in all such passages, in both the poetry and the objects described.

Architecture In all his travels, among all the fine edifices in the many styles of architecture which he saw, Byron has made no criticism of any building or group of buildings that is worthy of his talent. Churches, mosques, cathedrals, temples, a dungeon or two, as many amphitheatres and arches, and an occasional palace, attracted his interest enough for an appreciation here and there. But any mention of the kind is rarely more than a laudation,[2] although these are sometimes of sufficient critical or interpretative nature to demand attention. Of all branches of art he knew and appreciated architecture least.

Places of worship of any and all faiths seemed to interest him most.

Of Constantinople you will find many descriptions in different travels ; but Lady Mary Wortley errs strangely when she says,

---

[1] *Childe Harold* IV, 161-3.
[2] Byron's attachment to Newstead Abbey inspired three celebrations in his poetry, nothing more, except brief references to the place. See " Elegy on Newstead Abbey " in *Hours of Idleness*, " Newstead Abbey," 1811, and *Don Juan* XIII, 55 f.

" St. Paul's would cut a strange figure by St. Sophia's." I have been in both, surveyed them inside and out attentively. St. Sophia's is undoubtedly the most interesting from its immense antiquity, and the circumstance of all the Greek emperors, from Justinian, having been crowned there, and several murdered at the altar, besides the Turkish Sultans who attend it regularly. But it is inferior in beauty and size to some of the mosques, particularly " Soleyman," etc., and not to be mentioned in the same page with St. Paul's (I speak like a *Cockney*). However, I prefer the Gothic cathedral of Seville to St. Paul's, St. Sophia's, and any religious building I have ever seen.[1]

Of the amphitheatre at Verona and the reputed tomb of Juliet he says:

The amphitheatre is wonderful—beats even Greece. Of the truth of Juliet's story they seem tenacious to a degree, insisting on the fact—giving a date (1303), and showing a tomb. It is a plain, open, and partly decayed sarcophagus, with withered leaves in it, in a wild and desolate conventual garden, once a cemetery, now ruined to the very graves. The situation struck me as very appropriate to the legend, being blighted as their love.[2]

The Church of St. Mark, the ducal palace, and the dungeon by the " Bridge of Sighs " make up the whole subject of an unfinished poem on Venice, in the metre of *Christabel.* Of the palace and church he says:

> It is a princely colonnade !
> And wrought around a princely place,
> When that vast edifice displayed
> Looks with its venerable face
> Over the far and subject sea,
> Which makes the fearless isles so free !
> And 'tis a strange and noble pile,
> Pillared into many an aisle :

[1] *L. & J.* I, 281-2.
[2] *L. & J.* III, 386-7. Cf. *ibid.* IV, 4 f., 13.

Every pillar fair to see,
Marble—jasper—and porphyry—
The Church of St. Mark—which stands hard by
With fretted pinnacles on high,
And Cupola and minaret :
More like the mosque of orient lands,
Than the fanes wherein we pray,
And Mary's blesséd likeness stands.[1]

The tomb of Cecelia Metella is celebrated in a few stanzas of *Childe Harold*, but the author is interested more in the tenant than in the tomb.

There is a stern round tower of other days,
Firm as a fortress, with its fence of stone,
Such as an army's baffled strength delays,
Standing with half its battlements alone,
And with two thousand years of ivy grown,
The garland of Eternity, where wave
The green leaves over all by Time o'erthrown ;—
What was this tower of strength ? within its cave
What treasure lay so locked, so hid ?—A woman's grave.[2]

A stanza upon the Pantheon, apostrophic as it is, is his best criticism of architectural subjects.

Simple, erect, severe, austere, sublime—
Shrine of all saints and temple of all Gods,
From Jove to Jesus—spared and blest by Time—
Looking tranquillity, while falls or nods
Arch—empire—each thing round thee—and Man plods
His way through thorns to ashes—glorious Dome !
Shalt thou not last ? Time's scythe and Tyrants' rods
Shiver upon thee—sanctuary and home
Of Art and Piety—Pantheon !—pride of Rome ![3]

---

[1] Dec. 6, 1816, not published till 1901.
[2] Canto IV, 99.
[3] Canto IV, 146.

But it was reserved for St. Peter's to excite his greatest admiration among buildings and to hold it undiminished to the end.

But lo! the Dome—the vast and wondrous Dome,
To which Diana's marvel was a cell—
Christ's mighty shrine above His martyr's tomb!
I have beheld the Ephesian miracle—
Its columns strew the wilderness, and dwell
The hyæna and the jackal in their shade;
I have beheld Sophia's bright roofs swell
Their glittering mass i' the Sun, and have surveyed
Its sanctuary the while the usurping Moslem prayed;

But thou, of temples old, or altars new,
Standest alone—with nothing like to thee—
Worthiest of God, the Holy and the True!
Since Zion's desolation, when that He
Forsook his former city, what could be,
Of earthly structures, in His honour piled,
Of a sublimer aspect? Majesty—
Power—Glory—Strength—and Beauty all are aisled
In this eternal Ark of worship undefiled.

Enter: its grandeur overwhelms thee not:
And why? it is not lessened—but thy mind,
Expanded by the Genius of the spot,
Has grown colossal, and can only find
A fit abode wherein appear enshrined
Thy hopes of Immortality—and thou
Shalt one day, if found worthy, so defined
See thy God face to face, as thou dost now
His Holy of Holies—nor be blasted by his brow.[1]

[1] *Childe Harold* IV, 153-5. Cf. *Prophecy of Dante* IV, 50 f., for an equally fine tribute.
For a full study of Byron in his relation to art see Manfred Eimer, *Byron und die Kunst.*

CHAPTER IX

SELF-CRITICISM

I really cannot know whether I am or am not the Genius you
are pleased to call me, but I am very willing to put up with the
mistake, if it be one. It is a title dearly enough bought by most
men, to render it endurable, even when not quite clearly made
out, which it never *can* be till the Posterity, whose decisions
are merely dreams to ourselves, has sanctioned or denied it,
while it can touch us no further.—*L. & J.* VI, 88.

It is a mere truism to say that Byron was not the best
judge of his own works. Customarily he is dismissed somewhat contemptuously as a self-critic, because he condemned
for a while his own writings as a part of " the System,"
and preferred temporarily his own imitation of Horace to
his other poetry. But this opinion, as we shall see, is not
just to him.

He has not expressed himself adequately on his literary
character—on his talent, on his style of writing, on his
works as a whole, or on any single production of his. His
letters to his publishers are full of changes and corrections
of works then in the press, which Moore calls "the fastidiousness of his self-crtiticism."[1] But all such revisions and
amendments possess only a minor importance as criticism.[2]

---

[1] *Life* II, 334.
[2] One or two examples will suffice to show their character. The
first is a note to Dallas on *Childe Harold*, the second is a whole letter
to Lord Holland on the *Drury Lane Address*.
" *Lisboa* is the Portuguese word, consequently the very best.
Ulissipont is pedantic ; and as I have *Hellas* and *Eros* not long before,
there would be something like an affectation of Greek terms, which I
wish to avoid, since I shall have a perilous quantity of *modern* Greek

SELF-CRITICISM   275

In general, he comments more fully upon those works which
excited discussion at the time.   His self-criticism, then, is
in a manner drawn from him, and more often it is defensive in character, elicited as it was by objections to his
productions, brought to his notice by his publisher.   The
dearth of affirmative criticism is not altogether surprising.
He was the poet of impulsive self-expression, not of calm
self-contemplation, and the exercise of the latter power is
necessary to produce the best self-judgments.

He seems to have had a native lack of confidence in
his self-judging powers, which he never entirely overcame,

in my notes, as specimens of the tongue; therefore Lisboa may keep
its place."—*L. & J.* II, 44.

" Still 'more matter for a May morning'. Having patched the
middle and end of the Address, I send one more couplet for a part of
the beginning, which, if not too turgid, you will have the goodness to
add.   After that flagrant image of the *Thames* (I hope no unlucky wag
will say I have set it on fire, though Dryden, in his *Annus Mirabilis*,
and Churchill, in his *Times*, did it before me), I mean to insert this—

    As flashing far the new Volcano shone
    And swept the skies with $\begin{Bmatrix} meteors \\ lightnings \end{Bmatrix}$ not their own,
    While thousands throng'd around the burning dome,
            Etc., etc.

" I think ' thousands ' less flat than ' crowds collected '—but don't
let me plunge into the bathos, or rise into Nat. Lee's *Bedlam* metaphors.
By the by, the best view of the said fire (which I myself saw from
a house-top in Covent-garden) was at Westminster Bridge, from the
reflection on the Thames.

" Perhaps the present couplet had better come in after ' trembled
for their homes,' the two lines after;—as otherwise the image certainly
sinks, and it will run just as well.

" The lines themselves, perhaps, may be better thus—(' choose,
or ' refuse,'—but please *yourself*, and don't mind ' Sir Fretful.')—

    'As flash'd the volumed blaze, and $\begin{Bmatrix} sadly \\ ghastly \end{Bmatrix}$ shone
    The Skies with lightnings awful as their own.

The last *runs* smoothest, and, I think, best; but you know
better than *best*. ' Lurid ' is also a less indistinct epithet than ' livid
wave,' and, if you think so, a dash of the pen will do.

" I expected one line this morning; in the mean time, I shall remodel
and condense, and, if I do not hear from you, shall send another copy."—
L. & J. II, 148-9.

and in consequence to have trusted to public opinion for estimates of his own works,[1] as of the works of others.

My own opinion upon it is what it always was, perhaps pretty near that of the public.[2]

I really am no judge of those things; and, with all my natural partiality for one's own productions, I would rather follow any one's judgment than my own.[3]

I am apt to take even a critic, and still more a friend, at his word, and never to doubt that I have been writing cursed non-sense, if they say so.[4]

Remember, I can form no opinion of the merits of this pro-duction, and will abide by your Synod's.[5]

It is now two years nearly that MSS. of mine have been in your hands *in statu quo*. Whatever I may have thought (and, not being on the spot nor having any exact means of ascertaining the thermometer of success or failure, I have had no *determinate* opinion upon the subject), I have allowed you to go on in your own way.[6]

A little surprisingly, perhaps, in view of the usual notion of his wilful nature, he was accustomed to venture a part of a work or a work of a certain type, and to take a cue from its reception whether or not to proceed.[7]

There, for the present, this poem stops: its reception will determine whether the author may venture to conduct his

---

[1] " I won't quarrel with the public, however, for the ' Bulgars ' are generally right."—*L. & J.* IV, 237. A comparison of him in this respect with Scott, with whom he is associated more intimately and sympathetically than with any other poet, is interesting:—" It is a singular fact, that before the public, or rather the booksellers, had given their decision, he no more knew whether he had written well or ill, than whether a die thrown out of a box was to turn up a size or an ace."—Lockhart, *Life of Sir Walter Scott* V, 22.

[2] *Drury Lane Address, L. & J.* II, 173.

[3] *Giaour* and *Bride of Abydos, L. & J.* II, 281.

[4] *Ode to Napoleon, L. & J.* III, 70.

[5] *Marino Faliero, L. & J.* V, 66.

[6] *L. & J.* V, 312 f. Cf. *ibid.* III, 337, V, 78, etc.

[7] The fact will partially explain the number of fragments among his works, for most of which he had a real fondness, apparently.

readers to the capital of the East, through Ionia and Phrygia: these two cantos are merely experimental.[1]

I suppose *Lara* is gone to the Devil,—which is no great matter, only let me know, that I may be saved the trouble of copying the rest, and put the first part into the fire.[2]

If you would tell me exactly (for I know nothing, and have no correspondents except on business) the state of the reception of our late publications, and the feeling upon them, without consulting any delicacies (I am too seasoned to require them), I should know how and in what manner to proceed.[3]

I wish the first part to be published before the second, because if it don't succeed, it is better to stop there than to go on in a fruitless experiment.[4]

But there is evidence of a growth of self-confidence as his genius matured and of independence of his former complaisant regard for public opinion. After his departure from England in 1816 he showed a tendency, naturally, to identify the reading public with the "invisible infallibles," as he styled them,—the critics of his works. Upon a manifestation of a popular disapproval of a work, he did not accept the verdict quietly, as he had done earlier, but went "growling back to his jungle," and in his growl there is sometimes good criticism of the work. But the opinions drawn from him in this way are perhaps as much the result of his native combativeness as of any acquired feeling of security in his self-judging powers. The last few years of his life, he wrote, as he says, from habit, not for fame, and showed a tendency to forestall or ignore public opinion by pronouncing upon a work as soon as he had finished it.

---

[1] Preface to *Childe Harold* I and II.
[2] *L. & J.* III, 98 f.
[3] *L. & J.* IV, 248.
[4] *L. & J.* V, 414. Cf. *ibid.* IV, 260, Preface to *The Prophecy of Dante*, Advertisement to the *Morgante Maggiore*, *Don Juan* V, 159, *The Age of Bronze*, xviii, etc. And cp. *supra*, 117-8, footnotes.

I am pretty confident of the *tale* itself ; but one cannot be sure.[1]
You shall submit the MS. to Mr. Gifford, and any other two
gentlemen to be named by you, (Mr. Frere, or Mr.
Croker, or whomever you please, except such fellows as your Galley Knights
and Sothebys ;) and if they pronounce this canto to be inferior
as a *whole* to the preceding, I will not appeal from their award,
but burn the manuscript, and leave things as they are.[2]

Come what may, I never will flatter the million's canting in
any shape ; circumstances may or may not have placed me at
times in a situation to lead the public opinion, but public
opinion never led, nor ever shall lead, me.[3]

The reviews (except one or two—Blackwood's, for instance)
are cold enough ; but never mind those fellows : I shall send them
to the right about, if I take it into my head.[4]

As to myself, I shall not be deterred by any outcry ; your
present public hate me, but they shall not interrupt the march
of my mind.[5]

Every publication of mine has latterly failed ; I am not discouraged by this, because the writing and composition are
habits of my mind, with which Success and Publication are
objects of remoter reference.[6]

The best evidence of this growth, however, is in his individual works, as will be seen in subsequent pages.

**His Talent and Works
as a Whole**

It can hardly be doubted that
Byron believed himself to possess
genius,[7] but he makes no state-
ment concerning its general character.   After the success of

---

[1] *The Corsair, L. & J.* III, 2.
[2] *Childe Harold* IV.—*L. & J.* IV, 165 f.
[3] *L. & J.* IV, 327.
[4] *L. & J.* V, 325.
[5] *L. & J.* VI, 140.
[6] *L. & J.* VI, 173.
[7] Cf. "Whether I am a Genius or not, I have been called such by
my friends as well as enemies and in more countries and languages
than one, and also within no very long period of existence."—"Detached
Thoughts," *L. & J.* V, 460. Cf. *ibid.* VI, 88, etc.

English Bards and Scotch Reviewers, he justly thought his powers satirical and censorial,[1] and maintained a lively belief in them as such for life. The " *Juans* " are full of references to " my muse," but he never sets forth this goddess in her lineaments.

Before he has proceeded far in his juvenilia he pronounces his muse to be " *vastly prolific,*"[2] which is undeniable, though at the time the statement anticipated the evidence. He adjudged accurately the particular quality of his satirical gifts.

As to mirth and ridicule, that is out of my way ; but I have a tolerable fund of sternness and contempt.[3]

After one of his many determinations to quit writing he says :

I have had my day and there's an end. The utmost I expect, or even wish, is to have it said in the *Biographia Britannica,* that I might perhaps have been a poet, had I gone on and amended.[4]

After the success of the Tales, amid the distress of the separation, and in the bitterness of his feelings against England, there is some explanation of his surprising belief that his poetical " *mania* " was associated only with the East.

With those countries, and events connected with them, all my really poetical feelings begin and end. Were I to try, I could make nothing of any other subject, and that I have apparently exhausted.[5]

Five years later he says of the evidence of genius in his make-up :

---

[1] See Chapter IV. Cf. *Beppo,* 79, etc.
[2] *L. & J.* I, 105.
[3] *L. & J.* III, 58. " Tenderness is not my forte."—*L. & J.* II, 255. Cf. *ibid.* III, 101.
[4] *L. & J.* III, 64.
[5] *L. & J.* III, 274. Cf. *ibid.,* 407.

t

I have been reading Grimm's *Correspondence*. He repeats frequently, in speaking of a poet, or a man of genius in any department, even in music, (Grétry, for instance,) that he must have *une ame qui se tourmente, un esprit violent*. How far this may be true, I know not; but if it were, I should be a poet " *per excellenza* "; for I have always had *une ame*, which not only tormented itself but everybody else in contact with it; and an *esprit violent*, which has almost left me without any *esprit* at all.[1]

And of the unsuccessful experience of *The Liberal* he confesses :

My talent (if I have any) does not lie in the kinds of composition which is most acceptable to periodical writers.[2]

It has been seen that Byron at one period of his life condemned in totality the spirit and temper of his own romantic works.[3] But such was unavoidable, with only a little critical self-examination, in view of the subject he was championing in his animosity against the literary leaders of the day. No single work of his was ever out and out condemned by him.[4] On the other hand, hurried as his works were, he was accustomed to hazard none which did not, for the moment, at least, have his critical approval.[5] But his criticism of his poetry as a whole is of little consequence. It is often made impulsively, it is nowhere comprehensive, and it is too subject to change to be everywhere trustworthy.

---

[1] *L. & J.* V, 196.
[2] *L. & J.* VI, 172.
   For expressions upon his muse in *Don Juan*, purporting to be definitive, see cantos IV, 74, XII, 55, XIII, 89, XIV, 13, 54, XV, 64, 97, XVI, 2, etc.
[3] See Chapter VII, 181 f. Cf. *L. & J.* I, 186, V, 77, VI, 88-9, etc.
[4] *English Bards and Scotch Reviewers* came nearest such a fate (see Chapter IV), but he disapproved of it as a critical record only, not as an expression of his powers as a poet.
[5] Cf. *L. & J.* III, 251.

With gentlemanly disdain he declares in 1813:

I don't care one lump of Sugar for my *poetry*.[1]

His comparison of his works with Southey's and Wordsworth's is not the high praise that it may seem to-day,
still it evinces his assurance of superiority.

> When Southey's read and Wordsworth understood,
> I can't help putting in my claim to praise.[2]

And in spite of his seeming indifference, he is hopeful of
immortality.

> Whether my verse's fame be doomed to cease,
> While the right hand which wrote it still is able,
> Or of some centuries to take a lease,
> The grass upon my grave will grow as long,
> And sigh to midnight winds, but not to song.[3]

But his concern for Pope commits him to a disapproval
of his own poetry in great part, and a denial of any popular
character in it.

Your publishers seem to have used you like mine. M. has
shuffled, and almost insinuated that my last productions are
dull. Dull, Sir!—damme, dull! I believe he is right.[4]

I am astonished to see how *little* I have trained on. I wrote
better then than now; but that comes from my having fallen
into the atrocious bad state of the times—partly.[5]

I defy you to show a work of mine (except a tale or two) of
a popular style or complexion.[6]

At present I am paying the penalty of having helped to spoil
the public taste, for, as long as I wrote in the false exaggerated

---

[1] *L. & J.* II, 283.
[2] *Don Juan* I, 222.
[3] *Don Juan* IV, 99.
[4] *L. & J.* V, 51.
[5] *L. & J.* V, 77. The comparison is with *Hints from Horace.* Cf.
ibid., 222.
[6] *L. & J.* V, 243.

style of youth and the times in which we live, they applauded me to the very echo; and within these few years, when I have endeavoured at better things and written what I suspect to have the principle of duration in it, the Church, the Chancellor, and all men—even to my grand patron Francis Jeffrey Esq., of the *E. R.*—have risen up against me and my later publications. Such is Truth! Men dare not look her in the face, except by degrees: they mistake her for a Gorgon, instead of knowing her to be a Minerva.[1]

The later "*Juans*" bring reassurance and a proud unconcern.

> Even I—albeit I'm sure I did not know it,
> Nor sought of Foolscap subjects to be king,—
> Was reckoned a considerable time,
> The grand Napoleon of the realms of rhyme.

> But Juan was my Moscow, and Faliero,
> My Leipsic, and my Mont Saint Jean seems Cain:
> "*La Belle Alliance,*" of dunces down at zero,
> Now that the Lion's fallen, may rise again:
> But I will fall at least as fell my Hero;
> Nor reign at all, or as a *monarch* reign.[2]

> I write the World, nor care if the World read,
> At least for this I cannot spare its vanity.
> My Muse hath bred, and still perhaps may breed
> More foes by this same scroll: when I began it, I
> Thought that it might turn out so—*now* I *know* it,
> But still I am, or was, a pretty poet.[3]

The Translations Popular opinion is under a strange misapprehension in regard to Byron's imputed preference for his *Hints from Horace* over his other

[1] *L. & J.* VI, 88 f.
[2] Canto XI, 55-56.
[3] Canto XV, 60.

works, particularly *Childe Harold*.[1] In reality this preference was felt only at the time of his return from the pilgrimage, and was natural under the circumstances. The
poem was a continuation of the kind of work that had
brought him success, while *Childe Harold* was new to both
the author and the age, and would but subject him to attack
from his old enemies.[2] But before the " *Romaunt* " came
from the press, his delusion had vanished under the sound
judgment of his friend Dallas and of his publisher Murray.[3]

His claim for the *Hints*, even at the time, is certainly
modest enough. It is only a part of the " 4,000 lines, of

---

[1] The error is traceable to Moore. In dismissing the subject he says :
—" It would seem, indeed, as if, while the imaginative powers of his
mind had received such an impulse forward, the faculty of judgment,
slower in its developement, was still immature, and that of *self*-judg-
ment, the most difficult of all, still unattained."—*Life* II, 17. The
strange fact he characterizes as, "An error or caprice of judgment,
unexampled, perhaps, in the annals of literature."—*Life* II, 19. And
later when the preference is existent only in Moore's own imagination,
it " can only, perhaps, be accounted for by that tenaciousness of early
opinions and impressions by which his mind, in other respects so versa-
tile, was characterised."—*Life* IV, 296.

Miss Mayne says :—"What are we to think of this ? It is not alone
in literary history; authors have frequently preferred their failures
to their triumphs ; but such an extraordinary misjudgment as Byron's
remains inexplicable. For in nearly every other case, there has been
some personal reason to explain the unreason. The loved inferior has
in some way touched the writer's heart, has been, autobiographically
or locally, ' his ' book. But here was only a paraphrase—and poor
paraphrase."—*Byron* I, 188.

And W. M. Dixon, in a way that is characteristic of students of
Byron's criticism, reasons from this erroneous instance to his entire
critical ability :—"When it is added that he preferred his own poor
imitations of Pope to ' Childe Harold,' nothing need be added to prove
that Byron's literary judgment was so unreliable as to be utterly
worthless."—*English Poetry from Blake to Browning*, 61.

[2] " My plaguy Satire will bring the north and south Grub Streets
down upon the *Pilgrimage*."—*L. & J.* I, 335, " He said again and
again, that I was going to get him into a scrape with his old enemies." —
Dallas, *Recollections*, 77.

[3] The works were to appear from different presses (Cf. *L. & J.* II,
1, 23, etc.). Within three months after Byron's arrival in England,
he was soliciting Dallas to have the *Hints* delayed until the Romance
could appear. See *L. & J.* II, 44, 54, etc.

one kind or another,"[1] written on his travels, and an "ineffable work "[2]— with a good deal of qualifying banter in his tone. And from his concluding sentence in his request to Dallas to adjust the Latin to the text, it is obvious that his attachment to the poem was not because of its literary merit.

> If you condescend to my school-boy erudition, you will oblige me by setting this thing going, though you will smile at the importance I attach to it.[3]

His later references to the production, rare at that, are only requests to print. For the period of Horace's " *nonum prematur* " he is silent on the subject altogether, which is not the attitude of a man towards an esteemed *chef d'œuvre* of his, which alone among his works of any importance is lying year after year unpublished.[4]

It would be more reasonable to attack Byron's self-critical faculty in his estimate of his translation of Pulci, if his utterances on the subject could be taken literally.

> I sent him also a translation, close and rugged, of the first canto of the Morgante Maggiore, to be published with the original text, side by side, " cheek by jowl gome," on account of the superlative merits of both.[5]

> I look upon the Pulci as my grand performance.[6]

> Why don't you publish my *Pulci* ? the best thing I ever wrote, with the Italian to it.[7]

But his allusions to the work again and again elsewhere are merely as to a translation,[8] and the excellencies he

---

[1] *L. & J.* I, 317.
[2] *L. & J.* II, 56.
[3] *L. & J.* II, 24.
[4] " I have some thoughts of publishing the '*Hints from Horace*,' written ten years ago,—if Hobhouse can rummage them out of my papers left at his father's."—*L. & J.* IV, 425.
[5] *Correspondence* II, 136.
[6] *L. & J.* V, 225, Cf. *ibid.*, 33.
[7] *L. & J.* V, 362.
[8] See Chapter V, 104 f.

ascribes to it are to be understood only as of that category.
He assumes responsibility for nothing else.

About the *Morgante Maggiore, I won't have a line omitted*:
it may circulate, or it may not; but all the Criticism on earth
shan't touch a line, unless it be because it is *badly* translated.
Now you say, and I say, and others say, that the translation
is a good one; and so it shall go to press as it is. Pulci must
answer for his own irreligion: I answer for the translation only.[1]

Moreover, he classified the two poems together, which could
be done upon no other likeness or basis than as translations.

And, pray request Mr. Hobhouse to adjust the *Latin* to the
English: the imitation is so close, that I am unwilling to deprive
it of its principal merit—its closeness. I look upon it and my
Pulci as by far the best things of my doing *if you* will not think
so, and get frightened for fear I should charge accordingly; but
I know that they will *not* be popular, so don't be afraid—publish
them together.[2]

The two works doubtless cost Byron more effort than
any other of his compositions of no greater length, because
of the restraint and application, which they required. He
esteemed other translations but lowly,[3] and it was not unnatural for him to have, in comparison, an exaggerated
notion of his own carefully-wrought works of the kind. He
regarded highly his few lines translated from Dante.[4] But
it cannot reasonably be held that he thought of any of
these poems in the same sense in which he thought of *Childe
Harold* and *Don Juan*. To do so would be to present him
as a greater enigma than is conceivable either of a great
genius or of " an inspired fool."

[1] *L. & J.* V, 17. Cf. *ibid.* IV, 402, 407, VI, 31, etc.
[2] *L. & J.* V, 255.
[3] See Chapter V, 104.
[4] " Have you gotten the cream of translations, Francesca of Rimini,
from the *Inferno* ? "—*L. & J.* V. 6. For Byron's minor translations,
see Franz Maychrzok, *Lord Byron als Übersetzer.*

Individual Works Byron's own line from *English Bards and Scotch Reviewers* on the *Hours of Idleness*, " A schoolboy freak, unworthy praise or blame," is not only about all he has to say of the work,[1] but is about the best thing said on the subject. His opinion of his " ferocious rhapsody," the satire, has been shown already.[2] Of the individual judgments contained in it he ever thought with regret, but on the performance as evidence of his powers he afterward reflected with pleasure.[3]

Fame first came to him from cantos I and II of *Childe Harold*, but his mention of them is brief.[4]

A poem on *Ariosto's plan*, that *is* to *say* on *no plan* at all,[5]

is its introduction to a prospective publisher. Of the fictive character of the hero, against the imputation that author and hero are one, he says:

I by no means intend to identify myself with *Harold*, but to *deny* all connection with him. If in parts I may be thought to have drawn from myself, believe me it is but in parts, and I shall not own even to that . . . . . . I would not be such a fellow as I have made my hero for all the world.[6]

---

[1] For scant criticism of portions of the volume while it is in process or creation see, *L. & J.* I, 113, 121, 122, 124, 186, 205, 259, etc.

[2] See Chapter IV.

[3] " Yesterday I re-read *E(nglish) B(ar)ds*;—bating the *malice* it is the *best.*"—*L. & J.* III, 77. Cf. *ibid.* I, 309, V, 374, etc.

[4] His first opinion of the poem is in Dallas's account. " I could not refrain from expressing some surprise that he had written nothing else: upon which he told me that he had occasionally written short poems, besides a great many stanzas in Spenser's measure, relative to the countries he had visited. ' They are not worth troubling you with, but you shall have them all with you if you like.' So came I by *Childe Harold's Pilgrimage.* He took it from a small trunk, with a number of verses. He said they had been read but by one person, who had found very little to commend and much to condemn : that he himself was of that opinion, and he was sure I should be so too."— *Recollections,* 74. " He varied much in his feelings about it, nor was he, as will appear, at his ease, until the world decided on its merit."—*Ibid.,* 77

[5] *L. & J.* I, 320.

[6] *L. & J.* II, 66.

"I told you his popularity would not be permanent,"[1] he reminds his publisher upon an intimation that interest in the poem is waning. There is a fine literal truth in his last criticism of the poem, before the final cantos are added.

If ever I did anything original, it was in *Childe Harold*, which *I* prefer to the other things always, after the first week.[2]

His most typical work was the succession of romances which followed the first parts of *Childe Harold* and made secure his fame. It was only with this series than he gave up other aims and began to consider himself seriously as a poet. His judgments of the tales severally are as brief proportionately as the time spent on their composition.[3]

The opinion he gives of *The Giaour*, the first of the kind, is as incidental and scrappy as the poem itself. On account of its fragmentary condition and hasty publication under Murray's urgency, he says facetiously:

I shall not open a pye without apprehension for some weeks.[4]

Because of its abnormal growth while in the press, it is a "snake of a poem";[5] upon its appearance it is "that awful pamphlet,"[6] but inasmuch as the hero is "certainly a bad character, but not dangerous,"[7] its moral import is above reproach. After its favorable reception he is outspoken in his approbation.

I do not rate the last in my own estimation at half *The Giaour*.[8]
For my part, I adhere (in liking) to my Fragment. It is no wonder that I wrote one—my mind is a fragment.[9]

---

[1] *L. & J.* III, 25.
[2] *L. & J.* III, 77. Cf. *ibid.* VI, 149, 151.
[3] See *L. & J.* II, 284, III, 56, etc.
[4] *L. & J.* II, 219.
[5] *L. & J.* II, 252.
[6] *L. & J.* II, 262.
[7] *L. & J.* II, 277.
[8] *L. & J.* II, 285.
[9] *L. & J.* II, 372.

The " Bride of Abydos," his " first entire composition of any length (except the Satire, and be damned to it),"[1] was " the work of a week, and scribbled stans pede in uno "[2] to divert his thoughts from some absorbing intrigue, which he but hints at darkly.[3] Consequently, he had no great faith in its merit or expectation of its success.

I am doing my best to beat " The Giaour "—no difficult task for anyone but the author.[4]

On the day of its publication it is

Horrible enough, tho' not so sombre quite as the Giaour.[5]

In the privacy of his journal a week later, he says:

It can't be good, or I should not have stumbled over the threshold, and blundered in my very title.[6]

The Corsair, written " con amore, and much from existence,"[7] he is " pretty confident of . . . but one cannot be sure."[8] But withal it is only

A devil of a long story . . . in the regular heroic measure.[9]

Lara was the subject of a little hesitation in regard to the manner of its publication,[10] but his criticism of it is definite.

I fear you stand almost single in your liking of Lara ; it is natural that I should, as being my last and most unpopular effervescence ; passing by its other sins, it is too little narrative, and too metaphysical to please the greater number of readers.[11]

---

[1] L. & J. II, 291.
[2] L. & J. II, 279.
[3] L. & J. II, 293.
[4] L. & J. II, 285.
[5] L. & J. III, 407.
[6] L. & J. II, 366. Cf. ibid., 300, and Correspondence I, 214, 219. For an account of the purpose for which, the poem was written, see L. & J. II, 308-9.
[7] L. & J. II, 382. Cf., ibid., 400.
[8] L. & J. III, 2.
[9] L. & J. III, 5. For his political views in the poem, see L. & J. III, 13.
[10] See L. & J. III, 103, 109, 113, etc.
[11] L. & J. III, 201. Cf. ibid., 110. Late in life he says of the com-

No further tales of his travel were written till after his marriage, and before the next two appeared—*Parisina* and *The Siege of Corinth*—his domestic tragedy had occurred. The crushing events of his life at the time are sufficient explanation of his slight mention of the two. Neither is " of much pretension, nor intended for it,"[1] as they were written but to stamp scenes that were fast fading from memory.

His estimate of the whole group is raised as they recede with time.

I am very sorry that I called some of my own things " Tales," because I think they are something better.[2]

The next of his tales is *The Prisoner of Chillon*, which was written after his departure from England, although it followed closely the appearance of *Parisina* and *The Siege*. But it and *Mazeppa* are the products of other travels, and on neither has he given us even a scanty judgment.

Byron's Continental tour in 1816 marks the beginning of a new attitude toward his own works. Thereafter they receive a little more critical attention, never full, without so much reliance upon public opinion. The change is observable first in such poems as *Childe Harold* III, and *Manfred*, written within a few months after his leaving England.

What he says first of the former poem is conservative enough, except as it is remembered that his last mention

position of *Lara*, it " was written amidst balls and fooleries, and after coming home from masquerades and routs; in the summer of the sovereigns."—*L. & J.* VI, 81.

[1] *L. & J.* III, 266. For the metrical variation in *The Siege*, see *L. & J.* III, 263. The following passage, doubtless refers to the poem, although, according to Mr. E. H. Coleridge (*Poetical Works of Lord Byron*, 357), the poem was not written at the time:—" And now to the last—my own, which I feel ashamed of after the others;—publish or not, as you like, I don't care *one damn*. If *you* don't, no one else shall, and I never thought or dreamed of it, except as one in the collection. If it is worth being in the fourth volume, put it there and nowhere else; and if not, put it in the fire."—.*L & J.* III, 246.

[2] *L. & J.* IV, 78.

of the early cantos was the highest praise he had given any of his works up to that time.

I have finished a third canto of *Childe Harold* (consisting of one hundred and seventeen stanzas), longer than either of the two former, and in some parts, it may be, better; but of course on that *I* cannot determine.[1]

A few months later, but still before the appearance of the poem, he says:

I suppose Murray has sent you, or will send (for I do not know whether they are out or no) the poem, or poesies, of mine, of last summer. By the mass! they are sublime—*Ganion Coheriza*—gainsay who dares![2]

And again:

It is a fine indistinct piece of poetical desolation, and my favourite. I was half mad during the time of its composition, between metaphysics, mountains, lakes, love unextinguishable, thoughts unutterable, and the nightmare of my own delinquencies.[3]

The Fourth canto receives the same commendation. After quoting the first stanza and part of the second, when he has " roughened off about rather better than thirty stanzas," he exclaims with evident satisfaction:

There! there's a brick of your new Babel! and now, sirrah! what say you to the sample?[4]

A month later, before he has finished the canto:

I look upon parts of it as very good, that is, if the three former are good, but this we shall see; and at any rate, good or not, it is rather a different style from the last—less metaphysical—

[1] *L. & J.* III, 336-7.
[2] *L. & J.* IV, 32. The reference in this passage is not absolutely clear. His poetry of the summer included such poems as *The Prisoner of Chillon* and *The Dream*, and several notable short pieces as well as *Childe Harold III*, but from the expression "the poem," from attendant notes, and from his opinion elsewhere, hardly any other than *Childe Harold* III can have been the production in his mind. Cf. *L. & J.* III, 365.
[3] *L. & J.* IV, 49. Cf. *ibid.*, 46.
[4] *L. & J.* IV, 144.

which, at any rate, will be a variety . . . . . Since this epistle was begun, the stanzas of canto fourth have jumped to *one hundred and four* ; and such stanzas ! By St. Anthony (who has a church at my elbow, and I like to be neighbourly) some of them are the right thing !¹

In a reflective way, which suits well the conclusion of so important a work, he says of the whole poem:

I look upon *Childe Harold* as my best ; and as I begun, I think of concluding with it. But I make no resolutions on that head, as I broke my former intention with regard to *The Corsair*. However, I fear that I shall never do better ; and yet, not being thirty years of age, for some moons to come, one ought to be progressive as far as Intellect goes for many a good year. But I have had a devilish deal of wear and tear of mind and body in my time, besides having published too often and much already. God grant me some judgment ! to do what may be most fitting in that and everything else, for I doubt my own exceedingly.²

The fact that he contemplated other cantos of the poem only a few months before his expedition to Greece,³ when his literary career was all but finished, corroborates his expressed opinion of the poem as the best of his works. Only *Don Juan* shares with it his consistent high regard to the end, and that was not of so long duration.

Manfred is the first poem of consequence in a new vein after Byron's departure from England. It is his first dramatic composition. His first comment on " this sort of dramatic poem " is a brief analysis.

---

¹ *L. & J.* IV, 150 f., 153. Cf. *ibid.*, 153-5.
² *L. & J.* IV, 168. Cp., *ibid.*, 236 f., and cf. :—" I don't feel inclined to care further about *Don Juan*. What do you think a very pretty Italian lady said to me the other day ? She had read it in the French, and paid me some compliments with due DRAWBACKS, upon it. I answered that what she said was true, but that I expected it would live longer than *Childe Harold*. '*Ah but* (said She) *I would rather have the fame of Childe Harold for* THREE YEARS *than an* IMMORTALITY *of Don Juan.*' The truth is that *it is* TOO TRUE !"—*L. & J.* V, 96-7.
³ See *L. & J.* VI, 157, *Correspondence* II, 251, etc.

I forgot to mention to you that a kind of Poem in dialogue (in blank verse) or drama, from which " The Incantation" is an extract, begun last summer in Switzerland, is finished; it is in three acts; but of a very wild, metaphysical, and inexplicable kind. Almost all the persons—but two or three— are spirits of the earth and air, or the waters; the scene is in the Alps; the hero a kind of magician, who is tormented by a species of remorse, the cause of which is left half unexplained. He wanders about invoking these spirits, which appear to him, and are of no use; he at last goes to the very abode of the Evil principle *in propriâ personâ*, to evocate a ghost, which appears, and gives him an ambiguous and disagreeable answer; and in the 3d act he is found by his attendants dying in a tower where he studied his art. You may perceive by this outline that I have no great opinion of this piece of phantasy: but I have at least rendered it *quite impossible* for the stage.[1]

The following month he describes it as

A drama as mad as Nat. Lee's Bedlam tragedy, which was in 25 acts and some odd scenes.[2]

The quality of the acts and the genre to which the whole belongs he pronounces upon specifically.

The 2 first acts are the best; the third so so: but I was blown with the first and second heats. You must call it " a poem " for it is *no drama*.[3]

It is not a drama properly—but a dialogue, still it contains poetry and passion—although I by no means look on it as the best—or conceive that it will be the most fortunate of compositions by the same writer.[4]

His last utterance on the subject sounds the note of independent thinking on the merits of his own works.

---

[1] *L. & J.* IV, 54-5.
[2] *L. & J.* IV, 65-6. Cf. *ibid.*, 80, 86.
[3] *L. & J.* IV, 100. Cf. *ibid.*, 110, 115, for a further estimate of special acts.
[4] *L. & J.* IV, 138.

You say nothing of *Manfred's* luck in the world ; and I care not —he is one of the best of my misbegotten, say what they will.[1]

The group of tragedies with which he thought to reform English drama, were written more under the predominance of a critical consciousness than any other of his poetical works. It was his attempt to set forth specifically and practically the dramatic creed which for a while he preached wholesale.[2] At the same time, there is no one point in connection with his works insisted upon so emphatically as his criticism that his plays were not intended for the stage.[3] And there is little evidence to show that he ever held, when the flush of composition was over, his individual efforts at model drama in very high esteem.[4]

Marino Faliero, as being his first of the kind, receives a little more mention than the others.

The fifth act is nearly completed, but it is dreadfully long— 40 sheets of long paper of 4 pages each—about 150 when printed ; but " so full of pastime and prodigality " that I think it will do.[5]

I *havé* " *put my Soul* into the tragedy " (as you *if* it); but you know that there are damned souls as well as tragedies. Recollect that it is not a political play, though it may look like it ; it is strictly historical; read the history and judge.[6]

[1] *L. & J.* IV, 147.
[2] See Chapter V, 106 f.
[3] He seems really to have had a " constitutional " antipathy to a representation. See his Preface to *Marino Faliero*, most of his other dramatic prefaces, *L. & J.* IV, 72 f., 136 f., *Correspondence* II, 43 f., 198, etc.
[4] " Many people think my talent ' *essentially undramatic,*' and I am not at all clear that they are not right."—*L. & J.* V, 218. "Ah that is a subject in which I have failed; I will write no more tragedies, I think."—Dr. Kennedy, *Conversations*, 158. Cf., Chapter V, 107, footnote 2. Cp., "With the extraordinary blindness to his true characteristics which marked Byron in every self-criticism except that of *Don Juan*, he was persuaded, and he earnestly sought to persuade Murray that in the tragedies he was doing his immortal work."—Ethel Colburn Mayne, *Byron* II, 187 f.
[5] *L. & J.* V, 51.
[6] *L. & J.* V, 67.

It is more like a play of Alfieri's than of your stage (I say this humbly in speaking of that great Man) ; but there is poetry, and it is equal to *Manfred,* though I know not what esteem is held of *Manfred.*[1]

Sardanapalus and *The Two Foscari* taken singly are only explained, briefly and in parts at that, not criticised.[2] The two plays were published in one volume with *Cain* in 1821. Of the trio he says:

I hear that the *Edinburgh* has attacked the three dramas, which is a bad business for *you* ; and I don't wonder that it discourages you. However, *that* volume may be trusted to *Time,*—depend upon it. I read it over with some attention since it was published, and I think the time will come when it will be preferred to my other writings, though not immediately. I say this without irritation against the Critics or Criticism, whatever they may be (for I have not seen them).[3]

It is the best word that he has to say of his plays.

Werner he links with the later mystery, *Heaven and Earth,* in his only critical notice of the play, and pronounces them good jointly.

The *Mystery* I look upon as good, and *Werner* too.[4]

The reader must not be misled into a wrong notion of his estimate of his plays, from his zeal for his " system." It was the system itself which he so applauded, not the individual plays written in partial illustration of it. His indifference to the subject in after life, in addition to his reported confession of failure, emphasizes his conviction that he had not done well in his dramas.

The dramatic piece, *Cain,* as it deserves, received more direct and single critical approval at his hands than any

[1] *L. & J.* V, 81. Cf. *ibid.,* 90.
[2] See *L. & J.* V, 299, 301, 372, etc.
[3] *L. & J.* VI, 64. Cf. *ibid.,* 25, 67.
[4] *L. & J.* VI, 49.

other of his dramatic works. As soon as it was finished he rightly associated its qualities with *Manfred.*

I think that it contains some poetry, being in the style of " *Manfred.*"[1]

I have a good opinion of the piece, as poetry : it is in my gay metaphysical style, and in the *Manfred* line.[2]

It is in the *Manfred* metaphysical style, and full of some Titanic declamation . . . . . . it is in three acts, and entitled " *A Mystery,*" according to the former Christian custom, and in honour of what it probably will remain to the reader.[3]

Because of the attacks made against the play for its irreverence, his later declarations are defensive, in which he asserts its generic conformity and his own orthodoxy, and incidentally gives some fine character analysis.

I beg leave to observe, that there is no creed nor personal hypothesis of mine in all this : but I was obliged to make Cain and Lucifer talk consistently, and surely this has always been per mitted to poesy. Cain is a proud man : if Lucifer promised him kingdoms, etc., it would *elate* him : the object of the Demon is to *depress* him still further in his own estimation than he was before, by showing him infinite things and his own abasement, till he falls into the frame of mind that leads to the Catastrophe, from mere *internal* irritation, *not* premeditation, or envy of *Abel* (which would have made him contemptible), but from the rage and fury against the inadequacy of his state to his conceptions, and which discharges itself rather against Life, and the Author of Life, than the mere living. His subsequent remorse is the natural effect of looking on his sudden deed. Had the *deed* been *premeditated*, his repentance would have been tardier.[4]

Cain is nothing more than a drama, not a piece of argument :

[1] *L. & J.* V, 360.
[2] *L. & J.* V, 361.
[3] *L. & J.* V, 368. See the same letter for an analytical account of the play. Cf. *Correspondence* II, 197, 202.
[4] *L, & J.* V, 470.

if Lucifer and Cain speak as the first Murderer and the first Rebel may be supposed to speak, surely all the rest of the personages talk also according to their characters—and the stronger passions have ever been permitted to the drama.[1]

Of his two remaining dramatic compositions, *Heaven and Earth* and *The Deformed Transformed*, the former, which is associated in critical mention with *Werner* above, is only " a lyrical drama on a scriptural subject,"[2] " less speculative than *Cain*, and very pious,"[3] while the latter is unmentioned in his works.

Parts of *Don Juan* were written and published even before Byron undertook the practical regeneration of English drama. The various cantos occupied him several years, and before his death he had indicated enough material to continue them almost indefinitely.[4] The poem is recognized as his last great—perhaps his greatest—achievement, and his criticism of it, therefore, well may conclude, except a few phrases on his shorter poems, his commentary on his own works.[5]

His first mention of the poem is a sensible characterization. It is of the first canto only.

I have finished the first canto (a long one, of about 180 octaves) of a poem in the style and manner of *Beppo*, encouraged by the good success of the same. It is called *Don Juan*, and is meant to be a little quietly facetious upon everything. But I doubt whether it is not—at least, as for as it has gone—too free for these very modest days.[6]

His surmise was correct. The " Synod " hesitated at the "immorality" of the poem, and Byron replied in its defense.

---

[1] *L. & J.* VI, 16.　Cf. *ibid.*, 31 f.
[2] *L. & J.* V, 475.　Cf. *ibid.* V, 474, and VI, 30.
[3] *L. & J.* VI, 31.　Cf. *ibid.* V, 473, and VI, 47.
[4] See *L. & J.* VI, 429.
[5] For a discussion of the type of the poem see Chapter V, 98 f.
[6] *L. & J.* IV, 260.

I maintain that it is the most moral of poems ; but if people won't discover the moral, that is their fault, not mine.[1]

By this time the second canto had been composed, and he was confident of the quality of the two parts, independently of critical opinion.

I care nothing for what may be said, or thought, or written, on the Subject. If the poem is, or appears, dull, it will fail ; if not, it will succeed.[2]
You shan't make *Canticles* of my cantos. The poem will please, if it is lively ; if it is stupid, it will fail ; but I will have none of your damned cutting and slashing.[3]

The tone of the work, as well, was accepted as more serious than he intended. He remonstrated against such an interpretation, two or three days before the cantos were published.

But a truce with these reflections. You are too earnest and eager about a work never intended to be serious. Do you suppose that I could have any intention but to giggle and make giggle ? —a playful satire, with as little poetry as could be helped, was what I meant : and as to the indecency, do, pray, read in Boswell what Johnson, the sullen moralist, says of *Prior* and Paulo Purgante.[4]

But the outcry which the poem raised affected him,[5] as appeared in the spirit in which he did the next three cantos, and in his opinion of them.

I have not yet sent off the Cantos, and have some doubt whether they ought to be published, for they have not the Spirit of the first : the outcry has not frightened but it has *hurt*

[1] *L. & J.* IV, 279.
[2] *L. & J.* IV, 281 f.
[3] *L. & J.* IV, 283. Cf. *ibid.*, 285, 294-5.
[4] *L. & J.* IV, 343. Cf. *Correspondence* II, 97, 108 f., 122, 125.
[5] The reader will recall that the Reply to *Blackwood's* was stimulated by an attack upon the writer of *Don Juan* I & II.

me, and I have not written *con amore* this time. It is very decent, however, and as dull, " as the last new Comedy."[1]

I told you long ago that the new Cantos were *not* good, and I also *told you a reason* . . . I told you that I wrote on with no good will—that I had been, *not* frightened, but *hurt* by the outcry.[2]

A year later, however, just after the appearance of the new parts, he has regained his confidence, and " Richard is himself again."

I tell you, it will be long before you see anything half so good as poetry or writing . . . . . . I have read over the poem carefully, and I tell you, *it is poetry.* Your little envious knot of parson-poets may say what they please : time will show that I am not in this instance mistaken.[3]

I read over the *Juans*, which are excellent. Your Synod was quite wrong ; and so you will find by and bye.[4]

You will be a long time before you publish a better poem.[5]

His letters convey little criticism of the next several cantos,[6] but there is no evidence that his opinion is falling.

I have carried *D. J.* through a siege to St. Petersburg, etc., and thence to *England* : how do you like that ? I have no wish to break off our connection, but if you are to be blown about with every wind, what can I do ? You are wrong, for there will be a *reaction,*—you will see that by and bye.[7]

This was when four new cantos had been completed, without comment, and " a fifth (the 10th) finished, but not transcribed yet ; and the *eleventh* begun."[8]

The poem itself contains the best he has to say of the work at the time.

[1] *L. & J.* IV, 402. Cf. *ibid.*, 366, 383.
[2] *L. & J.* V, 16. Cf. *ibid.*, 66, and *Correspondence* II, 125, 132, 145.
[3] *L. & J.* V, 351 f.
[4] *L. & J.* V, 359. Cf. *Correspondence* II, 198 f.
[5] *L. & J.* V, 471. Cf. *ibid.*, 467.
[6] See *L. & J.* VI, 101, 109, 139, etc.
[7] *L. & J.* VI, 121. Cf. *Correspondence* II, 231.
[8] *L. & J.* VI, 121.

> Such my present tale is,
> A nondescript and ever-varying rhyme,
> A versified Aurora Borealis,
> Which flashes o'er a waste and icy clime.[1]

In the whole latter portion he shows an even greater security and self-dependence,[2] a wider and clearer vision, and something of real calm and reflection. He is writing as a man eats and sleeps, that is, as a part of his life, not for notoriety or fame, hence there is in the movements of his pen an assurance and self-possession, and a trust in posterity,[3] that have not been present in such measure anywhere else in his works. He has attained the position— remarkable for him—over the entreaties of the Countess Guiccioli, the trepidations of his friends, the alarms of his publisher, the execrations of reviewers, the menaces of the public prosecutor, and his own constitutional self-mistrust.

> 'Tis time we should proceed with our good poem,—
> For I maintain that it is really good,
> Not only in the body but the proem,
> However little both are understood
> Just now,—but by and by the Truth will show 'em
> Herself in her sublimest attitude :
> And till she doth, I fain must be content
> To share her beauty and her banishment.[4]

---

[1] Canto VII, 2.

[2] Cf., from the poem itself,

> " Thus far, go forth, thou Lay, which I will back
> Against the same given quantity of rhyme,
> For being as much the subject of attack
> As ever yet was any work sublime,
> By those who love to say that white is black.
> So much the better !—I may stand alone,
> But would not change my free thoughts for a throne."
> —Canto XI, 90.

[3] Cf., with regard to the " north-west passage to my magnetic pole," " I think, as Gibbon says of his History, ' that, perhaps, a hundred years hence it may still continue to be abused.' "—*L. & J.* VI, 29.

[4] Canto IX, 22.

Don Juan will be known by and bye, for what it is intended, —a *Satire* on *abuses* of the present states of Society, and not an eulogy of vice : it may be now and then voluptuous : I can't help that. Ariosto is worse ; Smollett (see Lord Strutwell in vol. 2d. of *R(oderick) R(andom)* ten times worse ; and Fielding no better. No Girl will ever be seduced by reading *D. J.* : —no, no ; she will go to Little's poems and Rousseau's romans for that, or even to the immaculate De Staël : they will encourage her, and not the Don, who laughs at that, and—and— most other things. But never mind—Ça ira !¹

Not many of Byron's less important productions were recognized in his self-critical observations. But a few were incidentally glanced at in a way that must not go unrecorded.

The Waltz is merely " in the old style of *English Bards, and Scotch Reviewers.*"² An inferior poem like *The Devil's Drive* is " a wild, rambling, unfinished rhapsody."³ The *Monody on Sheridan* was only " written by request of Mr. K. for the theatre . . . . . [and] where I have not my choice I pretend to answer for nothing."⁴ The *Lament of Tasso* —" I look upon it as a ' these be good rhymes.' "⁵ *Beppo* " has politics and ferocity."⁶ *The Prophecy of Dante* is justly ranked highly—" the best thing I ever did, if it be not *unintelligible.*"⁷ *The Blues* are " a mere buffoonery."⁸ *The Irish Avatar* is " as pretty a piece of invective as ever put publisher in the way to ' Botany.' "⁹ *The Vision of*

---

¹ *L. & J.* VI, 155-6.
² *L. & J.* II, 176.
³ *L. & J.* II, 378—Byron uses the term *rhapsody* of any and all poetry, consistently with his idea of the origin of poetry in overwrought feeling. Cf. Chapter V, 86 f.
⁴ *L. & J.* III, 365-6.
⁵ *L. & J.* IV, 115. Cf. *ibid.*, 139.
⁶ *L. & J.* IV, 195.
⁷ *L. & J.* IV, 442.
⁸ *L. & J.* V, 338.
⁹ *L. & J.* V, 367. Cf. *ibid.*, 366, 377.

Judgment is as correctly pronounced, " one of my best in that line,"[1] " one of my best things,"[2] and, " in my finest, ferocious, Caravaggio style."[3] The *Age of Bronze* is but " calculated for the reading part of the million, being all on politics."[4] *The Island* is only " a little above the usual run of periodical poesy."[5] And the one lyric, perhaps his best, which he mentions in this way, is favored with as high praise as he has to bestow.

Do you remember the lines I sent you early last year. . . . . . I mean those beginning. " There's not a joy the world can," etc., etc., on which I rather pique myself as being the truest, though the most melancholy, I ever wrote.[6]

[1] *L. & J.* VI, 30.
[2] *L. & J.* VI, 77.
[3] *Correspondence* II, 203.
[4] *L. & J.* VI, 161. Cf. *ibid.*, 164 f.
[5] *L. & J.* VI, 164.
[6] *L. & J.* III, 274.

CHAPTER X

CONCLUSION

The purpose of this study has been to trace Byron's critical career in all its varied relations. But in working out the plan the more significant aspects or bearings may at times have been obscured in the numerous details, so that a brief summary may not be out of place.

Byron's equipment for criticism, from his nature, education, and travel, was far above the average. He esteemed the rôle of critic an honorable one. His first sustained effort of any kind was a critical triumph against the degrading practices of the time. He interested himself, for a while thereafter, actively in periodical criticism. And but for the sudden and unparalleled success of his occasional poetry, he probably would have adopted a critical career.

He is not, in total outline, in his criticism the confirmed reactionary that he is usually represented. He held principles of his art, in his more constant character, conformably with his practice, and expressed them deliberately and definitely. There was, as well, a substantial strain of conservatism in his nature, such as is often the basis of technique. He saw the wanton abuse of this principle by many of his contemporaries, distrusted his own liberal impulses, and expressed himself on the common tendency with the full " forty-parson power " that was his to command. But his utterances of the kind are not to be taken as constituting of themselves his whole critical creed.

The reformation of two great literary types is contemporaneous with Byron's critical activities—drama and criticism itself. He wrought consciously and valiantly for the betterment of both these forms, by the construction of severe models for the guidance of the one, and by combatting, often by its own methods, the evil practices of the other. The emergence, almost immediately after, of higher types in both forms is conclusive evidence of his influence and service in each.

Byron's professional critical " scribblement " is less creditable to his powers than any other part of his criticism. And yet only the controversial portion of it is the source of his unenviable reputation as a critic. At best this portion is but a " nine-days wonder." It occupied no longer time in its production, it was performed without prevision or plan, " in a passion and a Sirocco," as he with some exaggeration expressed it, and it was not even reread by him. Such work is not a just measure of the critic.

His best criticism is in isolated passages—pretty frequent at that—in his letters and journals and in his poetry. It is a part of the elemental impressionism of his nature, is interpretative in character, and wherever it is inspired by his creative talent, it is at one with his great poetry.

For no fault of his own Byron lives in somewhat scornful memory as a critic of his own works. He deplored the extravagance of the time, and in his appraisal of its effects on literature he included his own romantic work. But his opinions of his productions separately are very nearly permanent estimates.

Of the sum total of Byron's criticism, it may be said first that it is unusually strong and vigorous. It more often goes beyond the mark than wide of it. Its very strength and vehemence have brought against him the charge of exaggeration, of wildness, hence of unreliability. Such an attitude is illiberal in an age which applauds Swinburne's apotheosis of Victor Hugo, Carlyle's dictum that Macaulay had less intelligence than a hare, Voltaire's declaration that *Athalie* is the masterpiece of the human mind, and Schlegel's pronouncement that Calderon is the last summit of romantic poetry.

Byron's criticism, as a part of his far-reaching censoriousness, is largely destructive. He had the power of a Titan, and he used it wilfully and fearlessly, but with discretion nevertheless, that is, seldom where there was not cause for destruction.

His early death prevented his attainment of true and constant greatness as a critic. His nature was endowed with judicial elements, critical and censorious, he believed in the early subsidence of the poetical faculty, and before his death a real philosophical calm was beginning to appear. Criticism was now rid of its old shackles, largely from his own exertions, and was in the full progress of its new freedom. His " corruption " from a poet, in the event of any change in his vocation, could hardly have been into anything less than a powerful critic. Poetry may not have lost more in his untimely death than has criticism.

BIBLIOGRAPHY

The following list contains only a portion of the works consulted in the preparation of this book. The list is intended to be complete of the authorities specifically employed by quotation or reference. Titles are freely abbreviated, for the sake of space, in the citations in the notes. The special texts of Byron, used in the quotations and references, are indicated here by asterisks.

ANGELI, HELEN ROSETTI, *Shelley and His Friends in Italy*. London, 1911.

ARISTOTLE, *The Poetics*, Text and Translation by S. H. Butcher.

ARMSTRONG, J. L., *The Life of Lord Byron*. London, 1846.

ARNOLD, MATTHEW, *Essays in Criticism*.

BABBITT, IRVING, *Are the English Critical?*, in *The Nation*, March 21 & 28, 1912.

BAGEHOT, WALTER, *The First Edinburgh Reviewers*.

BEERS, H. A., *A History of English Romanticism in the Nineteenth Century*.

BETTANY, W. A. LEWIS, *The Confessions of Lord Byron*. London, 1905.

BLESSINGTON, The Countess of, *A Journal of Conversations with Lord Byron*. London, 1850.

BRANDES, GEORGE, *Shelley and Lord Byron*. 1893.

BRECKNOCK, ALBERT, *The Pilgrim Poet: Lord Byron of Newstead*. London, 1911.

BREWSTER, W. T., *The Logic of Literary Criticism*.

BRYDGES, SIR EGERTON, *Letters on the Character and Poetical Genius of Lord Byron*. London, 1824.

BROGLIE, LOUISE DE, Countess of Haussonville, *Les dernières Années de Lord Byron.* Paris, 1874.

BURGESS, GEORGE, *Cato to Lord Byron on the Immortality of His Writings.* London, 1824.

*BYRON, GEORGE GORDON NOEL (Lord), *The Poetical Works*, edited, with a memoir, by Ernest Hartley Coleridge. New York, 1910.

—— *Poetry* I—VII, edited by Ernest Hartley Coleridge. London.

*—— *Letters and Journals* I—VI, edited by Rowland E. Prothero. London, 1901.

*—— *The Poetical Works*, edited by Paul Elmer More. Boston, 1905.

*—— *The Poetical Works*, edited and annotated by Thomas Moore, Lord Jeffrey, Sir Walter Scott, Bishop Heber, Samuel Rogers, Professor Wilson, J. G. Lockhart, George Ellis, Thomas Campbell, and Rev. H. H. Milman. London, 1845.

—— *Verse and Prose*, edited by Fitz-Greene Halleck. Hartford, 1849.

—— *Letters 1804—13*, edited by William Ernest Henley. New York, 1897.

*—— *Correspondence* I—II. Chiefly with Lady Melbourne, etc., edited by John Murray. New York, 1922.

CARLYLE, THOMAS, *Reminiscences.*

CARPENTER, F. I., *Selected Poems of Lord Byron*, with Biographical and Critical Introduction. New York.

CASTELAR, EMILIO, *Vida de Lord Byron.* Habana, 1873.

CHEW, SAMUEL C., Jr., *The Dramas of Lord Byron.* Baltimore, 1915.

CLINTON, GEORGE, *Memoirs of the Life and Writings of Lord Byron.* London, 1826.

COLERIDGE, ERNEST HARTLEY, Article on Byron in *Encyclopedia Britannica.*

COLERIDGE, SAMUEL TAYLOR, *The Complete Works*, edited by Professor W. G. T. Shedd. New York, 1884.

COLVIN, SIDNEY, *John Keats : His Life and Poetry, His Friends and Critics and After-Fame*. New York, 1917.

COURTHOPE, W. J., *History of English Poetry* I—VI.

DALLAS, R. C., *Recollections of the Life of Lord Byron from the Year 1808 to the End of 1814*. Philadelphia, 1825.

DAWSON, EDGAR, *Byron und Moore*. Leipzig, 1902.

DIXON, WILLIAM MACNEILLE, *English Poetry from Blake to Browning*. London, 1894.

DUFF, J. WRIGHT, *Byron's Selected Poetry*.

EDGCUMBE, RICHARD, *Byron : The Last Phase*. London, 1909.

EIMER, MANFRED, *Die persönlichen Beziehungen zwischen Byron und den Shelleys*. Heidelberg, 1911.

ELZE, KARL, *Lord Byron*. Berlin, 1881.

ENGEL, HERMANN, *Byrons Stellung zu Shakespeare*. Berlin, 1903.

ESTEVE, EDMUND, *Byron et le Romantisme francaise*. Paris, 1907.

FINDEN, *Illustrations of the Life and Works of Lord Byron*, with Original and Selected Information, by W. Brockedon. London, 1833.

FERGUSON, JOHN CLARK, *Lectures on the Writings and Genius of Byron*. 1856.

FROUDE, J. A., *A Leaf from the Real Life of Lord Byron*, in *Nineteenth Century*, 1883.

FUESS, CLAUDE M., *Lord Byron as a Satirist in Verse*. New York, 1912.

FUHRMANN, LUDWIG, *Die Belesenheit des Jungen Byron*. 1903.

GALT, JOHN, *The Life of Lord Byron*. London, 1830.

GAMBA, COUNT PIETRO, *A Narrative of Lord Byron's Last Journey to Greece*. London, 1825.

GERARD, WILLIAM, *Byron Re-Studied in His Dramas.* London, 1886.

GRAHAM, WILLIAM, *Last Links with Byron, Shelley, and Keats.* London, 1898.

GRIBBLE, FRANCIS, *The Love Affairs of Lord Byron.* New York, 1910.

GUICCIOLI, The Countess, *My Recollections of Lord Byron and Those of Eyewitnesses of His Life.* New York, 1869.

HAZLITT, WILLIAM, *Collected Works* I—XII, edited by A. R. Waller and Arnold Glover. London, 1902.

HERFORD, C. H., *The Age of Wordsworth.*

HOBHOUSE, JOHN CAM (Lord BROUGHTON), *Recollections of a Long Life* I—V. London, 1910.

HODGSON, REV. JAMES T., *Memoir of the Rev. Francis Hodgson* I—II. London, 1878.

HORACE, *Ars Poetica.*

HOWITT, MARY, *An Autobiography* I—II, edited by her daughter, Margaret Howitt. London, 1889.

HUNT, LEIGH, *Autobiography*, revised by his eldest son, London, 1861.

—— *Lord Byron and Some of His Contemporaries ; with Recollections of the Author's Life, and of His Visit to Italy.* London, 1828.

INZE, OTTOKAR, *Katalog der Byron-Abteilung des Englischen Seminars.*

JEAFFRESON, JOHN CORDY, *The Real Lord Byron.* Boston, 1883.

KEATS, JOHN, *The Poetical Works and Other Writings* I—IV and Supplement, edited by Harry Buxton Forman. London, 1883.

KENNEDY, JAMES, *Conversations on Religion with Lord Byron and Others.* London, 1830.

KINGSLEY, CHARLES, *Thoughts on Shelley and Byron.*

KÖHLER, *A Glance at Lord Byron as a Dramatist.*

LAKE, J. W., *The Life of Lord Byron.* Paris, 1828.

LAMARTINE, A. DE, *Le dernier Chant du Pélerinage d'Harold.*

LANDOR, W. S., *Poetry.*

LE BAS, CHARLES WEBB, *A Review of the Life and Character of Lord Byron.* London, 1883.

LEIGHTON, ALEXANDER, *The Life of Lord Byron.* Edinburgh, 1861.

LEONARD, WILLIAM ELLERY, *Byron and Byronism in America.* Boston, 1905.

LESCURE, M. DE, *Lord Byron, Histoire d'un Homme.* Paris, 1866.

LOCKHART, J. G., *Life of Sir Walter Scott* I—X. Boston and New York, 1901.

MACAULAY, THOMAS BABBINGTON, *Lord Byron.*

MACKAY, CHARLES, *Medora Leigh: a History and an Autobiography,* edited. London, 1869.

MATTHIAE, OTTO, *Characteristics of Lord Byron.* Berlin,1875.

MAYCHRZOK, FRANZ, *Lord Byron als Übersetzer.* Breslau, 1895.

MAYNE, ETHEL COLBURN, *Byron* I—II. London, 1912.

MCMAHAN, ANNA BENNESON, *With Byron in Italy.* Chicago, 1906.

MEDWIN, CAPTAIN THOMAS, *Conversations of Lord Byron at Pisa in 1821 and 1822.* London, 1824.

MILES, ALFRED H., *The Poets and the Poetry of the Century* I—X.

MILLEDGE, FRANK ALLEN, *Byrons Beziehungen zu seinen Lehrern und Schulkameraden und deren Einfluß auf seine literarische Tätigkeit.* Erlangen, 1903.

MILLER, BARNETTE, *Leigh Hunt's Relations with Byron, Shelley, and Keats.* New York, 1910.

MINTO, WILLIAM, Article on Byron in *Encyclopedia Britannica.*

MITFORD, MARY RUSSELL, *Correspondence with Charles Boner and John Ruskin.* London and Leipzig, 1914.

MOORE, THOMAS, *The Works of Lord Byron : with His Letters and Journals, and His Life* I—XVII. London, 1832—3.

—— *Memoirs, Journal, and Correspondence,* edited by the Rt. Hon. Lord John Russell. London, 1856.

MOORMAN, F. W., *Byron,* in *Cambridge History of English Literature.*

MORE, P. E., *The Wholesome Revival of Byron,* in *Atlantic Monthly,* December, 1898.

MURRAY, JOHN, *Lord Byron and Lord Lovelace,* in *Monthly Review,* February, 1906.

NAPIER, MACVEY, *Selections from the Correspondence,* edited by his son. London, 1879.

NICHOL, JOHN, *Byron.* London, 1880.

NOEL, RODEN, *Life of Lord Byron.* London, 1890.

NORTON, ANDREWS, *A Review of the Life and Character of Lord Byron.* London, 1826.

PARRY, WILLIAM, *The Last Days of Lord Byron.* Philadelphia, 1825.

PHELPS, W. L., *The Beginnings of the English Romantic Movement.* Boston, 1893.

PITCAIRN, ROBERT, *Harrow School.*

PÖNITZ, ARTHUR, *Byron und die Bibel.* 1906.

PRESCOTT, W. H., *Byron's Letter on Pope,* in *North American Review,* October, 1821.

PUGHE, F. H., *Studien über Byron und Wordsworth.* Heidelberg, 1902.

ROBERTS, R. ELLIS, *Samuel Rogers and His Circle.* London, 1910.

ROBINSON, H. CRABBE, *Diary.*

ROE, JOHN C., *Some Obscure and Disputed Points in Byronic Biography.* Leipzic, 1893.

ROGERS, SAMUEL, *Table Talk.* London, 1856.

SAINTSBURY, GEORGE, *A History of Criticism* I—III.

—— *A History of English Prosody from the Twelfth Century to the Present Day* I—III.

—— *A History of English Literature of the Nineteenth Century.*

SCHIRMER, WALTER F., *Die Beziehungen zwischen Byron und Leigh Hunt.* 1912.

SCHMIDT, OTTO, *Rousseau und Byron.* 1890.

SCOTT, SIR WALTER, *The Character of Lord Byron,* in *The Pamphleteer,* 1824.

—— *Miscellaneous Prose Works* I—XXVIII. Edinburgh, 1835.

SECCOMBE, THOMAS, *The Age of Johnson.*

SHELLEY, PERCY BYSSHE, *The Letters* I—II, collected and edited by Roger Ingpen. London, 1909.

SMILES, SAMUEL, *Memoir and Correspondence of the Late John Murray* I—II. London and New York, 1891.

STEPHEN, LESLIE, *The First Edinburgh Reviewers.*

—— Article on Byron, *Dictionary of National Biography.*

SWINBURNE, ALGERNON CHARLES, *Essays and Studies.* London, 1875.

TAINE, H. A., *A History of English Literature.*

TRELAWNY, JOHN, *Records of Shelley, Byron and the Author.* New York, 1887.

TRENT, W. P., *The Authority of Criticism and Other Essays.* New York, 1899.

W. M., *Was Byron a Dandy?,* in *The Academy,* July 30, 1898.

—— *Byron as Self-Critic,* in *The Academy,* August 11, 1900.

WATKINS, JOHN, *Memoirs of the Life and Writings of the Right Honorable Lord Byron.* London, 1822.

WEISER, KARL, *Popes Einfluß auf Byrons Jugenddich-tungen.*

WHIPPLE, E. P., *Characteristics of Lord Byron,* in *North American Review,* January, 1845.

WILLIAMS, J. FISCHER, *Harrow.* London, 1901.

WINCHESTER, C. T., *Some Principles of Literary Criticism.*

WILSON, JOHN, *et al., Noctes Ambrosianae.* 1819—35.

WORDSWORTH, WILLIAM, *The Prose Works* I—III, edited by Alexander B. Grosart. London, 1876.

ZABEL, ERNST, *Byrons Kenntnis von Shakespeare und sein Urteil über ihn.* 1904.